When Stocks Crash Nicely

WHEN STOCKS CRASH NICELY

The Finer Art of Short Selling

Kathryn F. Staley

HarperBusiness
A Division of HarperCollins*Publishers*

Library of Congress Cataloging-in-Publication Data

Staley, Kathryn F.
    When stocks crash nicely : the finer art of short selling /
Kathryn F. Staley.
        p.   cm.
    Includes bibliographical references.
    ISBN 0-88730-497-4
    1. Short selling.
HG6041.S73   1991   90-26890
332.63'228—dc20   CIP

International Standard Book Number: 0-88730-497-4

Library of Congress Catalog Card Number: 90-26890

Printed in the United States of America

91 92 93 94 CC/HC 9 8 7 6 5 4 3 2 1

To Clarence Taylor

Bears can make money only if the bulls push up stocks to where they are overpriced and unsound.

Bulls always have been more popular than bears in this country because optimism is so strong a part of our heritage. Still, overoptimism is capable of doing more damage than pessimism since caution tends to be thrown aside.

To enjoy the advantages of a free market one must have both buyers and sellers, both bulls and bears. A market without bears would be like a nation without a free press. There would be no one to criticize and restrain the false optimism that always leads to disaster.

Bernard Baruch

Contents

Preface   *xiii*

PART 1
FACTS AND PRACTITIONERS   *1*

1. **Overview: Wealth with Risk**   *3*
   Who Sells Short?   *4*
   Why Opportunities for Short Selling Exist   *5*
   Analytical Techniques: How to Detect the First
   Tremors of the Quake   *7*
   Who Can Benefit from Short Selling Wisdom?   *11*
   Mechanics and Risks   *13*
   Current Market Statistics and Growth Prospects   *15*
   Caveats   *19*

2. **Short Sellers**   *21*
   Hedge Funds and Investment Advisors   *21*
   Short Sellers: The Alter Ego of Wall Street   *25*
   An Expanding List of Short Sellers   *38*

PART 2
CATEGORIES AND EXAMPLES   *39*

3. **Bubble Stocks**   *41*
   Dirty Carpets: ZZZZ Best   *41*
   Harrier: It Just Didn't Add up   *42*
   Second Derivation: Medstone   *51*

4. **High Multiple Growth Stocks: High Risk, Low
   Return**   *59*
   Computers and Cabbage Patch Dolls: Coleco   *60*
   Marble and Brass in a Grocery Store: J. Bildner &
   Sons   *63*
   Lending to Franchisees: Jiffy Lube   *71*

5. **If You Can't Read It, Short It**   *83*
   CUC International   *84*
   National Education   *87*
   Current Nominations for Unreadable Financials   *94*

6. **Money Suckers: Coining Money to Live**   *99*
   The Nine Lives of Integrated Resources, Inc.   *100*
   Cable Companies: We're Gonna Make a Whole
   Bunch of Money Real Soon   *114*

7. **Check Kiting, Corporate Style**   *121*
   Cheyenne Software: Respectable Ratios by
   Acquisition   *121*
   The Weasel Launches a Hot Air Balloon   *123*
   Insurance Companies: Who's on First?   *134*

8. **If You Can't Fix It, Sell It**   *143*
   Harcourt Brace Jovanovich Escapes Maxwell's
   Money   *144*
   Texas Air: Flying with Frank   *150*
   Kay Jewelers Sells Out (or Tries to) at the Annual
   Sale   *155*
   Service Corporation: Short the Acquirer   *158*

9. **Industry Obsolescence: Theme Stocks**   *163*
    The Arizona Land Race   *164*
    American Continental: What's All the Ruckus
    About?   *165*
    Sun State Savings Acquired on Margin   *172*
    Valley National: Uncharacteristic Wall Street
    Battle   *175*

10. **All of the Above: Crazy Eddie**   *185*
    An Identifiable Story Stock   *185*
    A Private Family Bank or an Electronics Chain?   *187*
    Does a Medical School Count as Vertical
    Integration?   *188*
    Wall Street Hysteria and Home Shopping   *189*
    The Plot Develops   *191*
    The Big Break   *193*

PART 3
HISTORY AND GENERAL LESSONS   *199*

11. **Shortcomings**   *201*
    Three Short Sins   *201*
    And a Multitude of Small Follies   *205*
    And Last of All   *210*

12. **History and Controversy**   *213*
    History   *213*
    Witch Hunts and Regulation   *224*

13. **Six Pillars of Fundamental Short Selling**   *231*
    The Short Seller's Random Walk for Ideas   *231*
    1. The Pessimist's Guide to Financial Statements   *233*
    2. In Search of Greed and Sleaze   *240*
    3. The Bigger Puzzle   *247*
    4. Who Owns It?   *248*

5. Check the Water Temperature   248
6. Pay Attention   249
Concept Recap   250
Conclusion   250

Appendix Margin Accounts and Short Selling   253

Preface

The first time I shorted a stock it was with trepidation; I thought the very act would cause havoc in my margin account, or deflate my net worth, or worse, bring out the capitalist patrol to grill me on my un-American trade. The stock crashed nicely. I was hooked.

I spent increasing hours on weekends reading prospectuses and 10Qs, looking for the Achilles' heels of puffed-up balance sheets, searching for evidence of greed and sleaze.

Then I was introduced to several card-carrying professional short sellers, and my education continued in the backwaters of the equity market. Black humor, sharp intelligence, and true contrarian sensibilities characterized the group of people who always, by choice, are out of line with the Wall Street masses.

The analytical process that the short sellers used was distinguished by accumulation of prodigious amounts of information, followed by intuitive leaps to a valuation conclusion. Since my equity training was conventional MBA/CFA–style analysis, the short seller technique of learning from the mistakes that corporations made was beguiling.

The lack of published information on short selling as well as the current dearth of fundamental financial analysis prompted me to accumulate what I've learned from short sellers in this book. I had the fortune of good files and good friends to help me in my attempt to organize and document an unstructured approach to analyzing stocks. All the stocks mentioned, with the exception of Coleco and ZZZZ Best, are stocks I was short and followed at the time with less objectivity than the text would suggest.

My particular thanks to the short sellers whose ideas and analytical methods appear in this book, as well as to the money managers who shared their thoughts on short selling.

I was lucky enough to have able readers for the manuscript. Dr. Richard McEnally offered valuable suggestions on structure and content. Portions were also reviewed during development by Sue Hardman, Bob Rhodes, Aki Groon Pampush, Charles Leonard, and Alex Arapoglou.

In collecting data on case studies, I was assisted by Jim Chanos, Scott Bessent, Bill McGarr, Caroline Halama, Mark Fichtel, Rick Nelson, Robert Schwerin, Sue Hardman, and Mary Ellen Keim. Mary Ellen Templeton at the Emory University Library and the staff at Georgia State also helped accumulate documents, as did Dan Goldin at the University of North Carolina. Tim Brown at Emory helped with the charts. The stock price charts and short interest data following many of the case studies were compiled from public information.

Deborah Lamb made the speed and accuracy of the manuscript possible with her persistent help on charts, tables and figures, brokerage practices, SEC procedures, proxies, and company research, as well as her accurate editorial comments on drafts.

Martha Jewett at Harper Business and her editorial eye allowed the process of a book to be painless and humorous.

And last, my husband, colleague, and friend, Clarence Taylor, listened to stock stories and read chapters beyond any human capacity. To him this book is dedicated.

PART 1
FACTS AND PRACTITIONERS

1

Overview: Wealth with Risk

When Integrated Resources finally went belly up, when Home Shopping Network matched its spectacular ascent with an equally spectacular descent, when Bank of New England took major bites from its equity capital with real estate write-offs, a small group of people on Wall Street benefited. This is a book about the people who profit from collapse, who specialize in detecting disaster, and about the methods they use to track the demise of companies, like equity seismographers watching for the first tremors of an earthquake.

Short sellers unearth facts from financial statements and from observation to ascertain that a stock is overpriced. They act with conventional wisdom—they buy low and sell high, but they sell before they buy. When the stock of Crazy Eddie, a retail electronics chain, expanded like a balloon gone berserk, short sellers studied the company and saw that inventories were growing faster than sales, that management made more money than the stockholders, that competition was brutal in retail electronics in New York City. Wall Street continued to puff up the balloon in a frenzy of enthusiasm, so the short sellers sold stock they didn't own—at high prices, $40 a share. When the stock collapsed and Crazy Eddie Antar himself (founder and ex–corporate chief) disappeared, they bought it cheap for $2 to close the trade and make profits of $38 a share in less than a year.

A short sale is the sale of a security that the seller does not own but promises to deliver by borrowing it from someone else, in order to profit from the subsequent price drop. Selling long, the opposite, is selling a security that is owned, thus long in the account of the seller. Like sellers of stock who own it before selling it, short sellers expect the price appreciation to be limited. They also bet that the price will go down after the stock is sold.

Who Sells Short?

Specialists on the exchanges, market makers, and block traders all sell short to provide market liquidity. When a large order causes temporary trading imbalances that would result in volatile prices, trading professionals create supply by selling short.

Arbitrageurs also buy one security and sell another one short to realize profits on temporary price disparities in markets or like securities.

Institutions, money managers, and individuals sell short to speculate on price declines. Short sellers who sell in anticipation of price decline are generally information-based traders; that is, their valuation studies show that a security is overpriced, and they are trading on that information. Their bets contribute to pricing efficiencies in the market.

Portfolio managers also sell short to hedge another holding. If the outlook for the airline industry is mixed, the managers might sell one airline stock and buy another to hedge the outlook on the industry while profiting from individual security characteristics.

Bernard Baruch, Joseph Kennedy, and many other financial titans of the first decades of the twentieth century were adept at selling short; in fact, they used the technique as casually as buying and selling stocks and bonds. Before 1983 no solely short funds existed, and short selling was primarily the venue of hedge fund managers and sophisticated individuals. Short selling—fundamental, information-based, non–computer-motivated short selling—is practiced as a full-time profession by only ten or fifteen people in the United States. Since 1988, additional short managers have expanded the ranks. Mystery surrounds the group, increased by an occasional ground swell from executives maligning the practice and its cabal of disciples as unpatriotic, destructive, self-serving.

Short selling is perceived by professionals, as well as by casual investors, as risky and speculative. A frequent criticism of short selling as an investment alternative states that stocks can go only to zero on the downside, to infinity on the way up. Short sellers respond that they have seen a lot more stocks at zero than at infinity, like cat skeletons in trees. Because the risk is greater, short sellers must be more confident that their conclusions are correct and have strong evidence to support cases for price declines. Because reverses are terrifying and sudden, the burden rests on a solid, careful analysis completed before the stock is shorted.

Short sellers are usually hard-working, creative people who enjoy going against the grain and competing with the mind of Wall Street (represented by the prices of stocks); they enjoy solving puzzles that other people find frustrating, confusing, or unsolvable.

Why Opportunities for Short Selling Exist

Money managers and individuals alike find that it's tough to make consistent profits in the financial markets. Why then, do short sellers always find broad gaps in stock valuation that can lead to dramatic price drops?

Clearly, short selling is a niche, and a small one relative to the stock market as a whole, and that situation creates inefficiencies in stock pricing. Several studies in security price behavior suggest that there is theoretical justification for short selling. Brokerage houses add to pricing discrepancies with buy-side vigor and with reliance on computer analytical models.

Edward M. Miller, professor of financial economics at the University of New Orleans, proposed an amendment to the efficient market theory when he suggested that "prices are bounded by limits set by the buying and short-selling of informed investors."[1] The upper limits of securities prices are set by short sellers who will stop the ascent of the price if the potential return is great enough to augment the costs of being short. The short seller's ability to sell becomes the critical variable in the upper price boundary. Since, Miller argues, there are many restrictions on short selling (institutional prohibitions, transaction costs, borrowable shares), stocks trade not at one efficient price but within a band of prices. The dynamics of Miller's theory of the bounded efficient market suggest that portfolio managers are well advised to look for mispriced stocks to sell, since more overpriced than undervalued stocks can be identified.

Research by Robert Hagin and Henry Latane provides evidence that negative earnings surprises affect stock prices to a greater degree than positive earnings surprises and that the effect persists over time.[2] The common wisdom that there's no such thing as one bad quarter has a statistical basis. Hagin coined the phrase "torpedo stocks" to describe the effect on a portfolio of a negative earnings surprise. "Stocks become torpedos when very high earnings expectations give way to earnings disappointments. . . . The higher one's expectation for earnings growth, the deeper the disappointment if the expectation is not realized."[3]

Recent academic research on speculative bubbles shows what short sellers have known for centuries: evidence exists that bubbles form and then collapse. Colin Camerer reviews the research, both theoretical and experimental, on bubbles in an article for the *Journal of Economic Surveys.*[4] Economists are attempting to discover why prices vary from intrinsic value. One theory suggests that fads linger in the security market because institutional investors are too averse to risk and too aware of short-term relative performance to bet against the fad and sell.

A bias against selling that exists in the market allows pricing disparities to remain; brokerage houses add to that bias. Most brokerage stock recommendations range from buy to hold, with few analysts willing to rank stocks as sells. Analysts are constrained by corporate finance relationships or by the desire to keep access to a company open.

Donald Trump's March 1990 attack on analyst Marvin Roffman and Roffman's subsequent firing by Janney Montgomery Scott, Inc., give credence to an analyst's fear of honesty. Company executives have gotten more aggressive in defending their stocks against adverse sentiment, and lawsuits have proliferated in response to the occasional Wall Street analyst's frank statement of negative opinion. Sy Jacobs at Mabon, Nugent & Company was placed in "investor relations Siberia" because of his sale recommendation on Household International, Inc.[5] Charles Peabody at Kidder, Peabody & Co., Inc., was cut off by Valley National Bank and NCNB after offering negative opinions. Richard Sweetnam at Kidder, Peabody raised the ire of executives at California Energy with his short sale recommendation. Some executives apparently feel an open market should not provide a forum for discussion or dissent, so the quality of analysis and information declines with the restrictions on speech.

Brokerage house estimates also tend to be over optimistic, thereby providing potential for negative surprises with greater regularity than positive surprises. The concentration on optimism makes for more inefficiency in short-term stock prices and gives prices a positive bias.

Analytical Techniques: How to Detect the First Tremors of the Quake

Terminal short sellers (as they are called to distinguish them from technical or computer model shorts) spend their days identifying publicly traded companies with flaws that may cause bankruptcy or major income reversals, companies that are overvalued relative to the present value of their potential stream of income. Securities sold short in their portfolios are sometimes not bought back for years—until the prices in the market reflect the perceived condition of the company or the flaw becomes apparent to Wall Street.

How do short sellers work? What signs do they look for to capture the price anomalies? How do they then analyze the securities and where do they find the data?

Short sale candidates cluster in three broad categories:

- companies where management lies to investors and obscures events that will affect earnings;
- companies that have tremendously inflated stock prices—speculative bubbles;

- companies that will be affected in a significant way by changing external events.

Short sellers are always alert to publicly traded corporations that fall into these three categories. No computer screen or set of screens and no consistent mechanical method can capture this universe. And that's what makes short selling lucrative—it takes too much work for most people to fool with it.

So how do short sellers find the stocks? They read hundreds of financial statements. They talk to everybody about everything: to baby-sitters about tennis shoe trends, to children about toy purchases, to doctors about new equipment or drugs. They talk to brokers, money managers, and company executives about competitors and suppliers. They read newspapers, business journals, and trade papers like the *Poultry Times* and *Gaming and Wagering Business.* They listen for stocks that people are excited about and pay attention to trends in regional real estate and retail purchases.

When they find an industry that appears to be overvalued, they begin to look for more specific company evidence. Clues that something is amiss in a corporation are the starting point of a short seller's quest. These trail signs are grouped around several characteristics:

- accounting gimmickry: clues that the financial statements don't reflect the true state of corporate health;
- insider sleaze: signs that insiders consider the company a personal bank or think the stock should be sold;
- fad or bubble stock pricing: usually marked by a stellar price rise over a short period;
- a gluttonous corporate appetite for cash;
- overvalued assets or an ugly balance sheet.

If one or more of those characteristics is apparent in a company, short sellers proceed in the quest for comprehensive information. To piece together the story of a corporation, short sellers do labor-intensive work. A framework for stock analysis follows this rough outline:

1. Short sale analysis is dependent on financial analysis—cash flow proformas, balance sheet strength, and the quality of

earnings. Start with at least two years of company financials and analyze the numbers using the fundamentals of financial analysis: balance sheet and rate of return ratios, income statement analysis, cash flow breakouts. Overlay traditional analysis with an especially tough look at quality of assets and earnings. Work from the 10Qs and 10Ks because the versions of the quarterly and annual reports filed with the Securities and Exchange Commission (SEC) have more data and less puff.

2. Use the proxy and the SEC insider filings to track management's salary, stock activity, and attitude toward the company and its stockholders.

3. Check in the marketplace to see what the execution of the business strategy looks like: look at the products, the competitors, the suppliers of production inputs.

4. Follow the trading patterns, the short interest, and the ownership by watching price and volume, 13D filings, and institutional ownership.

5. Read anything in the media—magazines, newspapers—and the Wall Street research pool to determine consensus.

6. Watch everything about the company over time to see what happens, how earnings and price progress, what changes.

The main precept of short analysis is bulk. Short sellers accumulate volumes of disparate facts and observations, then they make an intuitive leap based on the information at hand. Frequently, the signs point to large problems that won't be revealed in total until after the collapse. Crazy Eddie had slowing inventory turnover. Short sellers didn't find out until after the stock collapsed that the building inventory was bogus. So short sellers have to be able to make a logical leap without complete information. They have to trust their experience and judgment and know where to look for signs and what the impact of those signs might be.

Where does the material come from? The financial documents and proxy can come from the company, from a service that microfiches SEC documents, or from a library that subscribes to a microfiche service.

Insider transactions and 13D's are also reported to the SEC. *Barron's* and the *Wall Street Journal* print the largest ones. Several services, *Vickers,* and the *Insider Chronicle* copy all of them from the SEC and have on-line computer subscriptions as well as weekly or monthly hard copy subscriptions.

Short interest is disclosed in the *Wall Street Journal* around the 20th of the month for the New York Stock Exchange (NYSE) and the American Stock Exchange (AMEX), the 25th for the National Association of Securities Dealers Automated Quotation System (NASDAQ). The *New York Times* and *Barron's* also carry a list. All newspapers get the information from the exchanges.

Brokerage reports, the least useful information on the list, can be obtained from the brokerage houses, sometimes, or from the company. Some business library databases also include brokerage reports on-line.

Any major public library has tremendous research resources, including computerized searching by company name for article citations and summaries, industry information, and price history. Dow Jones and Dialog on-line computer services also can search for articles and price history through a large pool of business publications.

The accounting-based analysis is not difficult to do, but it takes time, patience, and a suspension of belief. A Wall Street pundit recently commented that this level of fine-toothed work is too costly for brokerage analysts or institutional managers to perform because of the time and skill required. The lack of attention by other professional investors to these financial details provides the inefficiency in information dissemination that is so central to the short seller's art.

Insider information is never a problem with short sellers since management rarely talks to known vociferous critics. Typically, short sellers have an adversarial relationship with corporate insiders. One of the maxims of short analysis is that public information should provide all an analyst needs to know—careful reading of SEC-filed documents and observation of the execution of the corporate business plan in the marketplace should tell the story of the company.

There is a certain measure of the moralist in short sellers. As detectives on Wall Street, they enjoy revealing the emperor without his clothes, and relish the collapse of an overvalued empire. Some short seller targets in recent years have been highly touted corporate giants with well-developed personal selling skills, secure in their ability to finance shaky businesses with public funds. Charles Keating, Jr., of American Continental (chapter 9), the Zises brothers of Integrated Resources (chapter 6), Morley Thompson of Baldwin United (chapter 2), Fred Carr of First Executive (chapter 7), Gene Phillips of Southmark (chapter 13), and Frank Lorenzo of Texas Air (chapter 8) were all the gratifying quarry of short sellers.

Short sellers normally disagree with Wall Street as well and enjoy beating highly paid, highly visible Wall Street analysts. The conflict of interest inherent in the job description of a Wall Street analyst strikes short sellers as a consistent reason for flawed information. Analysts are paid to follow stocks, yet many rarely read financial documents closely. Short sellers are contemptuous of analytical skills that primarily regurgitate the management line.

Who Can Benefit from Short Selling Wisdom?

Any student of the markets should find the analytical techniques of short sellers interesting, particularly during a period when fundamental analysis is frequently supplanted by computers and technicians and when research departments are understaffed and overrun by investment bankers.

Anyone who buys stocks, loans money to corporations, or runs a company can benefit from the collective wisdom of short sellers. Identifying the tragic flaw in a business long before the company's demise is a timely skill in any economy and an irreplaceable one in a recession.

Institutional managers should find the discipline enticing on several levels: as an analytical methodology, as a means of enhancing returns through avoidance of torpedoes, and as a hedging technique.

As a methodology, short sale analysis is not significantly different from classic fundamental work. It places heavier emphasis on cash flow dissection and on the reality underlying reported earnings. It attempts to identify the long death rattle of a company in decline. In security analysis, managers are rarely trained by using examples of poorly run companies, yet it's easier to identify trouble spots if education includes examples of corporate mistakes. Short selling is, therefore, another tool in a tradesman's bag.

In his essay, "The Loser's Game," Charles Ellis writes, "Almost all of the really big trouble that you're going to experience in the next year is in your portfolio right now; if you could reduce some of those really big problems, you might come out the winner in the Loser's Game."[6] As an equity research skill, short selling gives analysts the ability to avert disaster in good times as well as in bad. And it gives them the ability to enjoy the joke when a sham is discovered, because the fun might not be at their expense. The art of selling trains analysts to avoid torpedo stocks or to profit from them.

Short sales should be considered by portfolio managers who want to hedge or to decrease the volatility of total returns by setting the market sensitivity of their portfolios with more precision. Since short positions have a negative correlation with a stock portfolio, a balanced portfolio of shorts and longs can even out the market effect, reduce risk, and afford returns based purely on stock selection.

Individuals can employ the analytical techniques of short selling to avoid owning stocks that will explode otherwise well-conceived portfolios and to escape the new issue frenzy of rabid retail brokers. Knowledge of professional methods of short selling saves money in the long run.

The main weakness of professional short sellers, an inability to judge the timing of collapses, is a strong argument for attention to short selling by any entity that owns stocks. Short sellers are consistently years too early when they sell stocks. Stockholders are always slow to sell even when the evidence is irrefutable and the future for profit bleak. The years of irrational price behavior in a deteriorating company provide stock owners with years to sell a problem stock. Portfolio managers or individuals who attempt to educate themselves about the reasons for escalating short interest in stock holdings can radically improve the returns by avoiding torpedo hits—they can use the weakness of the discipline as a strength.

Mechanics and Risks

Short sellers of common stocks borrow stock from a brokerage house to sell in the organized markets. They must put up 50 percent of the short sale price to satisfy the current Federal Reserve requirement. The broker, in turn, gets the to-be-borrowed stock from customer margin accounts or from another broker-dealer.

If the short sale is made on the New York Stock Exchange or the American Stock Exchange, the trade can be executed only on an up tick or a zero plus tick—the stock price must move up before a short sale can be made. The over-the-counter NASDAQ market has no tick rule.

After the short sale is made, the brokerage house uses the closing security prices to compute a gain or loss daily or weekly on the positions. If the price has moved down, the seller has use of the funds for security purchases, short sales, or money market purchases. If the price moves up, the seller must put up more collateral (see table 1.1).

Although most brokerage houses do not pay interest on the short sale proceeds, a few do pay interest at a negotiated percentage of the broker call rate. Most managed short funds or hedge funds receive 60 to 90 percent of the broker call rate on short credit balances. The borrower is also charged by the broker for all cash and stock dividend payments on the short positions.

To close a position, the seller must buy the stock and deliver the shares to the broker, who then returns them to the original owner. (The appendix has a detailed explanation of the brokerage and margin requirements.)

The short seller of common stocks runs two risks:

- the price moves up after the stock is sold, thereby requiring more cash infusions into the account; or
- the lender demands the return of the stock.

TABLE 1.1

A simplified example of a short sale

A client sells short 100 shares XYZ @ $100:

Sell 100 shs × $100	=	$10,000
Reg T Requirement 50%	=	$ 5,000 client deposit—equity
		$15,000 credit balance

If the stock declines to $80 per share:

	$15,000 credit balance
—	$ 8,000 current market value
	$ 7,000 equity

If the client chooses to cover the stock by buying it at $80.00 per share and to close out the margin account, the client would make a $2,000 profit plus the return of the initial investment of $5,000, for a total of $7,000, excluding commissions.

If the stock increases to $120 per share:

	$15,000 credit balance
—	$12,000 credit market value
	$ 3,000 equity

If the seller chooses to cover at $120, he would incur a loss of $2,000.

The brokerage house can ask for the return of the stock if the client who owns the stock sells it or wants physical delivery, or if the lending broker requires it for similar reasons. At that time, if the broker can't find another position to loan to the short seller, the customer will be forced to buy it at the current market price (a buy-in).

Short sellers fear most a sustained rally in a stock followed by a forced buy-in of their position, resulting in a loss out of their control. For that reason, short sellers tend to be secretive about positions in stocks with small floats (shares available for purchase, or outstanding shares minus insider and 5 percent positions), particularly in companies with floats below 10 million shares. Despite popular fears that short sellers band together to pound small companies into the ground, the reality is that a good idea is closely held by its originator. Any action that forces owners to sell may create a shortage of stock to borrow if the new owner takes delivery of the position. When short sellers go public with a stock sale idea by communicating the story to the press and the stock has fewer than 10 million shares outstanding, they are betting on an immediate collapse to give them the opportunity to cover the borrowed shares at lower prices. Generally, however, publicity accompanied by only a slight downturn in price can create more problems for short sellers than it solves, since the limelight may trigger buy-ins.

To avoid this risk, some short sellers short only large cap stocks (stocks whose market price times shares outstanding is greater than $500 million), and some never discuss positions or talk to reporters. The short interest columns in the *Wall Street Journal,* the *New York Times* and *Barron's* are the only public sources of information about short sellers' activities.

Current Market Statistics and Growth Prospects

Short selling is a small percentage of the overall market. Short sales as a percentage of New York Stock Exchange shares outstanding for December 1989 were .64 percent, up from .06 percent in 1960. Figure 1.1 shows short interest as a percentage of outstanding shares on the New York Stock Exchange. In 1960 the NYSE had an aggregate of 6,458,415,072 long shares versus an average of 3,375,522 short. In 1989 those figures were 82,797,111,076 versus 529,455,488.

The American Exchange short volume went from .06 percent in 1960 to an average of .54 percent in 1989, with 8,902,572,115 long and 47,950,923 short (figure 1.2). Short statistics were not available for NASDAQ until 1987. It averaged .56 percent short in 1989, when short interest was 219,232,226 versus total shares of 39,211,940,000.

Analysts have said that a high short interest number is bullish, since short sellers must cover and prices rise as the short sellers rush to cover shares. The short indicator as a market predictor has been under attack in recent years, however, because of the use of short sales in arbitrage positions and by institutions to hedge portfolio risk. Some analysts feel that this new dimension has skewed the historical relationships. Short interest is also higher in December as a result of year-end tax strategies.

FIGURE 1.1

New York Stock Exchange Short Interest

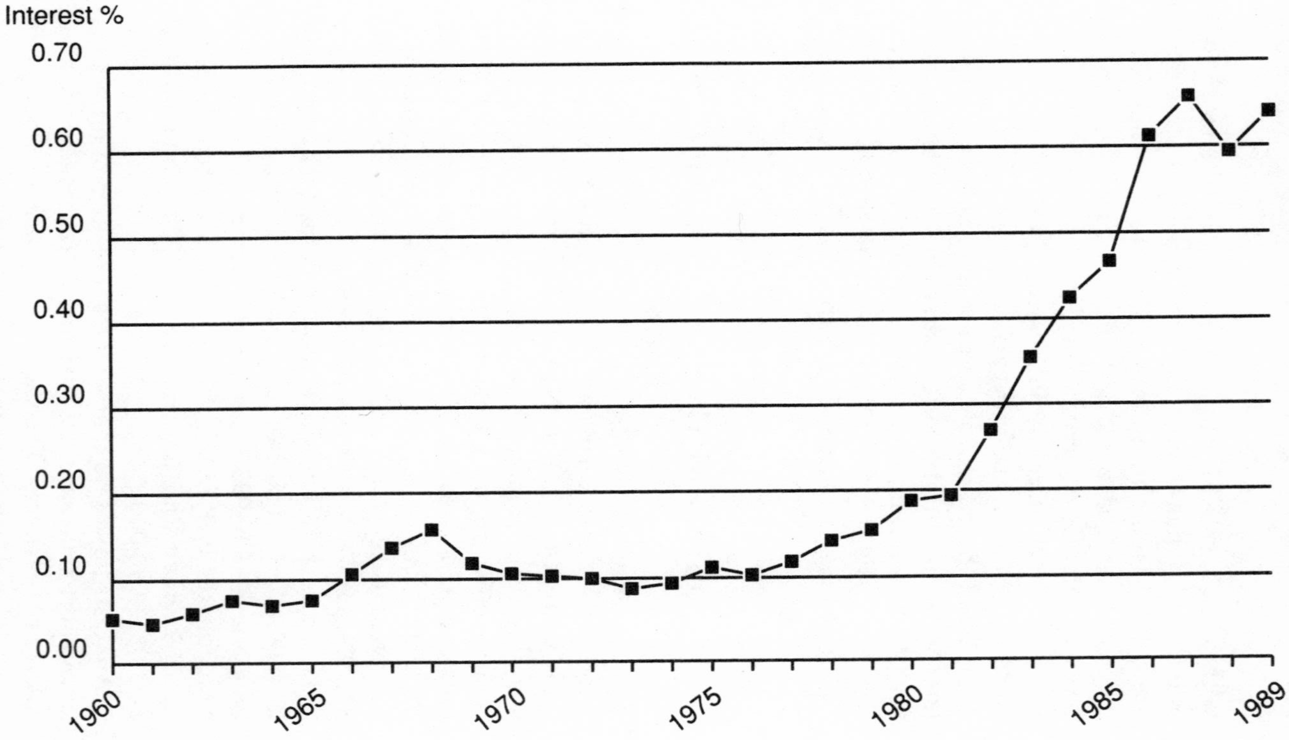

FIGURE 1.2

American Stock Exchange Short Interest

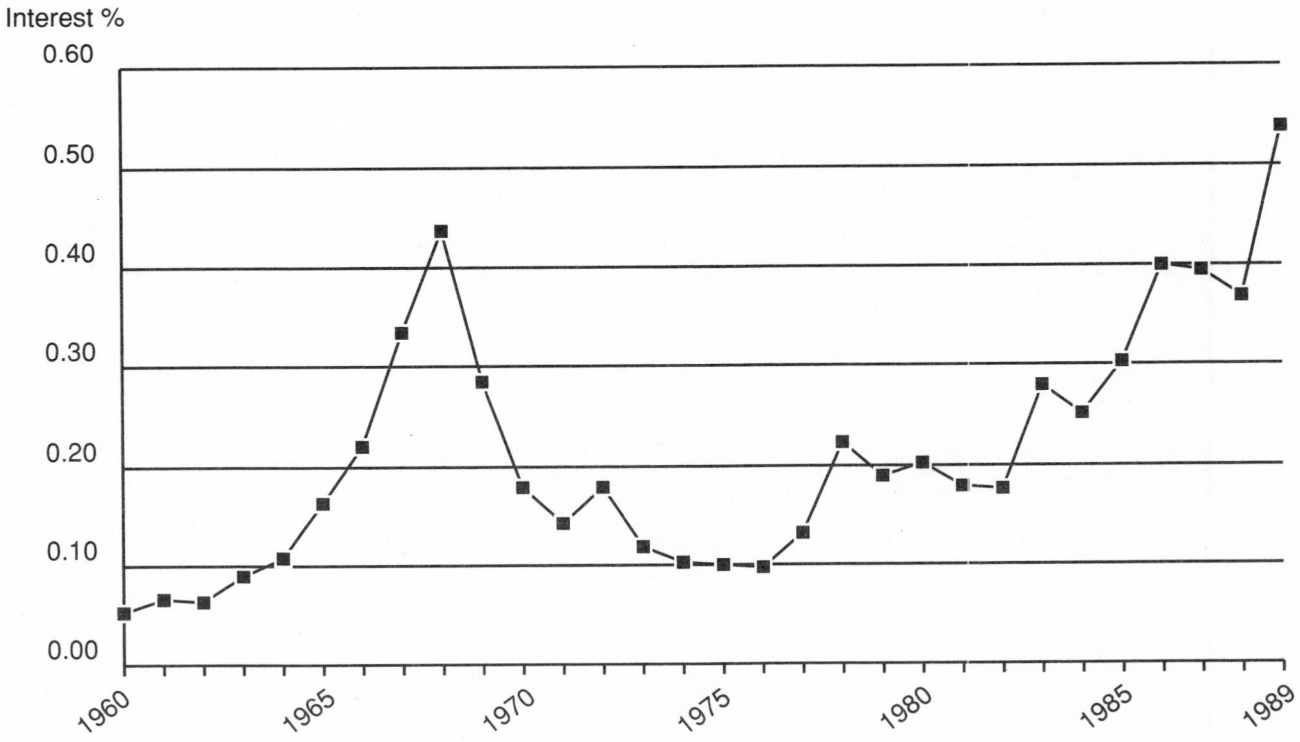

Managed funds dedicated to short selling totaled roughly $1 billion at the end of 1989. That amount is expected to grow with the recent private letter ruling (discussed in more depth below) on the legality of pension funds' shorting stocks. Money managed for pensions alone was $3.32 trillion in May 1989, with 48 percent of that total estimated to be invested in stocks.

The size of short positions is expected to grow for several reasons: the pension fund interest, the protracted bull market, and the interest of institutions in hedging or capturing market inefficiencies in portfolio returns. The growth of the "fund of funds" concept, diversified use of limited partnership funds with different investment styles, also adds substantial dollars to short funds under management.

A private letter ruling allowing a pension fund to participate in short sales was handed down in 1988. A private letter ruling applies only to the entity that asks for it, but it does establish a precedent. Two issues previously kept pension funds out of the short market: "unrelated debt financed income" and "unrelated business taxable income."

The "unrelated debt financed income" question meant that tax-exempt funds couldn't borrow money without jeopardizing their tax-free status. If borrowing stocks was construed as "acquisition indebtedness," pension funds couldn't short, but the Internal Revenue Service ruled that the short sale in an arbitrage transaction did not give rise to acquisition indebtedness if the trade was collateralized by cash or Treasury securities excluding the credit balance from the sale. If the manager did not short an amount in excess of the cash in the account, the short sale would not be considered a form of leverage.

The "unrelated business taxable income" issue questioned whether any income arising from short sales could be considered unrelated business taxable income. Interest on credit balances is generally thought to be excluded from this category. The recent rulings seem to put both issues to rest, therefore allowing pension funds access to another asset class.

The protracted bull market of the 1980s, together with the increasing volatility of price swings, turned the interest of portfolio managers toward short sales. The advent of computer screens also made short selling easier as managers discovered that the firm's normal earnings momentum or value screens could be inverted for short sales. With fewer earnings increases as the economy appears to flatten in growth rate and with a paucity of value ideas, aggressive managers are finding the short side tempting.

The institutional quest for inefficient sectors of the market supports the growing curiosity toward short portfolios. Computer models that once generated equity portfolios are now spitting out short and long portfolios with zero betas and maximum alphas, portfolios that attempt to capture incremental company return without market risk. The growth of the futures and index options market has, no doubt, changed conservative investment thinking. For example, exposure to portfolio insurance and hedging programs has increased manager and client comfort levels with more diverse asset classes and quantitatively driven strategies. It is part of this trend that short sales are no longer considered radical.

The growth in computer-driven short management for institutional investors is expected to exceed the growth in fundamental short management by a fair percentage. Some observers estimate current funds under management at close to $1 billion already. The implication for fundamental short sellers is that, although stocks may become harder to borrow, these programs also readily lend long positions for rebates.

As the short market becomes more crowded and perhaps more efficient, the decline in the number of fundamental analysts suggests that opportunities for profits in short sales will continue to exist.

Caveats

Short selling is not for the faint of heart or for the inexperienced investor. If a stock moves against the position holder, the effect on a portfolio and net worth can be devastating. Short selling for the amateur can be as hazardous as selling uncovered puts or calls. Investors need to understand the impact on their accounts as well as the consequences of getting bought in before they indulge in short selling.

Simple selling, however, is a discipline for even the faint of heart, and the skills are the same. How to make money by shorting and how not to lose money by selling are different sides of the same coin.

There is a certain sense of power, of being in control, of being, somehow, smarter or more independent that comes with successful short selling. The discipline gives the truly addicted stock gamesman the ability to play and to win in any economic environment: muddled corporate strategic plans are always evident, bubbles of hope exist even when the market is undervalued, villains are always somewhere nearby. Short selling is a game of wits, with the odds in favor of the analysts who do hard work and think for themselves, who turn jaundiced eyes on what passes for Wall Street wisdom.

Notes

1. Edward M. Miller, "Bounded Efficient Markets: A New Wrinkle to the EMH," *Journal of Portfolio Management* 13 (Summer 1987):4.

2. Charles P. Jones, Richard J. Rendleman, Jr., and Henry A. Latane, "Stock Returns and SUEs during the 1970s," *Journal of Portfolio Management* 10 (Winter 1984):18.

3. Robert L. Hagin, "The Subtle Risk of High Expected Growth— How to Avoid Torpedo Stocks," Kidder Peabody & Co., Incorporated Research, 30 March 1984, 1.

4. Colin Camerer, "Bubbles and Fads in Asset Prices," *Journal of Economic Surveys,* 3 (1989): 3.

5. Sy Jacobs quoted in Eric Berg, "Risks for the Analysts Who Dare to Say Sell," *New York Times,* 15 May 1990, C1.

6. Charles D. Ellis, "The Loser's Game," *Classics: An Investor's Anthology,* ed. Charles D. Ellis (Homewood, Ill.: Dow Jones-Irwin, 1989), 535.

2

Short Sellers

Professional short sellers usually have a zestfully unbiased attitude toward men and affairs. They are often men of biting humor. After all, their stock in trade is an ironic transubstantiation of values—a satiric commentary on the standards of men.

—Dana L. Thomas

Historically, significant money has been made selling short, but nobody talks about it much. In the last twenty years, hedge funds (limited partnerships composed of accredited investors that have few restrictions on strategy or investment instruments) have consistently used short sales to augment returns. Robert Wilson, whom John Train profiles in *The Money Masters,* is the acknowledged grandfather of the short selling hedge fund managers. Other great fund managers—George Soros, Michael Steinhardt, and Julian Robertson—are as comfortable with either side of the market as an ambidextrous person.

Hedge Funds and Investment Advisors

Among the hedge funds and investment advisors who sell short as well as buy equity positions, three types of strategies emerge: making sector bets (for example, selling banks exposed to real estate when real estate is expected to drop), playing tag-a-long, doing extensive stock analysis on both longs and shorts.

Macroeconomic Bets: Michael Aronstein of Comstock Partners

When a fund or manager bases investment policy on a top-down approach, broad stock bets mirror the impact of the economic environment on specific industries. The managers project macro-economic variables like interest rates and currency and pick stocks to reflect those scenarios.

Comstock Partners, Inc., practices an investment strategy in which macro factors dictate a subset of complementary companies to buy or sell. Comstock's short selling policy is a reflection of their general philosophy. Michael Aronstein says, "Generally, we have a strong feeling about certain comprehensive forces at work in the market. We look at companies, countries and industries that have the most to lose."[1]

He feels that the free and easy credit policies of the 1980s will affect a large variety of stocks in the 1990s, so Comstock has shorted baskets of financial stocks and shopping center developers as well as junk bonds. Comstock also uses fundamental company analysis to supplement the macro strategy, but Aronstein notes that when the evidence is compelling on a macro level, it's hardly necessary to analyze individual properties for numerical evidence.

Although there's never a shortage of "bad people, with bad ideas and bad intentions," Comstock insists that individual stock short sales fit with their economic consensus as well. First Executive and Integrated Resources are examples of well-rounded short sales in this category.

Follow the Leader

Tag-a-long, or follow the leader, is a popular investing technique on the short side as well as the long. It is easier for a hedge fund manager than for an individual because the individuals join the tag line at the back, just as the first players are exiting. The big funds that hedge with shorts are recipients of a level of information to which most people are not privy. Because they have high commission dollars to spend, portfolio managers are screened from idiot analysts by intelligent and savvy institutional brokers who relay information from the best analysts at their firms, as well as Street gossip from other institutional clients. The broker can tell the fund managers which analysts are reliable and can provide nuances of relevant information. Analysts have been continually restricted from negative public comments on companies they follow by their own firms and by the companies themselves. A good institutional broker can relay additional, unpublished, subjective information to the manager. So the fund managers can play in the short market without the huge level of financial analysis that the short fund managers execute. They scan the short interest tables in the *Wall Street Journal* and then gather information quickly through reliable equity brokers, the First Call system (the Electronic network for delivery of brokerage reports and daily comments), and colleagues. Tag-a-long players aggravate fundamental short sellers no end: stocks become more volatile, hard to borrow, buffeted by heavy-handed traders eager to get involved. No one will admit to being a tag-a-long player.

Fundamental Analysis

Julian Robertson of Tiger Funds

Detailed company analysis is practiced by most of the top performing hedge funds. Julian Robertson of Tiger Funds has been shorting stocks for thirty years. He uses the same fundamental approach to the short side as to the long—prodigious research, a bottom-up analytical methodology, and a long-term time horizon. The generic drug stocks are an example of his thought process. The public perceived that the stocks were enormous growth vehicles and moved the prices up to earnings multiples of thirty or forty times and ten times sales and book value. In reality, the companies had no franchise, no sales force, and produced commodity products. The product pricing and concomitant gross margins couldn't support the stock valuations with the built-in euphoria for earnings increases.

Robertson feels valuation bets on price alone make bad short sales: there must be either a fundamental change in the outlook for the company or a major misconception by the stock-buying public. He is known for his ability to match a long position in a good company with a short position in a deteriorating one—short Texas Air, long American Airlines, for example; he is equally adept at unhedged industry stock selection bets—long United, short Zenith Labs. Since he declines to predict the market, his funds have always been short with no specific weighting or maximum percentage allocation.[2]

Alex Porter of Porter, Felleman

Alex Porter at Porter, Felleman is another hedge fund manager who has been shorting stocks for several decades. He shorts to reduce the risk in the overall portfolio, as an insurance policy against a protracted decline. The trick, he says, is to be short the stocks you can stay short without pain or expense, particularly the stocks where financial legerdemain denotes something is seriously wrong. His analytical work is company-based; therefore his shorts are predominantly companies where management doesn't own much stock, where management is not realistic and forthright about their business, and where the company itself is leveraged or has a fatal balance sheet flaw. Porter also feels that the long side of the market is more aggressive and persistent about hyping stocks than the short side and that the lemming-like agreement on Wall Street is greater on the rise than on the fall of a stock price.[3]

Joe DiMenna of Zweig Funds

Joe DiMenna, general partner and portfolio manager of the Zweig Group of Funds, is another experienced fundamental player on both the short and the long side. Total short exposure at Zweig is dictated by two variables: the number of attractive short sale candidates their research uncovers and the net exposure to the market which their battery of indicators suggests (monetary policy, supply and demand of stocks, etc.). Fundamental analysis accounts for at least 75 percent of the decision.

DiMenna shorts five types of situations: frauds, earnings

disappointments, hyped stocks where he can shoot holes in Wall Street's consensus expectations, industry themes where macro forces are negative, and deteriorating balance sheets. He reassesses short positions continually and tries to determine the catalyst that will cause a stock to fall before he shorts. He generally won't short stocks with strong relative strength and earnings momentum solely on the basis of overvaluation. Typically, he waits for these stocks to break before getting involved. He avoids short candidates where the field is crowded unless the company is terminal.[4]

Short Sellers—The Alter Ego of Wall Street

In the last seven years, several funds have been founded that specialize in short selling. The Feshbach Brothers of California and one shy curmudgeon called McBear were the first two managers dedicated to short selling in 1981 and 1983, then Jim Chanos in 1985, followed by a covey of others in late 1988–89. The dedicated short sellers were different in two respects. First, their performance belied common wisdom—they were up in up markets, as well as up in down markets (see table 2.1). Second, their analytical methods were the logical extension of the hedge fund managers who did thorough fundamental work, not main line Wall Street–based earnings work or even quick turn Wall Street traders.

Short sellers are odd people. Most of them are ambitious, driven, antisocial, and singleminded; as individuals, they're least likely to own Rolex watches or a Presidential springer spaniel or other symbolic trappings of success and most likely to have a wry, slightly twisted sense of humor. As a group, they like to disagree and they like to win against big odds. Typically, they have an axe to grind, a chip on a shoulder. As in the general population, some of them are cretins and some aren't, but they are all smarter (most of them, in fact, are intellectual snobs) and more independent. Contrary to popular wisdom, they don't band together and bash stocks senseless. They normally are secretive and slightly paranoid. And they are frequently irreverent in their regard for business leaders and icons of Wall Street.

The Feshbachs: Stock Patrol on NASDAQ

The most famous short sellers are the Feshbach Brothers—Kurt, twins Joe and Matt, and non-Feshbach, Tom Barton. Feshbach Brothers, founded in 1982, was the first group formed to concentrate on short selling. They currently manage more money by a significant factor than any competitor—$600 million at last count, individual, institutional, and pension fund money. They made their mark early as small cap, stock police with a specialty in investigative frauds.

The Feshbachs look for terminal shorts with four characteristics:

- overvalued stock prices by at least two times Feshbach perceived valuation;
- a fundamental problem at the company;
- a weak financial condition—working capital problems or high long-term debt, for example; and
- weak or crooked management.

The Brothers perceive themselves as hype detectors serving an important watchdog function for the public. They enjoy the chase and the challenge of short selling and the camaraderie of being four against the world. Conversely, they also consistently

TABLE 2.1

Short Seller Investment Results

Year	DJI	S&P	Feshbachs	McBear	Chanos
1985	+33.62%	+31.6%	+43.50%[a]	−4.81%	−1.9%[b]
1986	+27.25%	+18.6%	+62.38%	+19.9 %	+35.0%
1987	+5.55%	+5.1%	+59.08%	+32.50%	+26.7%
1988	+16.15%	+16.6%	+21.77%	−6.45%	+14.9%
1989	+32.20%	+31.7%	+19.92%	+28.90%	+30.9%

[a]From 2/15/85 to 12/31/85
[b]From 10/1/85 to 12/31/85 only.

reap the wrath of bear baiters like the *OTC Review*'s editor, Bob Flaherty.

Their first short was Universal Energy, a stock the Feshbachs thought was manipulated by an insider/owner that crashed quickly and created a model for subsequent ideas. The Feshbachs' keystone is intense work and sometimes, informational overkill. They start with fundamental methods of analysis and overlay that process with information gathering from a wide range of sources.

They don't short a stock unless they expect it to decline in price by 50 percent, because they believe that the risk of short selling is too great for marginal plays. "We short stocks where the negatives so overwhelm the positives that, over time, the market can't just shrug off the bad news—eventually the stock price will reflect it," Joe says.

"Everybody has the same balance sheet and income statement that we do. The only thing we're looking for in an income statement or balance sheet is a story that appears to defy basic economic laws—a company that is spending more than it's making, for example. Those kinds of things are obvious, not subtle points at all," Feshbach continued. Kirschner Medical is an example of this principle. Any analyst could figure out that the company had over four hundred days of inventory, but the Feshbachs developed sources that said Kirschner had over $10 million in obsolete inventory. Overkill, perhaps, but the Feshbachs feel that detailed masses of information are part of their success. "The reason we put so much emphasis on phone calls to competitors, suppliers, and customers is that's where we get our edge—in discovering what drives the numbers. Everybody knows what the numbers are on a historical basis. If they don't, they're either illiterate or just lazy. Sometimes, they misinterpret them."

ZZZZ Best (chapter 3) was their most publicized short, but Circle K is representative of their current work. When a broker from Boston called the Feshbachs with Circle K, they hired an industry consultant to tell them how much the convenience store chain was worth per store. He came back with a number that precluded a short sale. Later, the consultant called to lower his evaluation because he had found that the sale/leasebacks of stores meant that Circle K didn't really have much to sell. He also discovered that many top people were leaving. The stock was still around $14 a share, so the Feshbachs went to work.

What they found was a highly leveraged company with ugly operating fundamentals, a rising off-balance-sheet liability, and a declining industry. The balance sheet had $1 billion in debt, half in junk bonds, half in bank debt. All the assets had been sold to the company's largest shareholder, Carl Lindner. Same-store sales were declining, and operating income was no longer covering interest.

They also found that Circle K had understated the liability for gas tank remediation. Ex-employees told them that Circle K bought locations sight unseen with no testing. So not only were the locations old and expensive to fix, but the transferred title meant that the new lender assumed the liability.

The Feshbachs developed a network of ex-employees, competitors, and suppliers who confirmed that operationally the company was flailing. First, they found that CEO Karl Eller had developed a relationship with the Steve's Ice Cream owner, Richard Smith; he used Smith as an unpaid consultant to run the company's day-to-day operations. Smith made a crucial mistake: he thought customers were insensitive to price, so he raised prices across the board and attempted to negotiate suppliers' contracts lower in an effort to raise margins to 40 percent. The customers walked and the suppliers told them to buy elsewhere. Same-store sales dropped, margins dropped, and customers were permanently alienated.

One other factor made the stock a great short. The industry trends were changing radically. When existing gas stations rebuilt convenience stores and could sell gas for less than Circle K could buy it, Circle K was in serious trouble. It was a national trend. Simultaneously, grocery stores started staying open 24 hours a day.

So, the company's internal environment and the industry external factors led the Feshbachs to short 1.4 million shares above $10. Then they shorted the convertible when it continued to trade at $70 (because of a 1991 put provision) after the stock trashed to $5. Circle K was institutionally owned and Wall Street covered. They bought in positions for around $1.

Since the Feshbachs have specific target prices, turnover is low.

When they take a position, they typically add to it as more data come in, and they only cover because they made a mistake or because the stock hits the target price—not with a 20 percent decline for a quick profit.

The Feshbachs don't find company visits or Wall Street analysts productive places to gather information. Talks with management are not fruitful: "The company didn't get to be a good short without management's help." On Wall Street: "That's the place to get the bull story, not the bear story. The bias negates their usefulness to us in a lot of incidents."

Although their current staff of fifteen analysts plus assistants and support people has the expertise to cover any industry, some segments have been more lucrative than others. Banks and savings and loans have been money makers for years, not just six months: American Continental, Commonwealth Savings of Houston, Sunrise Savings and Loan, Sun State Savings and Loan, and Bank of New England are companies that the Feshbachs have made good money shorting.

The buyout frenzy of the 1980s provided massive opportunities for the Feshbachs. Their stock analysis is similar to what investment bankers use to determine private market value, so their methodology kept them out of trouble. The Sony acquisition of Guber Peters caught them short, but Joe Feshbach likens that to a natural disaster—there was no way to anticipate the buyout at those ludicrous prices.

The proportion of NASDAQ stocks in their portfolio has changed for two reasons in the last year. First, small caps have been listing on the American Exchange and moving out of the over-the-counter market. Second, high debt is predominantly a feature of the big cap market.

The most difficult part of short selling is timing, and the Feshbachs don't presume to have an answer to what determines the optimal trigger point. Joe uses the example of CopyTele: what is an appropriate indicator that the stock is finally ready to give up the ghost? (CopyTele has no earnings or revenues and only the promise of a product.) They believe that to sell short you have to be certain that you see an important factor that other people don't see. "But," Feshbach continues, "it's not enough to see it if it doesn't make a difference in the way the company is ultimately valued. You have to see those mechanics begin to impact the income statement and the balance sheet." You have to visualize how the change evolves through the health of the company. The Feshbachs feel that talking to competitors and suppliers reveals the climate and how long it might continue and gives insight into possible triggers. Joe Feshbach says, "You look for something that is obviously misperceived, obviously important, and obviously detrimental. At that point, if you're comfortable that it's already started to happen, that it's not discounted in the price, and that it is substantial enough to get you to the price target, then you ought to get started." He cautions that the first position isn't necessarily the biggest because stocks go up and you want to be able to average up. But the time you really want to add to the position is when those factors become overwhelmingly apparent and the stock is still up.

As the often-accused pundit of the supposed group of stock-bashing bears, Joe Feshbach says that all investors share information and develop research relationships. He's not aware of a single incident where short sellers got together and "agreed to pummel a stock. We like to hear new ideas but we don't view it as any different from a portfolio managers' dinner in New York where six guys get together and throw out their best ideas. If that's illegal, there won't be room in the jails for any criminals."

The Feshbachs feel the most important characteristic in a short seller is the ability to remain analytical when other people panic. They credit Dianetics for contributing that characteristic or set of responses to their management style. Joe Feshbach comments,

> We don't flip out when a stock goes up. The whole purpose of Dianetics is to eliminate reactive patterns whereby a person operates on a stimulus response basis and isn't being analytical. That's the starting point. Money managers make the same mistake over and over—that's part of whole reactive pattern. We try to get to the bottom of errors we make. We've developed a check list of good short criteria and a training manual based on successful and unsuccessful actions. We have learned by doing, and not everybody just by doing it, learns it. We attribute that to Dianetics.[5]

The Oldest Living Short Fund Manager

"McBear" launched his fund in mid-1983 at age 40. After a Stanford MBA, he worked as a special situations analyst, as a director of research, and managed money for wealthy individuals. As the oldest short manager, he jokes that his age gives him greater experience with the credit cycle. Consequently, his signature short ideas are based on extensive credit work. His formative short was Caterpillar Tractor in 1984. The financials read like a disaster. Cat's main customers were the Saudis, oil drillers, national mining companies, and the notorious South American countries—once flush, they were now all broke or cash short. In spite of the dismal reality, Street analysts were estimating $4.00 in earnings per share. The stock was widely owned and frequently featured by strategic thinkers as a portfolio necessity. The Street missed by $9 a share that year—Cat lost $5. McBear identified kindred plays and shorted drillers, mining companies, machine tools, and all the bets connected to the sinking Cat. The Street was predicting a cyclical turnaround. "Understanding Cat gave me the insight into understanding the structural problems at that time in the economy. Inflation-driven industries had huge capacity and the Street felt the problems were cyclical, not structural, and expected a turn in late 1983 or '84 but the economy missed a cycle."

In what he believes to be the current turn in the credit cycle, he has been particularly adept with the real estate, bank, and LBO phenomena. McBear believes the economy is in a protracted credit contraction. He was first to short the New England banks and, if a company levered up and made a large acquisition, he's looked at it. The stub stocks Harcourt Brace Jovanovich; U.S. Gypsum; and Carter, Hawley, Hale—deals that didn't work from day one, he says—are large portfolio shorts for his fund.

Ames is a good example of the current work of McBear and his associate. They first got interested in Ames when the company bought Zayre in October 1988 and added substantial debt to the balance sheet. Since the purchase was made below book and Zayre had ugly margins, Wall Street simply added the revenues

together, applied peak margins from Ames to the result, subtracted the new interest, and came up with $1.40 to $1.45 in
earnings. When Ames bought Zayre, sales were $2.1 billion with
operating margins of 2.2 percent in fiscal 1987. The balance sheet
was clean. Zayre's sales were $2.9 billion and the purchase price
was $778 million. The discount retail environment was under
pressure with Walmart's aggressive pricing and expansion plans,
so McBear felt the margin history was the key to the company's
health. "You get a window on a stock before the facts are announced when analysts can say anything they want and they do.
The institutions like to listen and believe because they've been
in a bull market so long. An Ames analyst could say Zayre will
work out, but sooner or later came the time of reckoning." So
they started tracking the margins through time, quarter by quarter from 1985—the peak year at 4.8 percent. Wall Street was
using 3 percent and implying that number was conservative. "It
was unbridled optimism that peaked on the convertible deal in
October 1989 with the stock at $18," says his associate.

The 1989 quarters supported their thesis that the debt wasn't
serviceable with the company's margin history. The company lost
money every quarter and showed negative comps at Zayre. The
Street, with the exception of the Goldman, Sachs analyst, continued cheerful about the operating and financial leverage. In
addition, Ames immediately had heavy cash drain from refur-
bishing seedy Zayre stores, closing overlap stores, cleaning up
inventories. All the depreciation and amortization appeared to be
going to necessary capital expenditures, throwing off Street analysts' cash flow projections. Zayre customers were also accus-
tomed to heavy promotions and Ames's policy was consistent
low prices, so Zayre's regular revenue base disappeared. Murphy's Law worked in the bears' favor. The expected Christmas
1989 sales never materialized, vendors weren't paid after Christmas, and the company filed for bankruptcy in April 1989, a victim
of acquisition mania.

McBear understood the effect of the acquisition of Zayre and
the potential impact on the equity of Ames, together with the
dynamics of the problem and how the problem develops. "A
problem takes more than three months to solve that took five
years to evolve."

McBear keeps a low profile relative to his peers because he gathers important information by visiting companies. He feels Wall Street analysts are a poor conduit for company insights because they screen out relevant facts. A good listener asking thoughtful questions can learn critical facts about business trends. He uses the example of Cross and Trecker: the company was leading analysts to a $1.20 earnings estimate at one point, while the Street still estimated $4.00.

He is scorching in his contempt for Wall Street investment bankers who have shepherded their clients into breakneck acquisitions. He feels that part of the satisfaction of short selling is going against Wall Street. Corporate management is rarely the target, unless there's fraud. It's generally Wall Street that has engineered the ascent of the stock. "Many corporate managers are odd lotters," he comments. "They are under relentless pressure from investment bankers and they are herded into mistakes. They do things when everybody else does them, like institutional money managers. If it's in vogue to buy oil companies or to make acquisitions, they all do it." He thinks Wall Street research has always been bad, but it's worse now because investment bankers are controlling the process. He implies that investment bankers have about the same value to society as drug dealers. Last summer he thinks it was clear when the credit cycle peaked because investment bankers could say anything and the analysts would complacently repeat it. Back in 1983, concept stocks, high-multiple, high-growth stocks were hot and you could, to some degree, understand the rationale of stock valuation even if you didn't agree with it. "But the summer of '89 wasn't a concept market—the numbers just didn't add up. Investment bankers said one plus one equals three and the prospectus put it in writing. It was the end of a cycle with extreme exaggeration, a truly speculative market."

The environment of Wall Street creates enough slippage for short sellers to make money. "The market is inefficient," he says, "because there is a bias to buy. There are six professional short sellers and twelve thousand investment advisors, a hundred buy reports for every sell, and, therefore, a natural upward bias to stocks. It's particularly true in a bull market. It's always somebody else's money. Like Texas Air, investors lost a lot, so what, it was a bunch of commissions. It creates pain for short sellers in the short run but a lot of opportunity."[6]

Jim Chanos: Financial Puzzle Artist

James S. Chanos of Kynikos Associates, Ltd., made an early showing when he called the Baldwin-United bankruptcy at age 24 when he was an analyst fresh out of Yale at Gilford Securities. He is doomed, as a result, even as he ages to the sobriquet of youth. He moved on to Deutsche Bank Capital Corporation in 1983 to specialize in sale recommendations and overpriced securities. When he left their employment in 1985, he started his own short fund and now manages over $250 million.

Chanos's specialty is solving complex financial puzzles. He shorts large capitalization financial companies with a high probability of bankruptcy. His average holding period is nine months, but his longest holding was Integrated Resources at over five years. The median equity market cap of the stocks in his portfolio is $900 million. He doesn't short frauds with small floats because of size constraints. In contrast to some of his competitors, he has not had a problem with buy-ins because of his use of large cap stocks. Chanos maintains a concentrated portfolio of about thirty stocks with ten positions accounting for more than 50 percent of his portfolio.

Typically, he likes to short stocks with secular problems where he can make a "reasonably strong argument based on the valuation of the business (much like the private market players look for discount to value), that the equity value of the enterprise is $0. When the stock trades to its warrant value, our analysis shifts to the valuation of the warrant. If there's a lot of debt, the warrant value may be nothing or we may cover at $2 or $3."

Chanos does not visit companies and seems to use Wall Street as a corporate emissary or interpreter.

> In a one-time corporate visit, they're not going to tell you anything they're not already telling the street. And if they do, you probably shouldn't be hearing it anyway because it's probably non-public. You can get a very good sense of what the company story is by using First Call and analyzing five years of data. We also attend

some corporate presentations when management comes to town—
one of the advantages of being based in New York. We tend to
focus on the numbers. We're not big on hiring detective agencies
or talking to ex-employees. We think a lot of traditional money
managers tend to get sloppy. It's easy to do. One common short-
coming is to rely on management or Wall Street analysts. When
they both get blindsided, you're left holding the bag. So to that
extent we'd rather not rely.

Analytically, Chanos says he doesn't do anything that's very
different from other managers, but his use of return on invested
capital as a key financial indicator is unique. "Using this, we've
been able to find companies that are not what they appeared to
be." His calculation is earnings before interest and taxes divided
by average total capital, defined as total liabilities plus equity
minus current liabilities plus short-term debt or, to say it another
way, the return on all interest-bearing liabilities plus equity plus
deferred taxes and short-term debt. "That ratio will reveal a lot
of wormy companies and poor businesses. It's a tough number to
screw around with."

Financial companies have been particularly lucrative for
Chanos because of the potential for rampant earnings manipulation, which, he says, attracts its fair share of scoundrels. Chanos
notes that the "leverage inherent in some of these companies is
incredible. When the accounting gets murky, people tend to shy
away from rigorous analysis and rely on management and just
take earnings per share at face value. Therein lies the opportunity."

Chanos's analysis of Baldwin-United illustrates his persistence
with puzzles and his ability to persevere in the face of marked
hostility, both from the company and from peers. Baldwin was
a high flyer with a large Wall Street following in the summer of
1982. Prudential Bache, Prescott Ball, Merrill Lynch, and Smith
Barney all had the stock rated a buy with a euphoric perception
of earnings momentum. Chanos took the time to read the annual
convention statements, understand the tax accounting, and follow a complex trail of affiliated company financial transactions
that convinced him the stock was next to worthless. The stock
went from $20 to $50 with his sell recommendation in place—and
then into bankruptcy for the largest insurance company scandal

of the decade. The Street analysts at the time were concentrating on earnings momentum, Morley Thompson's publicity releases, and the perceived hot market for single-premium deferred annuities. Chanos did painstaking spread sheets on cash flow, never an easy task with subsidiaries moving assets.

The arguments on Baldwin revolved around Wall Street's belief that Thompson's superior strategies could create earnings from his convoluted financial stratagem. He convinced the analysts that his investment plan was newfangled corporate arbitrage, very sophisticated, very complex. The docile crowd of analysts regurgitated the information in buy recommendations and long reports. Everybody loved a winner, shuffling his companies like cards.

In the summer of 1982, part of the Street elation was the MGIC Investment Corporation acquisition. Merrill analyst Carol Neves was cheered by the "continuous source of taxable income" from MGIC, "so that BDW [Baldwin-United] can fully utilize the substantial tax credits being generated by its most successful product, SPDAs [single-premium deferred annuities]."[7] Robert Back at Prescott, Ball and Turben had the stock "rated a very strong long-term purchase . . . at $62 per share, only 4.8x our conservative 1983 estimate."[8]

Chanos wrote his first report in late August 1982. It was a sell recommendation based on the leverage, the cash flow, the quality of earnings, and the potential decline in revenues from rate declines and possible tax legislation. He stated the heretical opinion that Baldwin was losing money on its annuity business and that assets purchased by affiliates from MGIC were a serious liquidity problem for insurance portfolios as well as a rate-of-return problem, since real assets were sold to purchase money-losing real estate. Cash flow, he said, was the real issue here, not reported earnings.

A brouhaha ensued. Chanos was excoriated publicly, threatened privately, and repudiated by management. Buy, said Paul Mackay at Bache, short interest is over one million shares, "creating a unique trading opportunity."[9] Insurance assets can easily cover all SPDA's from current liquid investments, said the company.

Chanos persisted with another report in December 1982 after

the stock had doubled. He pointed to declining fundamentals at MGIC, which would weaken cash flow and use of tax benefits. Then he went over cash flow again, in detail.

In March 1983 Baldwin announced it couldn't pay $900 million in short-term debt and subsequently filed for Chapter 11.

Chanos has continued to mine financial companies and complex financial statements for ideas and has made money from the stock collapses of the Zises of Integrated Resources, Gary Driggs of Western Savings and Loan, Charles Keating of American Continental, Fred Carr of First Executive, Frank Lorenzo of Texas Air, David Maniatis of Sun State Savings and Loan, as well as from Prime Motor Inns, Harcourt Brace Jovanovich, and Valley National.

Commenting on a variety of short selling issues, Chanos laughs about frequent small company criticism that a cabal of sellers exists. He says he talks to the Feshbachs maybe three times a year as friendly rivals. Chanos and the Feshbachs control the two largest pools of capital dedicated to short selling. Any interchange with other sellers is no different from talking to friends about good ideas. He feels the SEC is vigilant about stock price manipulation and would certainly be aggressive about investigating collusion among the short community to drive share prices down. He notes that, because of the "uptick" rule, it is impossible for short selling to cause a listed stock to decline in price. Both NASD and the SEC view short sellers as another good source of information.

He feels the potential pension fund entry into short selling is a looming issue, one that should shake up business and make it tougher. Personally, Chanos prefers dealing with private clients who want to preserve capital, are farsighted, and add to the investment process. Chanos uses his partners' business experience and their contacts as part of the research process. "These people are interested in building wealth versus making a few extra basis points," he surmises.

Chanos thinks he has a good relationship with the Street and that he talks to them more than any other short seller for two reasons: first, he shorts stocks that are covered by the Street, and second, he runs money for the Street, principals at brokerage firms, as well as brokerage firms. He sees international short

selling as the biggest new opportunity. While financial disclosures are semiannual, valuation more than makes up for it because the stocks are conceptually, not analytically, priced.
Chanos thinks that short selling is still in its infancy—akin to the
state of risk arbitrage and leveraged buyouts in the late 1970s.
The proliferation of short funds managed by newsletter writers,
and traditional money managers doesn't bother Chanos over the
long run. "Very few people have the stomach to take a fundamental short position. If a short position goes against most people, their first reaction is to cover, rather than sell more stock."[10]

An Expanding List of Short Sellers

Dedicated short funds continue to spring up in the investment
world. As the ranks grow, it remains to be seen if the returns
falter with the probable growing efficiencies on the short side.
The wizened veterans don't seem too concerned about competition, since they feel opportunities always appear for people pre-
pared to dig.

Notes

1. Interview with Michael Aronstein on 25 June 1990.

2. Interview with Julian Robertson on 2 May 1990.

3. Interview with Alex Porter on 24 April 1990.

4. Interview with Joseph DiMenna on 6 June 1990.

5. Interviews with Joseph Feshbach on 1 and 14 June 1990.

6. Interview with "McBear" on 2 May 1990.

7. Carol P. Neves, "Baldwin United," Merrill Lynch Pierce Fenner &
Smith Securities Research Division, 16 April 1982, 1.

8. Robert W. Back, "Baldwin-United Corporation," Prescott Ball &
Turben, 11 June 1982, 4.

9. Paul A. Mackey, "Baldwin-United Corporation," Bache Halsey
Stuart Shields Incorporated Institutional Research, 25 August 1982, 2.

10. Interview with James S. Chanos on 2 May 1990.

PART 2

CATEGORIES AND EXAMPLES

3

Bubble Stocks

Short sellers look for different things in a sale candidate, as their doppelgangers do on the long side. Everyone would agree, however, that a perfect short is a stock with a large float to allow ease of borrowing and no buy-ins, a high price for maximum return, and no business or assets to keep the risk nominal.

Even a company with no revenues and no assets can produce the appearance of hope and future earnings for an optimist. Many of these are research and development technology or medical products companies with a purported new hot product in the pipeline. Shams are created by stockholders, brokerage houses, or corporate executives who relentlessly push the valuation higher without regard for the underlying financials, inflating the prices beyond expectation of future value. Management, in some cases, may believe in their ephemeral product and the public's evaluation of it or, as in the case of ZZZZ Best, they may be conning the public and the SEC.

Dirty Carpets: ZZZZ Best

The Feshbach Brothers are masters of the bubble company, as evidenced by their detective work on ZZZZ Best—the carpet cleaning company with no revenues. ZZZZ Best, whiz kid Barry Minkow's hot growth company, had a market value of $200 million in the spring of 1987. Business was great for the company, and they announced a contract to clean two large buildings in Sacramento for $8 million. Carpet cleaning competitors told Feshbach analysts that the two largest cleaning contracts to date capped at a price of $3.5 million (the MGM Grand and the Las Vegas Hilton) so the Feshbachs smelled a skunk, started looking, and shorted aggressively. The stock price rallied despite rumors of false billing in late May. By July ZZZZ Best was bankrupt, and in March 1989 the amazing Minkow was sentenced to twenty-five years for fraud: no contracts, no revenues, and a money laundering scheme. The Feshbachs, meanwhile, went home happy and richer.

Some professional short sellers feel this segment of the market is the natural preserve of individual investors. Since the stocks are frequently hard to borrow in sizes large enough to make a meaningful addition to portfolio returns, the stocks take more work in fighting for reliable information than they provide in returns. Individual investors, however, can show dramatic returns since they can borrow enough stock to impact a diversified short portfolio. The stocks are often inefficiently, even absurdly, overpriced.

Harrier: It Just Didn't Add Up

Harrier, Inc., a new medical products company, is a good illustration of how short analysis logically proceeds and what short sellers look for in their framework of inverted value analysis. At first look in July 1988, the company, headquartered in Utah, appeared to be pure puffery—no assets, no sales, no products, and a $30 (presplit) stock price. With 2,808,000 shares outstanding, that represents a market capitalization (or public value) of $84 million.

The March 31, 1988 10Q provided the balance sheet, income statement, and "unaudited condensed statements of changes in financial position," as it was called, in tables 3.1–3.3. The top of the balance sheet provided some insight into the company—the date was wrong: instead of 1988, the top of the column read 1987. Apparently, the SEC-filed document was produced so haphazardly that the dates weren't proofread. The next point of note,

FIGURE 3.1

Harrier, Inc.

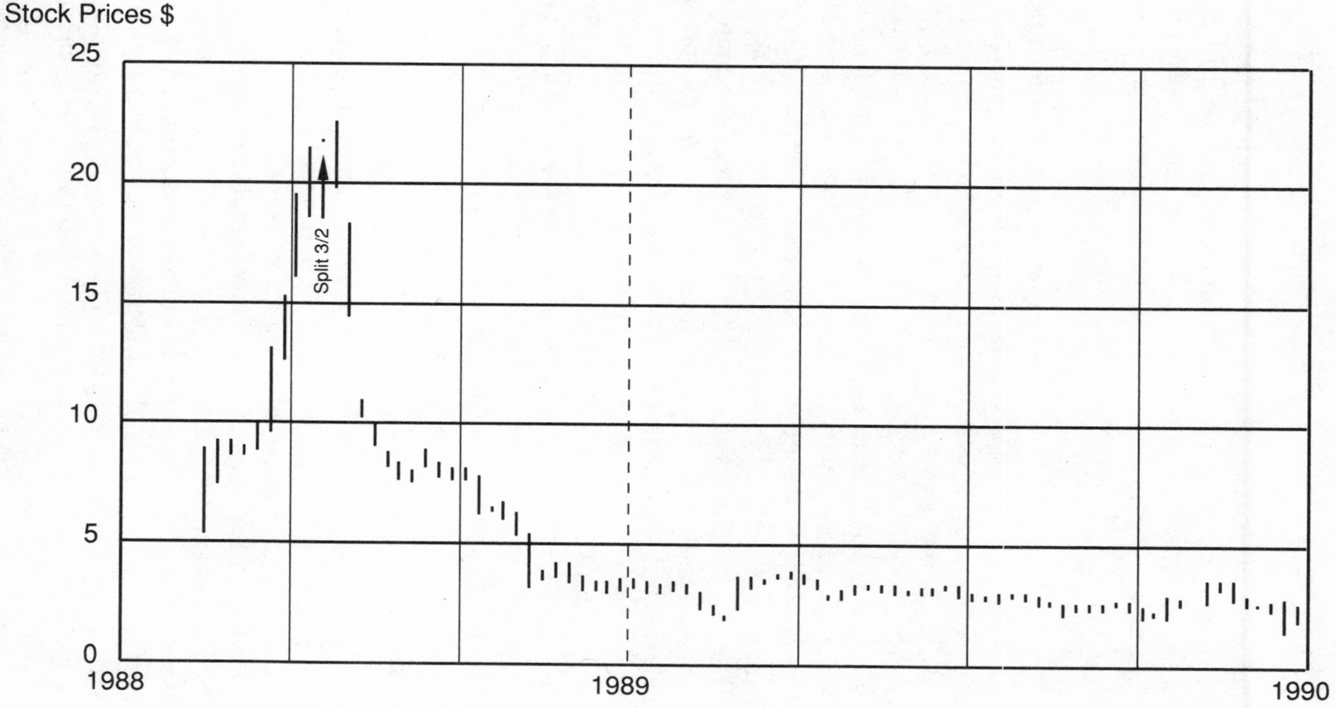

Stock Prices $

again from the balance sheet, was that Harrier had assets of about $2.5 million on March 31, 1988, up from $307,000 in June 1987, and stockholders' equity of $1,672,457. In other words, the market valued $1.7 million of book value at $84 million. The opportunity existed, therefore, to sell $1.7 million worth of goods for $84 million.

The market, then, put the present value of Harrier's potential stream of revenues in excess of $82 million. The next step for a short seller was to look at the income statement and see if the seeds of exponential earnings growth were visible in high-flying Harrier. The income statement (table 3.2) showed some revenues, with high proportionate expenses for general and administrative and for consulting and management and low research and development costs. Someone was getting paid, although it wasn't the stockholders.

The big clue in the financials of Harrier was the Statement of Changes (table 3.3). The numbers literally didn't add up. I've never before seen financials where the numbers didn't add up. The total of working capital provided should have been ($27,379) not $2,025,121 in 1988 (just a small slip, about equal to their asset size) and $1,746,846, not $194,346 in 1987. Everybody had computers and spread sheets and calculators and accountants and bookkeepers, even in 1988, and the numbers still didn't add up.

Prospectus: Going Public

The next step after the verification of dramatic overvaluation is to backtrack through the past financial documents for evidence that supports or contradicts the conclusion.

Starting at the beginning, a careful reading of the initial public offering prospectus gave a history as compelling as a Charles Dickens subplot. The SEC-required document is a favorite of short sellers for the detail and depth of company information; its existence in cases like Harrier is testimony to stockholders' preference for being led to slaughter blindfolded and smiling with misplaced hope.

Harrier was founded October 8, 1985, when a group of people assembled by Merlin Fish paid $21,500 for stock in a blind pool. The original owners were a former California client of Merlin, a

TABLE 3.1

Harrier's Balance Sheet

	March 31, 1987	June 30, 1987
Assets		
CURRENT ASSETS:		
Cash	$ 550,510	$ 104,758
Accounts receivable	359,325	—
Inventory	490,960	29,598
Interest receivable	9,221	—
Investment in marketable securities	104,095	—
Total Current Assets	1,514,111	134,356
EQUIPMENT, net	23,407	—
OTHER ASSETS:		
Product rights and technology, net	397,330	171,618
Other assets, net	14,311	1,918
Notes receivable from related parties	35,000	—
Receivable from related party	10,000	—
Certificate of deposit	500,000	—
Total Other Assets	956,641	173,536
	$2,494,159	$307,892
Liabilities and Stockholders' Equity		
CURRENT LIABILITIES:		
Accounts payable and accrued expenses	$321,702	$15,451
OTHER LIABILITIES:		
Note payable	500,000	—
Total Liabilities	821,702	15,451
STOCKHOLDERS' EQUITY:		
Preferred stock	—	—
Common stock	2,798	2,109
Capital in excess of par value	2,669,839	721,963
Accumulated earnings (deficit)	(1,000,180)	(431,631)
Total Stockholders' Equity	1,672,457	292,441
	$2,494,159	$307,892

The balance sheet at June 30, 1987 has been taken from the audited financial statements at that date, and condensed. Source: Harrier, Inc., Form 10Q (Alpine, Utah: Harrier, Inc, 31 March 1988).

TABLE 3.2

Harrier's Income Statement

	For the Three Months Ended March 31		For the Nine Months Ended March 31	
	1988	1987	1988	1987
SALES	$ 489,210	$ —	$ 540,797	$ —
COST OF SALES	352,865	—	380,899	—
GROSS PROFIT	136,345	—	159,898	—
EXPENSES:				
Professional fees	15,953	767	41,277	31,536
General and administrative	125,635	4,251	310,636	9,690
Amortization and depreciation	12,324	72	29,170	216
Consulting and management compensation	173,104	107,921	541,288	144,556
Marketing	2,051	—	50,613	125,000
Research and development	48,731	—	48,731	—
Total Expenses	377,798	113,011	1,021,715	310,998
INCOME (LOSS) FROM OPERATIONS	(241,453)	(113,011)	(861,817)	(310,998)
OTHER INCOME (EXPENSE):				
Interest income	9,229	36	25,517	4,092
Interest expense	(13,096)	—	(13,132)	—
Gain on sale	—	—	15,523	—
Sale of license rights	250,000	—	250,000	—
Consulting income	15,360	—	15,360	—
Total Other Income (Expense)	261,493	36	293,268	4,092
INCOME (LOSS) BEFORE TAX PROVISION	20,040	(112,975)	(568,549)	(306,906)
PROVISION FOR TAXES (BENEFIT)	—	—	—	(42)
NET INCOME (LOSS)	$20,040	$(112,975)	$(568,549)	$(306,864)
EARNINGS (LOSS) PER SHARE	$. 01	$ (.06)	$ (.22)	$ (.26)

Source: Harrier, Inc., Form 10Q, 31 March 1987.

TABLE 3.3

Harrier's Statements of Changes in Financial Position

	For the Nine Months Ended March 31	
	1988	1987
WORKING CAPITAL PROVIDED:		
Working Capital Provided (Used) by Operations	$(539,379)	$(306,648)
Issuance of common stock for cash 500,000		2,052,500
Issuance of common stock for cash in redemption of warrants	12,000	—
Issuance of common stock for assets	—	994
Issuance of long term debt	500,000	—
Total Working Capital Provided	2,025,121	194,346
WORKING CAPITAL USED:		
Stock offering costs	115,935	3,737
Organization costs	—	—
Product technology costs	262,343	182,244
Patent	3,225	—
Note receivable from related parties	35,000	—
Addition to equipment	25,114	—
Receivable from related party	10,000	—
Addition to long term certificate of deposit	500,000	—
Total Working Capital Used	951,617	185,981
TOTAL INCREASE IN WORKING CAPITAL	$1,073,504	$8,365

Source: Harrier, Inc., Form 10Q, 31 March 1988.

real estate developer from Charleston, S.C., Merlin's brother, who owned a construction company in South Carolina, and a furniture company manufacturer's representative from Utah, who loaned them 200 square feet, apparently part of his home, for an office.

In May 1986 Harrier had its first public offering, 25 million shares at $.01. The prospectus was lurid in actual prospect; no where could one find the promise of the subsequent lofty price level. The proceeds were for "unspecified use."[1] No business had been identified for investment, and the management didn't have the time, resources, or experience for analysis of such an opportunity. Of the proceeds, $170,000 would be available to invest. The funds probably wouldn't be adequate and the competition was hot, but the company slipped in under the February 1986 Utah Securities Division Rule 11.1, which prohibited "blank check" offerings—public offerings of companies that existed without a stated business purpose. The new stockholders provided 92.08 percent of the capital for 69.93 percent of the stock. And, by the way, the underwriters got 19 percent of the new funds.

A New Life with New Products

In December 1986, on its way to respectability, Harrier had a 50-to-1 reverse split. In February 1987 new management and significant stockholders came on board to propel the shell to unprecedented heights. Two executives from a Swiss X ray manufacturer tried to merge their company, Kehrli AG, into Harrier. Both companies were disappointed to find that the Swiss company's financials wouldn't meet reporting standards in the United States.

As a last resort, Jurg Kehrli and Armando Ulrich, the Swiss executives, exchanged a package (including rights to market X ray equipment, one of each model of the X ray equipment, rights to the Bioptron Lamp, and rights to a Hungarian therapy process) for 994,000 shares of stock, or 58.3 percent of the shares outstanding. Harrier was satisfied that it had acquired valuable marketing rights, important technologies, and the skills of two pros to assist the company with still-undetermined products and strategies for the blind pool.

The Swiss brought three new technologies. The first was a Hungarian polarized light that appeared to have an effect on cell membranes. The result was the biostimulating effects of the Bioptron Lamp, which was supposed to improve the healing process in burns, other surface wounds, and, perhaps, wrinkles. It looked like a hand-held hair dryer and "stimulated cell renewal without stressing the skin or body."[2]

The second technology was biodynamics, acquired from the late Dr. Walter Ott of Zurich. Biodynamics had many potential new product applications, including supersaturated water (ten times the oxygen in the water) and Diesel Cleaner.

Thymus compounds, "proprietary polypeptide fractions that serve to stimulate immunotherapeutic responses in the body to fight certain types of cancer" would be the most expensive of the three technologies to develop, requiring large amounts of capital, presumably from joint ventures with pharmaceutical companies.[3]

After spending an additional $125,000 on the marketing plan for the Kehrli X ray equipment, Harrier dropped the product, and Kehrli returned $17,000 to the company. Kehrli and Ulrich stayed on, without their equipment but apparently with their wallets.

The June 30, 1987 10K was a wonderful document. It revealed more specifics about the new product rights and processes. The 10K on biodynamics states, "This theory is based on discoveries in the use of centripetal force generated by eccentric motion to focus energy on an axis and to use that energy to accomplish certain phenomenon [*sic*] that may have commercial applications."[4] Huh? That includes biodynamic water, whatever that is.

Kehrli and Ulrich consulted with Harrier for $27,000 a month and received annual rent of $5,000 for Swiss premises, for a total of $329,000 a year. No free rent here. The price of the stock meanwhile continued to sprint ahead, reaching a high of $7 in the June quarter, $15 by September. It was a race (soon to be resolved) to see whether insiders made more on fees than stockholders on price appreciation.

By August 1987 Harrier had focused on the Bioptron Lamp, signed their first agreement, and sold 400,000 additional shares at $2.50 a share to a Liberian corporation. The first lamp agreement was announced with a flourish soon to be repeated many times: a Swiss corporation had the exclusive right to distribution in three countries and signed an initial purchase order of $2.4 million the first year, $2.8 million and $800,000 per quarter thereafter.

In September 1987 Harrier sold 200,000 shares at $3 a share to a new Swiss investor and by the March 31, 1988 10Q the shares outstanding were up to 2,808,000. March also brought another big contract from the Scandinavian countries, a minimum purchase of $6 million over three years with a minimum of $5 million in 1988.

Revenues for 1987 should have been a minimum of $2.4 million, with $7.8 million in 1988, if the previously announced contracts were added up.

A Little Help for Our Friends

Now that Harrier was a successful high-priced corporation, it began to help less fortunate friends. The March 1988 10Q notes that Harrier not only paid $448,000 to officers and directors, but also loaned $35,000 to several clients of its investment banker and bought $10,000 worth of stock in another investment banker client.

The most rousing recommendation of Harrier came from its investment banker, Merlin Group, in a 32-page report. The company's mission statement sets the tone: "the goal is to produce quality environmental and health care products which will meet the challenges of our modern times to reduce human suffering from disease and pollution."[5] The Bioptron Lamp is touted first for its potential worldwide market of 525 million users for ulcers, burns, and tension headaches and in sports medicine, plastic surgery, dermatology, neurology, gynecology, and dentistry—clearly, the most versatile medical discovery since aspirin. The Supersaturated Oxygen-Water and the Diesel Cleaner are also discussed in some detail as products with a wide range of applications—to save the world, a reader would surmise.

Partial Demise

On August 8, 1988 Alan Abelson at *Barron's* noticed Harrier and commented that even at $15, down from its post-split high of $22 in July, it seemed a mite overvalued. He noted the alliances with corporate artists—Henry Lorin, the "Abracadabra Man," for one. He also cast some doubt on the two top products, the Bioptron Lamp and the Diesel Cleaner. He suggested that the light from the lamp was the wrong end of the color spectrum to cure burns. The Diesel Cleaner, he said, would require the addition of another tank on a truck, the size of the existing fuel tank.[6]

The next day Harrier PR people came out with their best press release to date: "Harrier in Japan distribution pact."[7] Riding the wave of Japanomania, the company signed a $7.5 million contract. The stock failed to move with its usual bouncy step, but nobody who analyzes stocks expects press releases to be informational or relevant to actual earnings.

Simultaneously, Harrier gave the Kehrli-Ulrich team 600,000 more shares for rights to two new compounds, which supposedly strengthen the immune system and shrink tumors. The company also sold 157,500 shares for $1,050,000 to European interests.

The stock traded from $15 to $10 in the wake of Abelson's column; the insiders continued to sell.

In October 1988, prior to the release of the September 10Q, the price was still around $7. Harrier had continued to build its stock portfolio and now showed marketable securities of $555,000 out of total assets of $5.3 million. Accounts receivable were the other pillar of the balance sheet with $1.8 million, up from $42,000 in June. The stock headed resolutely for $3, where it rested for the next great marketing push of the Harrier team.

A quick romp through the 1989 10K a year later suggested sales were somewhat less than expected in the prior cheerful press releases: fiscal 1988 revenues were $582,825; those for 1989 were $2.164 million. Previously announced contracts had totaled $7.8 million for sales anticipated in 1988. Some of the marketing agreements had been terminated because of their failure to perform. The Bioptron Lamp was now targeted for treatment of acne, rather than burns, and perhaps for biological sewage purification. The SEC has requested information from the company's accountants for a "matter under inquiry," and the stock still trades around $3.

The main lesson of the Harrier frolic is: Always take a company seriously, even if its financials are kneeslapping, hootpromoting drivel.

Second Derivation: Medstone

One step removed from companies with no product are companies with a product accompanied by noteworthy claims by the investment banker or the company for proposed market share. Medstone International, Inc., a lithotripsy company that makes machines for non-invasive disintegration of kidney stones, is such an entity. The prospectus of Medstone, again, is the essential document. It alerted potential investors, or disinvestors, to critical product variables:

- the product wasn't patented;
- the competition was large and international with a significant installed base;
- the gross profit margins were 60 percent, maybe. Revenues and expenses weren't really matched in previous years, management said.

The prospectus stated the usual caveats: limited operating history, deficit net worth, working capital deficit, dependence on two key executives, nonrepresentative earnings history, one-product company. Some of the money from the offering ($1.4 million out of $11.3 million) went to senior officers to pay for prior services (stock wasn't enough?).

The stock was priced at $13 in early summer 1988 and traded immediately to $19 and on to the high twenties, a perfect "doctor stock"—doctors are reputed to be the marginal suckers on new drug or medical products companies for aggressive retail brokers. They promote the stocks to peers and friends and enthusiastically inflate the market value, especially if the product is remotely associated with their area of expertise. Medstone peaked from this ebullient assault around $42 in August.

The prospectus also mentioned, as it always does, that insiders couldn't sell for six months from the June 2, 1988 offering date without approval by the investment bankers. When key insider, founder, and president Richard Penfil sold 100,000 shares of stock in September before the deadline lapsed in December and Errol Payne, chairman of the board and founder, resigned, Medstone was a potential short. Jump-the-gun insiders should be more aware of product sales potential than Wall Street, after all.

Competitors Provide Comparison

Another company in a similar business (urology laser systems), Candela Laser Corporation, attempted to sell a secondary issue in October, after the Medstone initial public offering (IPO). Comparing prospectuses and business plans is a useful exercise with similar companies, particularly for the insight on valuation. The Candela story became particularly interesting when the offering was stopped because of an SEC inquiry about revenues: it ap-

FIGURE 3.2

Medstone International, Inc.

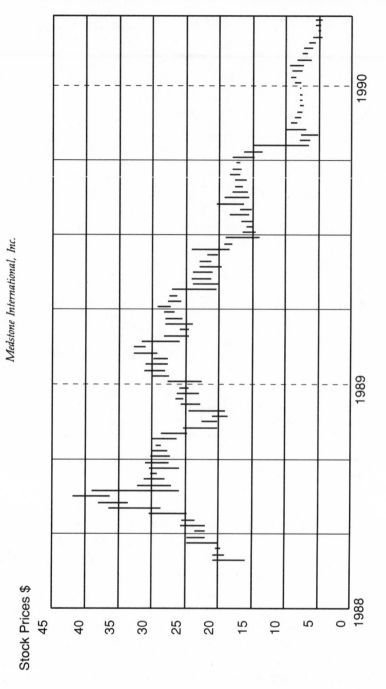

TABLE 3.4

Medstone International, Inc.
Short Interest

1988	
June	7,260
July	109,439
August	141,891
September	236,111
October	264,663
November	252,968
December	339,170

1989	
January	356,350
February	343,040
March	445,932
April	430,828
May	494,792
June	556,891
July	648,614
August	726,047
September	698,106
October	685,504
November	787,060
December	754,556

peared the company was too aggressive about when they booked sales of large machines.

Before the SEC problem, Candela was selling for $12.75 a share with 3 million shares outstanding before the offering, or a market valuation of $38.25 million. Candela had 149 employees, a sales force, several products, four patents, and an operating history. Their kidney shock treatment was an alternative method to lithotripsy for kidney stones and one which was perceived by some to do less damage to the surrounding soft tissue than the machines of Medstone and Dornier (the largest player).

Medstone was by this time trading for $29 with 4.5 million shares out, a market cap of $130 million. At the time of the offering, five months earlier, the company had one product (9 sold), no patents, 33 employees, and no mention of a sales force.

The September 1988 quarter was strong: $.52 vs. $.18 in earnings per share before extraordinary credit, and only 5 percent was from interest on the funds from the stock offering. Sales doubled.

Enthusiastic Support

The effusive puffery connected with Medstone came from one brokerage analyst in particular, who estimated earnings at $4.40 for 1989, up from $.33 in 1987. This drove the price higher, as retail clients followed in their zeal to participate in a winning kidney play. Only 6 times this year's earnings, the analyst said, with the group trading at 15 to 20 times. Buy now. Participate in the only dual machine, effective on both kidney stones and gallstones (he perceived the gallstone market to be the growth engine).[8]

An agreement with General Electric Medical Systems was announced with fanfare in December 1988. GE would sell Medstone's machine in Europe and the Middle East, providing parts, installation, and maintenance.

The 10K from December made a couple of interesting points. Sales to a single stockholder, Dr. Gaines W. Hammond, and to his affiliated companies, made up 13 percent of 1987 and 1988 revenues. The IPO document showed that he was an avid supporter of Medstone's work. He loaned the company $75,000 in November 1984. In connection with his first machine purchase in 1987, he "received a right of first refusal, exercisable until January 1989, to purchase and install any System for the treatment of kidney stones . . . within 100 miles of Spartanburg, South Carolina."[9] He also had the right to buy another machine at 80 percent of the price charged to third-party purchasers. He received $86,500 in consulting fees from Medstone in 1985 and an additional $123,000 at the close of the offering. It was a close relationship.

After a negative earnings surprise in the June 1989 quarter, a loss of $.04 a share vs. $.59, the stock price moved down and then stabilized above $15 after repeated table poundings by the rabid analyst. The 10Q showed troublesome inventory levels—$5.5 million vs. $385,000 in the previous June. Sales were down, more of a problem for a hot new company than no earnings. Sales expenses were up significantly, no doubt the burden of new marketing costs.

In August 1989 Richard Penfil resigned and the company reported "non-compliance regarding timely submission of required
reports governing the x-ray imaging system used in its shock-
wave lithotripter."[10] The stock didn't budge.

In October 1989 Medstone failed to get Food and Drug Admin-
istration (FDA) approval for its gallstone-shattering procedures,
and the stock dived from $16 to $6, despite the untapped Japanese market for kidney stone smashing. The third quarter was
another disappointment, a loss of $.34, the result of stopped
shipments pending a corrective action plan filing to the FDA.

Earnings for 1989 were a loss of $.45 per share with revenues
of $13.6 million, down from $23.2 million. Another president was
appointed in April 1990, the third in two years. Market valuation
was a little more realistic at $20 million as of April 1990.

Financial analysis of Medstone was common sense. The stock
was dramatically overvalued relative to a similar company. At a
million dollars a machine, how many machines must you sell to
make the valuation realistic, and how many can you sell with a
large experienced competitor—Dornier of Germany—ahead of
you in the field with a patented product and most of the installed
base, 250 machines? Part of the revenues were expected to come
from servicing machines and selling disposable components, yet
how many hospitals will buy a million-dollar machine that must
be serviced by a company that has only placed nine machines
when a dependable alternative exists?

The winning play was certainly a kidney straddle (or perhaps
a kidney smash): short Medstone and go long Candela Laser,
which traded as low as $4 after the offering was dropped when
Medstone was still priced in the stratosphere.

The lesson from Medstone: Consider shorting any stock with
color pictures of organs in the prospectus, particularly if an enthusiastic analyst whips eager individuals into a stock-buying
frenzy.

Notes

1. Harrier, Inc., Prospectus, 22 May 1986, 3.
2. The Merlin Group, "Harrier Inc.," May 1988, 11.

3. Ibid, 6.

4. Harrier, Inc., Form 10K, 30 June 1987, 4.

5. The Merlin Group, 7.

6. Alan Abelson, "Up and Down Wall Street," *Barron's,* 8 August 1988, 91–92.

7. Harrier, Inc., press release, 9 August 1988.

8. David H. Talbot, "Medstone International, Inc.," Arnhold & S. Bleichroeder, Inc., 21 December 1988, 1.

9. Medstone International, Inc., Prospectus, 2 June 1988, 28.

10. Medstone International, Inc., press release, 15 August 1989, 1.

4

High Multiple Growth Stocks: High Risk, Low Return

Sometimes Wall Street's favorites—growth stocks—mimic the ascent and overvaluation of their more humble siblings, the bubble companies. Every bull market has its new-concept, high multiple growth stocks. Concept or theme stocks are the companies that sell a product or service to fill a newly perceived need. In the 1960s, they were called one-decision stocks: you bought them and never sold them—thus one decision, to buy. Walmart and Compaq are examples of the best kind of concept stocks. The growth rate of corporate revenues continues to accelerate while the businesses' gross margins stay high, despite frequent additions to capital through equity and debt offerings.

By directing a cynical look at brokerage hysteria and enthusiastic price inflation the investor can determine which of the numerous innovators may succeed. The odds are with the short sellers; new business statistics show failure rates far in excess of success. The Wall Street game, however, is a little more complex. Wall Street awards preliminary kudos to companies just for trying or just for hiring the right investment banker or public relations agent. And that's what makes shorting concept stocks chilling, palm-sweating, white-knuckle hard work.

From the short point of view, the most important decision on a concept stock is: does this work? Is the prospective return worth the risk for the stockholder? The second question is: how soon will the new company run out of money? Shorts almost always judge correctly whether the business is seaworthy. On the timing of the demise, they're seldom right. Someone is usually available to buy stock, loan money, offer short-term bank debt long after the company financials are in nearly terminal condition. Add two years to a short's best projection and you may only have a couple more to wait.

Computers and Cabbage Patch Dolls: Coleco

In short history, Coleco Industries certainly deserves an honorable mention as a concept stock with terrible short timing. One of the mega-growth candidates of the early 1980s, the company was propelled to stellar stock heights with Street enthusiasm for a home computer in every pot. The stock moved from $19 to $65 from mid-1982 to 1983 with the excitement of a new idea. Coleco's Adam home computer was supposed to be cheap, (under $600), and sophisticated enough to play games, generate tax returns, and index recipes. It was due on the shelves before Christmas 1983.

The computer was unveiled with a fanfare that surprised even Wall Street with its devotion to hyperbole. In a smoky box at the Chicago Consumer Electronics Show in June 1983, the Adam nested in its prototypical glory. The computer needed to be rolling off production lines by September to meet expected demand at Christmas—the original delivery date was August 31.

Before too much time had passed, disagreement broke out on Wall Street. The stock price started to gyrate. Rumors began to circulate that delays, production problems, glitches in schedule were occurring. Analysts also started talking about jagged second-quarter financials: ballooning inventories from last year's ColecoVision video-game consoles, nonrecurring gains, odd asset classifications. The stock started slipping in earnest during the late summer.

FIGURE 4.1

Coleco Industries, Inc.

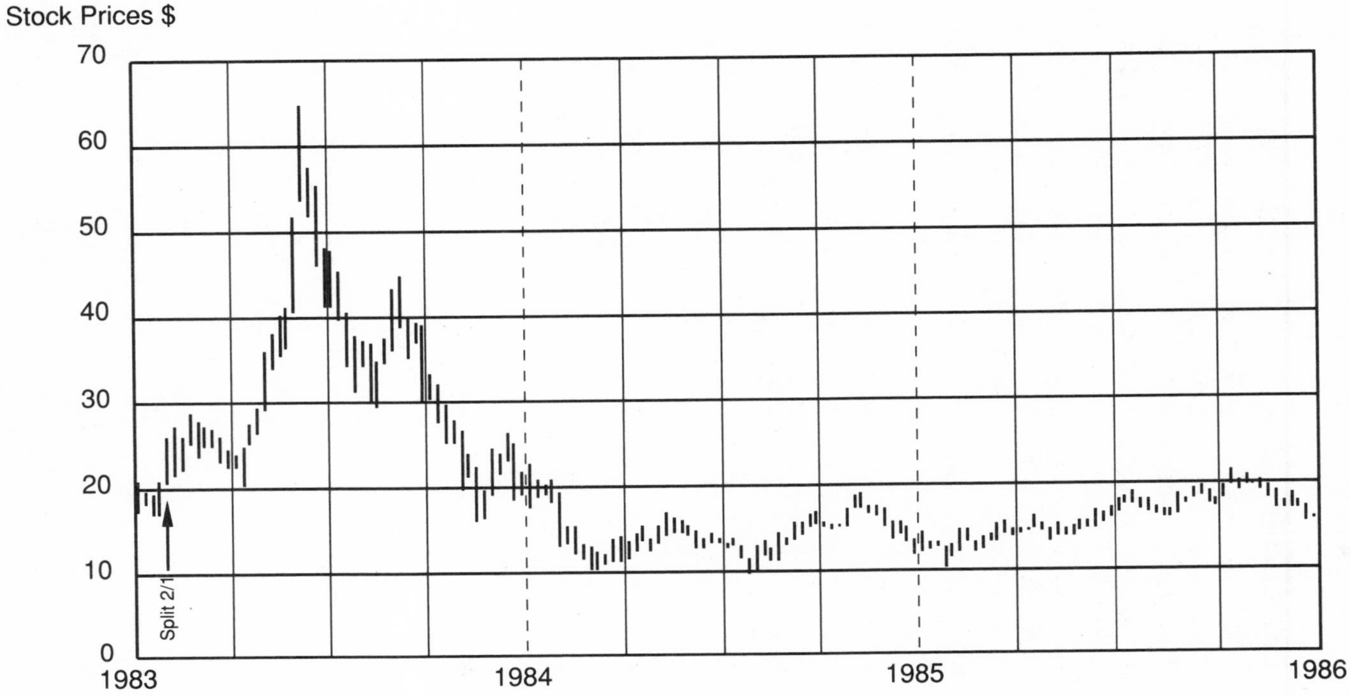

Stock Prices $

Coleco attempted to silence detractors first with daily press releases offering reassurance about production, revenues, and earnings. The stock would rally, then edge back down.

The positive company press slipped in late August: Coleco made an announcement that delivery would be stalled until mid-September. Then the company flubbed a demonstration on September 6. To calm the investment community, the company decided to sponsor a field trip to the factory for institutional investors and analysts. Short sellers were less than impressed with what appeared to be somewhat archaic methods of soldering circuit boards. Sure enough, computers sold on consignment were later returned for defects.

TABLE 4.1

Coleco Industries, Inc.
Short Interest

1983	
January	1,741,036
February	1,460,471
March	1,398,726
April	1,532,915
May	1,530,501
June	1,452,382
July	1,354,070
August	1,237,390
September	1,432,407
October	2,106,349
November	2,506,448
December	3,791,721

1984	
January	3,598,841
February	3,584,248
March	4,127,356
April	3,905,876
May	3,576,761
June	3,202,331
July	3,306,811
August	3,077,093
September	3,244,636
October	3,103,026
November	2,763,176
December	2,385,537

Next, the delivery date was pushed back to mid-October, and the number of units available for delivery was in question. Suppliers talked openly about canceled orders for production inputs. The September 30 10Q also showed a buildup in raw materials rather than finished goods or work in process—the production couldn't be spitting out Adams consistently.

But Coleco's demise did not occur in fall 1983. Although short sellers were right and momentarily jubilant, Cabbage Patch dolls—a fad from nowhere—bailed out the company and the stock price, for a while. The end was only postponed. In 1984, Coleco's management team ramped up production for their new hotter product, but the fad had passed by 1986. The company ceded to bankruptcy in 1988 with cash flow unable to support the continuous inroads of new-product optimism. Short sellers were right, but years after they made the call with assurance.

Marble and Brass in a Grocery Store: J. Bildner & Sons

J. Bildner was an upscale yuppie grocery store chain that went public in the fall of 1986. It had successful stores in Boston, all brass and marble and slick displays with delivery and gourmet carryout. The IPO prospectus stated that the mission was "to serve time-conscious consumers with high levels of disposable income"—in other words, a big 7-Eleven with great service and home delivery for investment bankers.[1] The stores featured imported tile, marble, European refrigerated cases, antique fixtures, and mahogany paneling and offered everything from video rentals to Brie to Pampers. It was the prospectus and its substantial information about the luxury grocery business that tipped the shorts. The Bildner escapade told shorts that anybody could get money for any business plan—for a little while. A vigorous IPO market is a tipoff to a sharp-eyed short that there is money to be made.

The Bildner deal got off to a rocky start when the stock offering was reduced from 1,875,000 to 1,450,000 shares at the bottom limit of the price range, $13 in a $13 to $16 proposed range.

The prospectus told readers that the company anticipated that

FIGURE 4.2

J. Bildner & Sons, Inc.

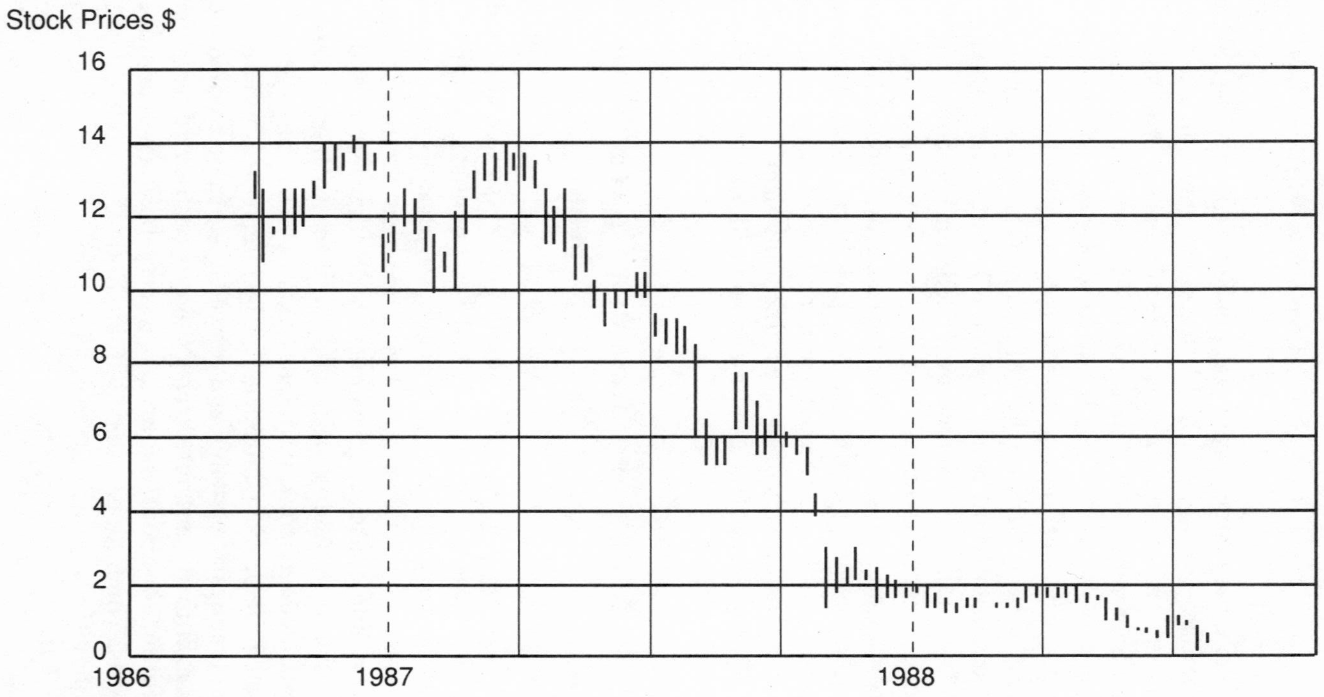

Stock Prices $

new funds for the ambitious expansion plan would last through calendar 1987. It warned that delays in opening stores could have "material adverse effect on . . . anticipated operating results."[2] The date was September 1986; eleven stores were running with twenty-four new stores scheduled to open, according to the strategic plan, by the end of 1987. Stores cost from $350,000 to $1,800,000 with net profit margins for the industry in 1986 running 1.38 percent, according to Value Line.[3]

The prospectus also mentioned in the Risk section that "successful growth of the Company's operations will depend on continued development of management skills" and that the current team had never had responsibility for a large operation.[4] James Bildner was 32, the senior vice-president of finance was 29, and assorted other officers ranged from 32 to 42.

The first indication that the marketing plan had gone awry was presented by a visit to one of the Atlanta stores. Located in a downtown Atlanta department store, this Bildner's had a produce counter featuring iceberg lettuce near the imported cheese and wine display, and the clientele was distinctly below the yuppie standard.

A check on proposed new locations showed the Bildner strategic marketing team to be the victim of an ebullient mall leasing agent (although there's no evidence that the Bildner planning staff was not a willing and compliant mark). Birmingham and Atlanta, in particular, had wildly inappropriate locations. In a town where everyone drives, no individual drives by choice to a mall after work, fights crowded parking lots for pricey carryout, and returns home in rush-hour traffic to eat in. Walk-in traffic may work in downtown Boston, but the South is not quite ready to shift from Kentucky Fried off the main six-lane drag to shiitake mushrooms through a maze of consumer traffic jams. In addition, the malls picked for locations were not necessarily in high-income locales.

A Few Small Problems

The next financial clue came with the January 25, 1987 10K. When the document came out in late spring the stock price was $11 to $13, after trading from $9 to $14.75 after the $13 offering. The 10K revealed three important points:

- the quality of earnings was poor;
- construction delays hurt the expansion plans; and
- cash burn was quicker than anticipated.

The quality of earnings is a major issue with short sellers. Companies repeatedly try to include nonoperating earnings in earnings to create the appearance of growth and financial well being. This subterfuge requires the analyst to read the footnotes and the management discussion of earnings in the 10Q—sometimes in extreme cases (Crazy Eddie in chapter 10), the verbiage is dramatically different in the quarterly report and press releases than in the 10Q.[5]

The quality of earnings issue is compounded by Wall Street's electronic ritual of tape watching for earnings. Typically, most institutional players and all brokers have machines that show asterisks for news releases. Everyone is prepped in advance for the time of probable release and expected quarterly earnings per share. When the number hits the tape, the response is instantaneous. If the company is followed by a number of brokerage houses, the stock moves up if the number is above target, down if it's below. And it sometimes takes hours or days (or years in the case of Integrated Resources) for brokerage analysts to get enough detail from the company to comment on the quality of earnings and the true margins. The company might be forthcoming and frank with specifics about earnings composition, but no one legally has to get a look until the 10Q or 10K is released. With the advent of fax machines, favorite analysts may get faxes way before hoi polloi. If the earnings report is a truly complex one, Street analysts may not catch the significance until the stock price alerts them to difficulties. Prime Motor Inns is a good example of this phenomenon.

In Bildner's case, the Consolidated Statements of Operations (table 4.2) showed earnings before taxes and extraordinary credit of $681,733 vs. $111,848 a year earlier—pretty good growth for a new company. A closer look at the expense lines suggested that "Other Expense, Net" was out of line—$34,781 vs. $280,339 in the previous year. A check to the footnotes, Note K (table 4.3) showed interest expense of $445,614 with ($111,036) in interest income and ($299,797) in other income for a net of the mysterious $34,781. So what's "other"?

The next step in the search for the missing "other" was the verbal explanation of earnings: "Other expenses as a percentage of sales were .1% in fiscal 1987, compared to 2.5% in fiscal 1986, and included a gain of $299,000 on the sale of one of the Company's cookie and ice cream stores in the fourth quarter of fiscal 1987."[6] Translated, that means the company booked a capital gain as a negative expense. With annual earnings of $529,733, quality of operating earnings was compromised. A more conventional and informative treatment would have been to disclose the profits from the gain as an extraordinary item, independent of operating profits. So operating earnings on sales of $31,289,870 were really $382,733, or 1.2 percent of revenues versus 2.2 percent with the gain (ignoring the tax treatment of the sale).

Next, the financials stated that the company had "experienced construction, design and licensing delays at new locations" and had deferred openings of seven stores to the next fiscal year.[7] For the first time, the company cautioned that it had made a substantial investment in New York City store locations, with no assurance of success. It also mentioned that local unions threatened problems in New York City.

New York City store checks showed one location close to both Fairway and Zabar's, two favorites of New York City shoppers for both price and quality, with a definite overlap in product. The strategic plan had failed to consider the large competitive threats across the street. The prospectus had noted that "the Company isn't aware of any competitor."[8] Most analysts on Wall Street don't do extensive site checks to determine the accuracy of execution of a company's plan. When they do, it's usually a company-sponsored trip to model locations or to a New York City location; motivated financial detectives can accumulate a bunch of relevant information easily by using their eyes. Store checks work. What you see may show variances in planned activities or weakness in strategy.

The 10K also mentioned that "the Company required more financing for expansion than originally anticipated."[9] Capital would be raised with an increased bank revolving credit agreement and with a new offering, a convertible subordinated debenture offered for $25 million in Europe, which should surely see Bildner through January 31, 1988. In a bull market, overseas convertibles are frequently an insight into the U.S. appetite for

TABLE 4.2

J. Bildner's Income Statement

	Fiscal Period Ended	
	January 25, 1987	January 26, 1986
Net Sales	$31,289,870	$11,353,935
Cost of Sales	16,444,774	6,263,031
Gross Profit	14,845,096	5,090,904
Store Operating Expenses	11,489,306	3,714,442
Selling, General and Administrative Expenses	2,639,276	984,275
Other Expense, Net	34,781	280,339
Earnings (Loss) before Income Taxes and Extraordinary Credit	681,733	111,848
Provision for Income Taxes	152,000	—
Earnings (Loss) before Extraordinary Credit	529,733	111,848
Extraordinary Credit—Utilization of Net Operating Loss Carryforward	87,000	—
Net Earnings (Loss)	$ 616,733	$ 111,848
Per Share Amounts:		
Earnings (Loss) before Extraordinary Credit	$ .11	$ .03
Extraordinary Credit	.02	—
Earnings (Loss)	$ .13	$ .03
Weighted Average Number of Common and Common Equivalent Shares	4,877,057	3,310,585

Source: J. Bildner & Sons, Inc., Form 10K, 25 January 1987.

TABLE 4.3

J. Bildner's Disclosure of Cookie Store Gain

	Fiscal Period Ended	
	January 25, 1987	January 26, 1986
Interest expense	$445,614	$297,406
Interest income	(111,036)	(17,067)
Other income	(299,797)	—
	$34,781	$280,339

Source: J Bildner & Sons, Inc., Form 10K, 25 January 1987.

a given security; Bildner was losing access to gold in traditional corporate finance veins. With the increased debt load, so went the margins, only in inverse direction.

Meanwhile, on the balance sheet, another red flag appeared: prepaid expenses and other assets rose, suggesting that Bildner was not expensing items from store openings quickly. Note C (table 4.4) showed evidence of aggressive capitalization of preoperating expenses, which included such lovelies as financial planning advice; clearly, there was a need, but the choice of consultants, if the future is an apt assessment for advice rendered, didn't make it easy to expense the costs over three years. The letter from President James Bildner in the Annual was optimistic, assured, naïve: "Over the past three years, we have successfully defined a new market—specialty food retailing—and today are on the leading edge of that niche. The coming year will be a time to build and fortify that leadership position through the innovation, energy and commitment of all of us at the company."[10]

Cockroaches: More Than One Bad Quarter

The April 1987 10Q continued the ebb. Cash was down. Prepaid expenses were up. Debt was up. Net income was only .3 percent of revenues, even without the burden of the yet-unissued convertible interest charge. Store checks disclosed that Atlanta stores were fairly empty, and informal customer surveys indicated unhappy shoppers, even in the better locations. Meat cuts were irregular, gourmet necessities weren't always available. Clerks weren't knowledgeable. The target market didn't have time or interest in trying repeatedly until J. Bildner got it right.

The company responded to the cash bind and the New York City problems by slowing its expansion plans. Analysts seemed pleased: no matter if earnings growth would be slower; the change would give the company time to get back in control. The new direction "reduces the risk of a major earnings interruption as the company pursues a somewhat less rapid growth strategy," the Kidder, Peabody analyst said.[11] The stock was cheap at $11, "given the company's 40% estimated 5-year normalized growth rate and prospects for earnings-per-share gains of 208% and 88%, respectively for the next two years, we believe these shares

TABLE 4.4

Bildner's Prepaid Expenses and Preoperating Expenses

Prepaid expenses

	January 25, 1987	January 26, 1986
Store preopening expenses	$1,516,880	$121,533
Deferred marketing development costs	205,307	—
Packaging and supplies	417,900	66,350
Other	177,773	49,513
Prepaid expenses and other current assets	$2,317,860	$237,396

Preopening expenses relate to initial direct store operating expenses, such as rent, promotion, labor, utilities, etc., incurred by an individual store prior to opening; also included is training for employees who will be staffing new locations.

Deferred marketing development costs relate exclusively to particular future marketing campaigns, are net of amortization and include prepaid advertising commitment fees, future promotional events, advertising time and space and costs for marketing production for radio and television. The Company's policy is to amortize these costs over the remainder of the length of a particular marketing campaign; the balance outstanding at January 25, 1987, is expected to be fully amortized by the Company's second quarter of fiscal 1988.

Preoperating expense

	January 25, 1987	January 26, 1986
Preoperating expenses (included in other assets)	$1,586,583	$457,975

Preoperating expenses are those expenditures incurred by the Company in creating and developing, and negotiating leases for a new store or multiple store locations by geographic region. These costs primarily consist of legal, outside consultants (including market and location study organizations), financial planning advice, travel, regional recruitment, administrative salaries and overhead costs related to these activities. Preoperating expenses, including those related to long-term lease agreements, are being amortized on a straight-line basis over three years. Additions and amortization for the year ended January 25, 1987, were approximately $1,485,000 and $357,000, respectively.
Source: J. Bildner & Sons, Inc., Form 10K, 25 January 1987.

offer considerable value for risk-oriented investors."[12] In other words, "the valuation is attractive," as the walls came down.

J. Bildner's management team made a concerted effort to pull things back together in mid-1987 when they hired a Federated executive from Atlanta-based Rich's to help run the growth. It was too late to salvage the leaky financials.

By fall, however, Bildner was admitting defeat, and expansion plans were scaled back to twenty-three new stores rather than the fifty originally planned. The company had two quarters of losses and planned to close a Birmingham store and sell more assets to raise cash. The resale market for used grocery fixtures made of mahogany and brass was somewhat lower than the cost to produce them.

In December 1987 Bildner announced the closing of the New York stores. New Yorkers had never warmed to the luxurious interiors and high prices; staffing, strikes, construction delays, and location joined to deliver small sales and larger losses.

Then, on July 12, 1988, Jim Bildner filed for bankruptcy under Chapter 11 with $45 million in debt and seven stores remaining.

The lessons from J. Bildner were three, all applicable to a torrid IPO market:

1. View the IPO document as a business person. Does the business make sense? Can prices be high enough to support the capital investment in glitzy store interiors? Can the necessary expansion be funded?

2. Watch for signs of potential failure, especially when the company gives you a benchmark. When the first financial clues appeared in print that J. Bildner's stock was not meeting the strategic plan, the stock was still high priced—$11 to $13 per share.

3. Don't be put off by a new and unexpected cash infusion. There's usually a greater financing fool. After you think it's obvious that the business plan has failed and the appetite for cash is geometric, Wall Street will find at least one more—maybe two—fools, to infuse large amounts of cash for an expected rate of return far below the risk they will take.

Lending to Franchisees: Jiffy Lube

Jiffy Lube, a quick oil change franchise company, was a growth stock and a short sale candidate with plenty of Wall Street assistance in blowing up the balloon. The story had all the drama and diversity of a multipart, made-for-TV accounting saga. Wall Street loved Jiffy Lube. The story was easy to tell, easy to sell.

Americans have less time, Americans need oil changes, local full-service gas stations are disappearing: buy Jiffy Lube, it solves a problem.

The corporate philosophy was a fine example of a poorly devised business plan: the company bet that a spectacular growth rate of franchises would swamp all competition, leave it in control of the field and, therefore, of pricing, and in the end, offer the company a high and sustainable rate of return.

The parent company received development fees for rights to geographical areas, franchise fees for opening stores, and then sold oil and parts to the franchisees and took a percentage of revenues for the privilege of the Jiffy Lube expertise. All of this is normal franchise procedure. It is not normal for the parent company to assume all of the risk of many of the franchisees. Jiffy Lube took back paper (debt) for franchisee start-up expenses, and they delivered inventories of oil and parts for credit. Eventually, the balance sheet tilted over like a human pyramid when one person too many is added. Getting there took several years and much agony for shorts who called the demise long before the event.

The Beginning

A *Barron's* article in December 1986 was the introduction to Jiffy Lube. The writer, Robert Barker, made some compelling points:

- "financial strength was nothing to write home about."
- competition was mounting;
- the stock was selling at forty times next year's earnings; and
- operating income was full of nonrecurring items.[13]

Not long after this article appeared, someone wrote to Wall Street Week asking for a play on quick-change oil companies, and the panelist answered that Jiffy Lube was one alternative. The stock price began its stellar climb, moving from $18 to $30 (pre-split) over a six-week period.

The stock-buying public soon warmed to Wall Street's vision of Jiffy Lube. They could see it on the highway near their suburban homes. They could understand the concept. It reminded them of a McDonald's, and the PR was quick to capitalize on that

FIGURE 4.3

Jiffy Lube Internationsl, Inc.

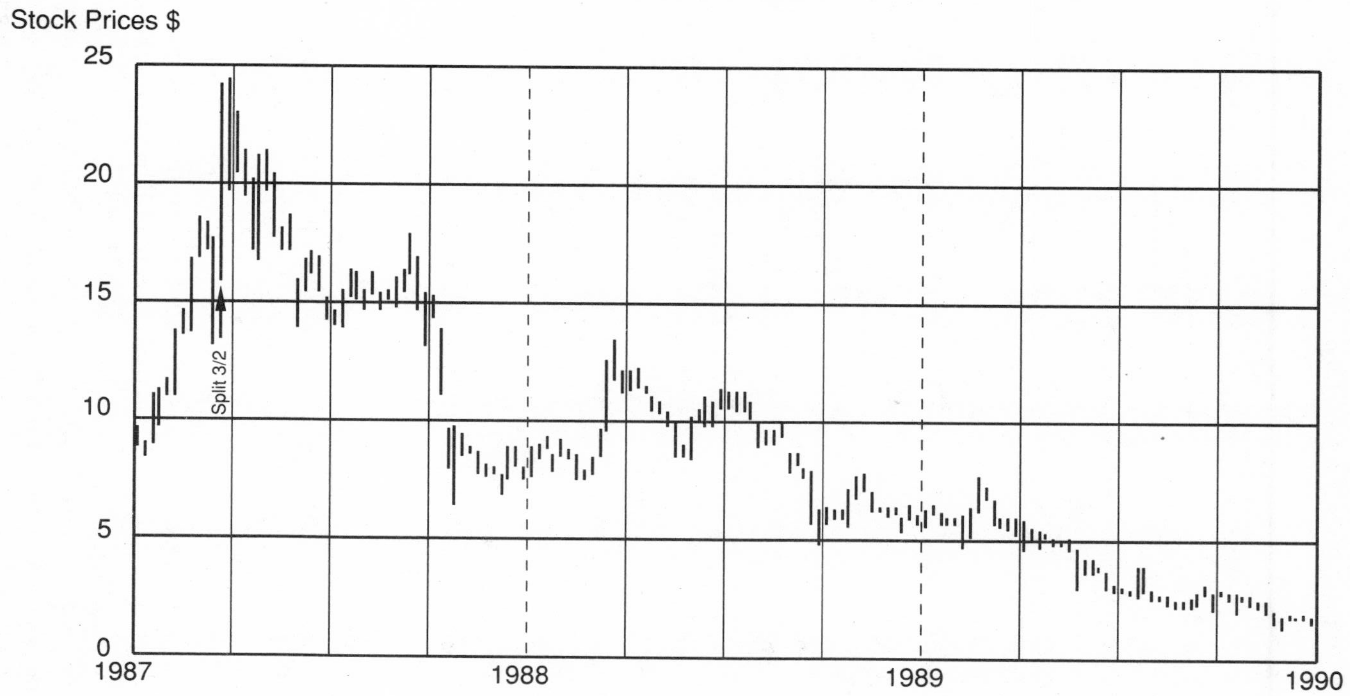

Stock Prices $

TABLE 4.5

Jiffy Lube International, Inc.
Short Interest

1987	
January	48,860
February	76,849
March	200,692
April	452,327
May	422,048
June	432,853
July	628,863
August	724,550
September	717,802
October	1,066,589
November	795,101
December	751,535

1988	
January	777,588
February	951,005
March	1,564,984
April	1,705,528
May	1,756,354
June	2,033,572
July	1,956,164
August	2,375,752
September	2,557,926
October	2,604,244
November	2,953,684
December	2,737,355

favorite franchisor stock as a selling comparison . . . hamburgers, oil change . . . the wave of the future, convenience, speed, cookie cutter stores.

Wall Street got behind the idea—Alex Brown, Shearson Lehman; the stock went on one-decision stock lists all over town. The analysts' voices could be heard rising in harmonious support like hounds baying at a hunt. In 1986 Alex Brown was already talking about quicklubes in Britain, France, and even Japan with earnings per share moving from $.32 in 1986 to $1.20 in 1988.[14] Some Wall Street growth company analysts with spreadsheet programs traditionally make earnings projections symmetrically up at an ever-increasing rate of growth.

The IPO prospectus dated July 22, 1986 foreshadowed the company's demise, as in the case of J. Bildner. Up front and out in the open under "Investment Considerations":

1. "Capital Adequacy. . . . The Company requires substantial amounts of capital to provide for the acquisition and development of Centers. . . ."

2. "Sources of Income. In the past three years the Company has experienced substantial growth in income largely as a result of income from area development fees and items such as gains on the sale of real estate and Company Operated Centers. These sources which are nonrecurring in nature and have enabled the Company to record a profit in such years, are expected to decline in magnitude. . . ."

3. "Financial and Operational Controls. Maintenance of accurate, consistent financial and operational controls over its own operations and its network of Centers is critical to the profitable expansion. . . ."

4. "Management. . . . Mr. Hindman has routinely facilitated the Company's funding of various projects by either loaning money directly to the Company or personally guaranteeing loans from others. . . ."

5. "Conflicts of Interest. Certain members of management are investors in area developments and franchises. The interests of such investors may conflict with the interest of the Company."[15]

You didn't even have to read past page 5 to get the gist of Jiffy Lube. Like shooting fish in a barrel, the shorts said.

The Middle

In March 1987 the stock split, and aggressive buyers moved the price up its obligatory bull market 25 percent on the announcement, to prove once again that the market really is driven by fools and euphoria. The stock peaked at $25 and change. The first sign of real trouble came in the prospectus from the next stock deal, dated June 4, 1987. Careful readers (this time one had to read to page 34) were rewarded with a peculiarly hard-to-follow sleight of hand. James Hindman, CEO and chairman of the board of Jiffy

Lube, was one of four partners in the aptly named BATH partnership, which in turn owned the franchising entity Lone Star. On March 26, 1987, before the quarter closed and the prospectus came out, Lone Star bought twenty-four centers and area development rights from Jiffy Lube for $6,015,000. Lone Star paid Jiffy Lube $2,765,000 in cash, $1,625,000 in deferred payment ten-year notes, and $1,625,000 in nonvoting stock of Lone Star. Jiffy Lube also arranged a line of credit for Lone Star and gave Lone Star reduced royalties on thirteen centers initially and on all centers after year six if sales were below a certain level. What that did for Jiffy Lube was:

- Increase revenues for the quarter by an unknown amount. Revenues for the quarter were $13,867,000, and the notes disclosed that of the $6,015,000 Lone Star sale the company recognized area development fees of $935,000, franchise fees of $90,000, and a gain on sale of assets of $658,998. With income from operations for the quarter of $2,048,809, the $1,683,998 that we know they booked was a significant addition to earnings.

- Add $2,765,000 in cash to the prospectus balance sheet, thereby boosting cash to $2,474,018—from no cash to some cash.

The Lone Star deal was thus a pretty productive transaction. Hindman sold 100,000 shares on the offering for $14.75 a share, or $1,475,000 total, no doubt covering any momentary outlay for his BATH. More on BATH and Lone Star later.

The next voice from the crowd was Ted O'glove's *Quality of Earnings* letter on July 23, 1987. O'glove noted that earnings from the 1987 fiscal year were poor quality. Nonrecurring revenues contributed appreciably to earnings. His figures for after-tax, per-share contributions from nonbase business were:

- initial franchise fees added $.10 a share;
- taxes and SG & A–adjusted area development and master license fees added $.13;
- "other" operating revenues added $.03;
- other income (interest on notes receivable and cash invested from the offering) added $.08;

- deferred (capitalized) expenses that should have reduced earnings by $.06; and
- the Hindman transaction mentioned above added $.06.

The sum of all these nonrecurring revenues and aggressive accounting procedures was greater than the reported earnings of $.28.[16] When nonrecurring earnings disappear, interest payments don't. The stock didn't budge.

Then the "Heard on the Street" column in the *Wall Street Journal* pounded the stock with short seller Jim Chanos questioning the bulls. High receivables, he said; average store sales dropping, too much credit to franchisees. Hindman responded that they had to get there first, capture the market, and the store sales weren't down, just more new stores in the count.[17] Alex Brown pulled back a touch—the stock is pretty high priced, they implied, but a good grower.

The stock price dropped with the crash of October 1987 to $8, and the bears were somewhat vindicated; some covered, some waited. It looked like a broken stock.

The End, But Not the Finale

In October 1987 Jiffy Lube announced a stock buy-back of 850,000 shares, not exactly the best use of capital for a company burning cash, but a popular corporate move after the crash to calm the bloodied stockholders.

Jiffy Lube, meanwhile, kept eating money and opening franchises. The December 31, 1987 10Q showed total debt up again, this time by more than $30 million, with net income of only $.10 a share versus $.09, down sequentially from $.12, and margins a tad pallid.

Most analysts look at earnings and revenues versus year-ago earnings and revenues. In a rapid growth company that adds outlets quarterly, sequential earnings can be equally interesting. Unless there's a pronounced seasonality to the product sales, revenues and net should go up each quarter.

The company also held thirty-one centers for resale. So the company had to sell unprofitable take-back centers as well as open new ones, doubling the burden of opening new stores. The franchise-for-sale section of a local newspaper or the *Wall Street*

Journal provides the equivalent of a store check in a retail store. If franchisees are selling franchises it means the parent has competition selling new units. If the company is advertising, the terms in the ad can be enlightening. An ad appeared in the *Wall Street Journal,* urging that "Entrepreneurs of all sizes, grab the Jiffy Lube opportunity. . . . No money down for owner/operators."[18] So the ads for centers for sale increased, offering giveaway terms.

The company made two other announcements that quarter that warmed bears' hearts: that the SEC disagreed with the recognition of area development fees, which would require restating past earnings lower; and that the company would purchase a new headquarters for $10,500,000. Grizzled analyst wisdom says sell the stock of a company building a new headquarters—owned, not leased: it's a top-of-the-earnings-cycle clue.

Jiffy Lube continued to run through cash at a prodigious rate. The Statement of Changes showed operating cash burn of $10.4 million for nine months with another $17 million used for real estate—a total of $27 million, versus operating plus real estate of $11.7 million for 1986.

In February 1988 Shearson, Lehman's prospectus on a previously announced best efforts limited partnership for the company came out: $50 million to invest in real estate for franchisees or the company, guaranteed by Jiffy Lube. The greater fool had arrived to throw money at the company, but unfortunately, the fools were the unwitting retail clients.

Rebirth

And then the stock price levitated again, in a palm-sweating, short-squeezing run-up in March to $13. That's 60 percent. Stock was impossible to borrow. Shorts got bought in. The price ticked relentlessly up. Options traded like water. When call option volume runs up, that signals takeover rumors to observers. Some shorts recaptured lost positions with synthetic shorts: buy a put, sell a call. The Wall Street grapevine said: Major oil company is buying JLUB for a fancy price, needs oil distribution, announced soon, probably Pennzoil. This is when one can hear the click and scratch of mechanical pencils, checking and double-checking valuations as the shorts do their version of telling the prayer beads: times revenues, times book, times earnings, times cash flow, times. . . .

And then the price settled back around $10 when the announcements failed to materialize. The June 30, 1988 10Q was reassuring to shorts. Centers for resale were up to an astounding seventy. Dogs that were returned to the parent because they weren't profitable were draining cash as the parent tried to turn them around and find a buyer. Total debt was up again, by $25 million, with an operating loss on the income statement for the first time.

Even more amazing was the nature of the new, soon to be long-term, debt. Jiffy Lube or their investment bankers had found insurance companies willing to buy a private placement of $58 million at reasonable rates, 10.97 percent on the ten-year, average life seven years, three maturities. Shorts called to find out buyers' names so they could short insurance companies willing to take on so much risk for so little return.

Jiffy Lube's stock price steadily declined after the operating loss with occasional price flurries when takeover rumors surfaced. Shearson pulled their rating on the stock, reducing it to a sell only ten days after an investment pool of Shearson executives filed to sell 100,000 shares.[19]

The September quarter continued the decline with one new twist. More debt, more centers for resale—up to eighty-one now, requiring new advertising to attract franchisees. For the first time the ugly specter of write-offs was raised: the company increased the credit loss provision because of "significant increases in the outstanding balances of accounts and notes receivable and to provide for possible losses on receivables with franchisees who are experiencing financial difficulties."[20] Since a large proportion of assets on the balance sheet were franchisee-backed, significant franchisee defaults could collapse the balance sheet, destroy the book value, and throw the company into default of debt covenants.

And Default, Finally

And that's exactly what the company announced on February 9, 1989: a write-off, or special charge as executives called it, of $39.2

million that threw Jiffy Lube into default of debt covenants. $10.6 million of the write-off was a charge for "resizing" Chairman Hindman's partnership (24 percent Hindman-owned), presumably the Lone Star/BATH arrangement that had created cash and earnings for the 1987 stock offering.

A TV station in Philadelphia added to the bad news when it aired a show on bad customer service at a local Jiffy Lube, dropping car counts in that market by 70 percent.

A comparative look at the Jiffy Lube balance sheets for year-end 1986 and 1988 tells the story of the company's demise. Franchisee-backed assets escalate from approximately 45 to 79 percent of total assets, while debt as a percentage of total capital declines slightly but nonetheless remains too high relative to dubious and illiquid assets. The company had no cushion to withstand the shock of weak sales or weak franchisee financial condition. The balance sheet, when analyzed with a healthy measure of skepticism, showed that assets might not be real and liquid.

The critical variable in franchise growth stories is obviously growth. If a company quits adding new franchisees, earnings and revenue growth halt. In a business like oil changes, cost of entry isn't very high so competition is fierce. A 10 percent price cut during a price war can decimate store margins. If the stores lose profitability, franchise growth slows, and franchisees slow payments to the parent (for the franchisor equivalent of a run on the bank—money out, none in). If the parent subsidizes all the growth of new stores, slow payments can kill already tenuous cash flow. And after cash burn escalates, the debt burden climbs and finally the asset side deteriorates as franchisees lose their ability to pay. The parent can't bail fast enough.

In retrospect, the bankers said the problem with Jiffy Lube was easy money. Given plenty of financing by banks, Wall Street, and insurance companies, the urge to spend was too compelling. In an effort to throw the growing cache of funds out the door, Jiffy Lube lost control, lent to increasingly weaker franchisees in bad locations, and also tried to expand more and more quickly. An austere money environment certainly begets more conservative business practices for the likes of Jiffy Lube.

Jiffy Lube continued its rush to restructure and return to profitability. Real estate went on the block. The new headquarters was slated for a sale/leaseback. Unprofitable stores were relentlessly slashed. The stock price settled around $2.50. Pennzoil infused cash for 80 percent of the stock, thereby diluting existing shareholders (and edifying short sellers who managed to stay short), and paid off Hindman handsomely for not working.

Jiffy Lube taught one bull market lesson soon to be repeated in the 1990s: in the long run, it's the equity and the junk bond holders who take the torpedo hit for poorly conceived business plans, not the insiders or the investment bankers.

Notes

1. J. Bildner & Sons, Inc., Prospectus, 22 September 1986, 3.

2. Ibid., 17.

3. *The Value Line Investment Survey,* 45, Part 3, No. 23, Edition 10, 23 February 1990, 1498.

4. Prospectus, 5.

5. The best books on detecting accounting gimmickry and quality of earnings problems are Bernstein's *Financial Statement Analysis* (Homewood: Richard Irwin, Inc, 1983), Thornton O'glove's *Quality of Earnings* (New York: The Free Press, 1987), and any book or article by Abraham Briloff. There are also several monthly services that detail ongoing problems.

6. J. Bildner & Sons, Inc., Form 10K, 25 January 1987, 18.

7. Ibid., 13.

8. J. Bildner & Sons, Inc., Prospectus, 22 September 1986, 19.

9. J. Bildner & Sons, Inc., Form 10K, 25 January 1987, 19.

10. J. Bildner & Sons, Inc., Annual Report, 15 May 1987, 8.

11. Barbara L. Kahn, "J. Bildner & Sons," Kidder, Peabody & Co., Incorporated Research, 12 May 1987, 1.

12. Ibid., 3.

13. Robert Barker, "Greaselock?", *Barron's,* 22 December 1986, 16.

14. Charles Glovsky, "Jiffy Lube International, Inc.," Alex Brown & Sons Incorporated Research, 29 October 1986, 1.

15. Jiffy Lube International, Inc., Prospectus, 22 July 1986, 4–5.

16. Thornton O'glove, *Quality of Earnings Report,* 23 July 1987, 66–67.

17. Randall Smith, "Heard on the Street," *Wall Street Journal,* 1 October 1987, 71.

18. *Wall Street Journal,* 6 October 1988, B10.

19. Stephen Taub, "Shearson's Nifty Lube Job," *Financial World,* 15 November 1988, 8.

20. Jiffy Lube International, Inc. Form 10Q, 30 September 1988, 16.

5

If You Can't Read It, Short It

Public financial statements are disclosures of the financial under-pinnings of publicly traded companies. The intent of the 10K is to explain the business of the company and give audited financial data supporting that business. Theoretically, shareholders should be able to understand what backs their equity in assets and liabilities, what earnings power drives the company, and whether the company can support that business with operating, financing, and investing cash flows. Footnotes to the financial statements should explain, expand on, and disclose additional information to the public.

Most companies write reports that are comprehensible to a person with a fair knowledge of accounting terminology. Some companies write reports that are impossible to follow, even for accounting experts. Experience suggests that if you can't under-stand it, officers are hiding something worse than you expect. It's almost an iceberg phenomenon: if you find five or six serious questions in financial statements, you can be sure that's only the tip. If a call to the company for explanation receives a garbled response that sounds suspiciously like the company official is eating intellectual graham crackers, you've got a live one.

The corollary to the graham cracker phenomenon is that most analysts are afraid to admit that they don't understand account-ing or accounting terminology. So the cycle is self-perpetuating: chief financial officers don't explain; analysts don't ask. *Barron's* or the *Wall Street Journal* should run nominations for the worst disclosure to increase the pressure for comprehensible information for investors.

CUC International

CUC was a hot growth stock with a catchy concept and geometric earnings growth. All the hot growth funds owned it confidently: earnings per share had grown from $.23 in 1984 to $.90 in fiscal 1988 (January 31, 1988 year end). The annual report had multiple bar charts and product matrices, but the financials were tough to read despite all the graphic assistance.

The main business and the largest source of revenue for the company was selling memberships to an electronic home shopping service. For $30 or $40 a year, a subscriber had the right to buy appliances and other consumer goods over the phone at discount prices. Most of the revenue came from these membership fees. CUC also had a telephone travel service: for a fee, agents would book cheap airplane tickets and hotels over the phone, arrange travel for individuals, and give them all the advantages of corporate buying power. Both services could be accessed by computer or by phone, depending on the type of membership, although the on-line service was primarily a promising source of future revenues.

CUC International first attracted attention when the insider selling stayed strong from March 1988 through the summer. Walter Forbes, president and chief executive officer sold 50,000 shares in June. Henry McCall, vice-chairman of the board, sold 200,000 shares in March. Short sellers keep their eyes on 144 lists to look for evidence of insider discontent.

The stock had the profile of a Wall Street growth stock—lots of hype and no one paying much attention to the financials. Typically, growth stock analysts (also called special situation analysts) are young and inexperienced and don't have the accounting expertise to follow the meandering of growth financials: they assume that there will always be plenty of money if the earnings per share keep coming out at regular intervals right where management tells them they'll be.

What's What?

The balance sheet was difficult (table 5.1). There were a covey of odd-sounding assets that suggested the company was managing earnings: what exactly were "Deferred Membership Charges"? What was the collection success? How real were those assets? What were prepaid solicitation costs and prepaid commissions? Clearly "Excess of Cost Over Net Assets Acquired" was goodwill, but were they amortizing purchased companies and contracts over the life of the contract or over forty years?

One way a company can manage earnings is to delay expensing the costs of doing business. The asset side of the balance sheet rises as prepaid expenses build, and net income stays consistent, always upward by a comfortable growth rate. Companies that have perfect growth rates should always be carefully studied for gimmickry on the balance sheet—in particular, burgeoning prepaid expenses and deferred costs. Thus CUC sparked greater interest when notice of increased insider selling was subsequently followed by consistent earnings growth and, finally, by rising assets.

The October 31, 1988 10Q showed Deferred Membership Charges and Prepaid Solicitation Costs escalating. A look at the footnotes provided some explanation. Note 2 showed that "Unamortized Membership Acquisition Costs" and "Deferred Membership Charges, net" were growing faster than revenues.

Management's discussion said that acquisition of membership was amortized over three years and that renewal rates were high enough to generate revenues greater than the charges. What that means in English is that management bought a one-year membership from another company and expensed the cost over three years. If the individual didn't rejoin, CUC would still have two years of expense and no revenues. No footnote in the financials gave an analyst a clear evaluation of what the liability to the company might be if renewal rates dropped.

Management was asked in an analyst meeting what that supporting schedule was. They answered, "It's in the footnotes." Questioner Sue Hardman, an accounting MBA from Indiana Uni-

TABLE 5.1

CUC's Balance Sheet
(Dollar amounts in thousands)

January 31	1988	1987
Assets		
Current Assets		
Cash and cash equivalents	$ 25,953	$ 14,810
Receivables, less allowance of $613 and $405	33,201	24,209
Prepaid expenses and other	3,468	3,288
Total Current Assets	62,622	42,307
Deferred membership charges, net	22,078	13,112
Prepaid solicitation costs	17,089	4,915
Prepaid commissions	6,267	8,127
Contract renewal rights, net	27,944	30,443
Excess of cost over net assets acquired, net	33,301	19,066
Properties, net	16,048	10,074
Other	1,519	4,416
Total Assets	$186,868	$132,460
Liabilities and Shareholders' Equity		
Current Liabilities		
Members' deposits	$ 4,997	$ 4,340
Accounts payable and accrued expenses	36,063	16,446
Federal and state income taxes	423	
Current portion of long-term obligations	1,404	5,011
Total Current Liabilities	42,887	25,797
Convertible subordinated debentures	12,000	22,000
Long-term obligations	3,767	5,120
Deferred income taxes	14,624	6,073
Other	1,229	1,268
Total Liabilities	74,507	60,258
Commitments and Contingencies		
Shareholders' Equity		
Common stock-par value $.01 per share authorized 50 million shares: issued 19,683,567 and 17,820,338	197	178
Additional paid-in capital	82,271	59,550
Retained earnings	32,420	14,997
Treasury stock—398,230 and 398,091 shares, at cost	(2,527)	(2,523)
Total Shareholders' Equity	112,361	72,202
Total Liabilities and Shareholders' Equity	$186,868	$132,460

Source: CUC International Inc., *Annual Report,* 31 January 1988.

versity and a long-time analyst, portfolio manager, and insurance maven with expertise in deferred items or acquisition costs for insurance companies, responded that she had read the notes and needed more disclosure. Management didn't jump at the opportunity to clear the water.

Thornton O'glove also had a crack at deciphering the confusing notes. His comment on reading the financials: "CUC's substantial buildup in unamortized membership acquisition costs and, to a lesser extent deferred solicitation costs should be closely scrutinized. *The Company should provide investors with an itemized list by category and dollar sum of all deferred (unamortized) membership acquisition costs and solicitation expenses* (emphasis mine). Meanwhile, we foresee continued erosion of CUC's price to earnings ratio."[1]

The stock, which had begun to drop in November, continued to decline when the company announced in March 1989 that it would reverse the aggressive accounting, write off the acquisition costs over one year, not three years, "to coincide with the initial membership period and to ensure recoverability on a more conservative basis," and restructure the company by taking a cash dividend out and increasing debt.[2] The accounting change resulted in a one-time charge of $1.50 and penalized earnings comparisons in the short run.

The more recent financials of CUC International are noticeably easier to understand, and the stock price is doing well again. Insiders don't seem as disposed to exit their positions.

The lesson of CUC is that if you don't understand the accounting, there's probably not enough disclosure by the company. If there's not enough disclosure, it may mean overly aggressive practices or it may mean fraud (see Crazy Eddie's mobile inventories in chapter 10).

National Education

National Education was another Wall Street darling, a comfortable concept stock with notable personage Barry Goldwater on the board. Unfortunately, the company's accounting stance didn't mimic his conservative political philosophy.

The company sold two types of education: re-education or

FIGURE 5.1

National Education Corp.

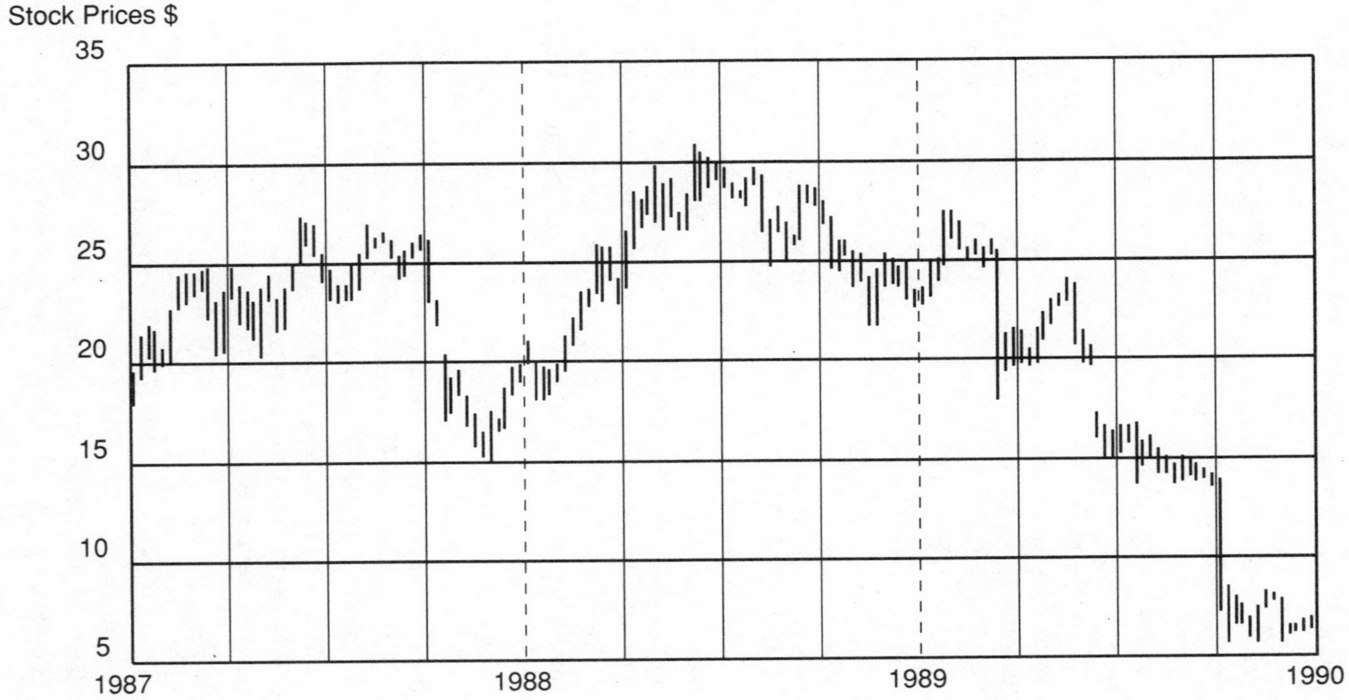

training for corporate and government employees (for example, a program to introduce a new computer system or product), and technical-vocational training. Popular wisdom said the stock was recession resistant, since more people would need to be retrained in a downturn. Demographics also favored the concept: a smaller labor pool meant that corporations would have to re-educate, reuse, and retrain existing employees. The eyecatcher, again, was the financial statements.

What Receivables?

The first clue was that Accounts Receivables were up significantly year over year: 90 percent year over year with sales up only 15 percent. Allowance for doubtful accounts, meanwhile, rose only 12 percent. Long-term receivables, or Contracts Receivable, were also up 100 percent. Receivables can be up by more than sales for several reasons:

1. The company acquired a company and the acquisition isn't yet under control; collections don't have the same billing cycle or terms for sales, for example. If the acquisition was a large one relative to sales, the relationship of year versus year in receivables is not comparable.
2. The company is booking revenues too aggressively—for example, a three-year contract recognized at the front end—so that receivables stay high because the rate of payment is slow.
3. The company changed its credit policy to easier terms or is giving incentives for sales, thereby jeopardizing future sales.
4. The company is having trouble collecting from customers.

Building accounts receivables is a cost to the company, since investing in business already booked hurts cash flow. Timely collections are sensible in a growing business because growth eats money by definition.

The first step in analyzing National Education's receivables was to check to see if any major acquisitions had skewed the receivables comparison. Note 2 on business combinations said that National Education acquired Spectrum on December 19, 1988, which was accounted for as a pooling-of-interest. Spectrum had provided $24 million of the $457 million of revenues for the combined companies—certainly not enough to increase receivables by $75 million.

The next step was to flip through the verbiage in the financial statements for disclosure, comment, observation—anything helpful to explain a large change. But they revealed nothing. National Education apparently didn't feel a $75 million increase merited a mention.

Note 1 (Summary of Significant Accounting Policies) was the next stop to see what accounting principles apply to the company's statements. Under Revenues and Costs, more confusion: National Education had a lot of different contracts, all booked with different assumptions. Of the three major types of training contracts:

- "Rental contracts revenues under ad hoc month-to-month arrangements are recognized when usage occurs," but "under resident library arrangements, customers agree to use training courses for a period of time and revenue is recognized for the contracted course usage." So when do they book it—up front or throughout the contract?

- "Custom contract revenues under time and materials contracts are recognized as costs are incurred, and revenues from fixed price contracts are recognized using the percentage-of-completion method." Not as cash is received.

- "Industrial contract revenues are recognized when cash is received with appropriate recognition of estimated expenses relative to servicing such contracts."[3]

The note tells the interested reader that National Education books revenue at different times under different assumptions, suggests that the company has some leeway in when to recognize revenues, and implies that the accounting methodology doesn't always match cash payment. How companies book revenues is a particularly quarrelsome issue for analysts: there are many ways to fool around, and technology and training companies are two categories of regular abusers. Revenues booked should have a consistent relationship with collection—if a company ships now and collects in sixty days, the Accounts Receivable schedule should consistently mirror that policy. So rising receivables versus sales or a lengthening number of days in receivables should always trigger a question: something has changed, it says. In National Education's case the resident library verbiage was especially troubling: how do they track use, and do they book two or three years at the outset of the contract?

The 1988 Annual also showed that an unusual charge in 1987 made the 1988 to 1987 comparison in earnings per share look good—$1.57 vs. $.03. In addition, the large acquisition of Advanced Systems in late 1987 with subsequent cost cutting on overhead from economies of scale gave the expense side a kick lower that probably wouldn't be duplicated in later years.

Acquired intangible assets (from the acquisitions) was a sizable balance sheet line of well over $89 million, with total assets of $422 million and stockholders' equity of $185 million. The notes said that the assets consisted of rental contracts, product and text materials, course development costs, and copyrights. These assets are being amortized over a period "not to exceed forty years." Educational manuals? Over a long period. How long? Not longer than forty years. Seems pretty aggressive with the massive amount of change in technology and software, some of the areas of National Education's expertise. Management has discretion on booking intangibles, creating a productive source of earnings management.

Management Changes His Mind

The real signal on National Education occurred when Jerome W. Cwiertnia, president, quit on March 16, 1989. He chose the conclusion of his presentation at the Shearson Selected Growth Conference. Cwiertnia had an advantageous employment contract: he got annual compensation of $695,251 including a special bonus applied to a tax loan—his aggregate loan was $176,734. He also received 150 percent of his salary times the number of years worked or $1.38 million if he was terminated. All of this was small relative to David Bright, the chairman of the board and chief executive officer (his termination pay was $7.373 million, a later bone of contention). But this corporate largesse came to

Cwiertnia in every instance *except for voluntary resignation under certain circumstances.* He resigned voluntarily. He potentially gave up millions and walked—unless, of course, the resignation was friendly and the terms of his contract included this particular circumstance. The stock dropped five points in twenty minutes and then rallied to $21-$22 in the months following. Analysts appeared unconcerned about Cwiertnia's contract, or the affability of his departure.

The confusing financials with mounting receivables and the resignation of a key person were enough evidence to short the stock. The vocational training business has come under repeated fire for spurious accounting practices, low collection rates, and bogus students—*Barron's* had an article titled "Schools for Scandal" on January 2, 1989. The smoke should have suggested that a casual analyst couldn't expect to decipher reality from financial statements in this particular industry sector.

Analysts on the Street, however, were reassured and comfortable. As a group they bah humbugged the accounting issue, rationalized Cwiertnia's resignation (change of life, wants his own company), and dismissed growing receivables (new billing system). Merrill Lynch analyst Arthur Rade commented on April 17, 1989 that he expected $1.90 for 1989; "quite attractive," he said, "growth averaging about 18%."[4] Morgan Stanley's Ram Capoor also liked the stock, stating that the change "reinforces our recommendation. . . ."[5]

Management met with analysts at the end of May and suggested that revenues and earnings might be a little light for the quarter. Everyone simultaneously dropped year estimates a nickel or a dime. The Shearson analyst appeared to be nervous about cash flow and accounting and kept the rating at 3–1 (Hold short term, buy long term).

Troubled waters didn't clear quite as quickly as the Street had hoped. *Barron's* ran an article in the June 5 issue that talked about student default rates at vocational schools. National Education had five schools listed with defaults over 40 percent. The stock hiccuped, the company reassured the Street that the numbers were old, analysts rustled nervously like sheep in a pen.

But that was not all. As they said on the Street, another shoe dropped (this sucker was a centipede) when the company announced on June 12 that the quarter would be below last year because of "account reassignments and lengthened sales cycle."[6] The stock traded to $16. Analysts affably lowered their year estimates to $1.50 and some went to "hold" on the stock, a trifle late for investors. Dean Witter's Fred Anschel refused to follow the herd, however. "Buy," he said; "target $24–$27."[7]

The stock dropped from $16 to $13 when the company announced a second quarter loss on July 19, 1989. It was much bigger than expected, even after the company's June meeting. Some analysts went to a "sell." Merrill's Rade said, "Adolescent crisis, rather than terminal illness," but clearly a loss of confidence had occurred.[8]

Cwiertnia Comes Back

Analysts again rallied around the company when David Bright quit (presumably because of the dog-like earnings), and Cwiertnia was reinstated. The honeymoon was short-lived, despite company reassurances that "the other shoe wouldn't drop."[9]

The 10Q when it came out showed prepaid marketing expenses up to $42 million, with accounts receivable down a little and operating cash burn of $21 million, versus $11 million from the previous year. National Education also charged off $4 million. The verbiage explained that "the second quarter results include an unusual charge of $4 million resulting from all issued and estimated future customer credits arising from the reconciliation of customer accounts following the conversion to a new management information system at Applied Learning."[10] The company topped previous obfuscatory verbiage with this explanation—what did they mean? Perhaps the receivables were bad because the computer system didn't track usage right? Eventually, the company admitted to receivables problems from booking 60 percent of revenues on the signing of a three-year contract in the Applied Learning division, resident library section. Tighter revenue recognition policies were instituted.

Throughout the six-month period, analysts seemed content to listen to management explanations and direction without asking tough questions. As a group, they lowered estimates and ratings at the prodding of company officials. They appeared to be unconcerned about employment contracts and the ensuing lawsuit by the deposed David Bright about payment of his contract. They failed to understand that the accounting issues masked important negative developments, whatever they were.

On February 1, 1990, the stock was at $4. Most Wall Street analysts no longer cover the stock; it went from the recommended list of major firms with eight analysts covering the stock to Siberia. Nobody remembered to change estimates or comment; it quietly slipped off lists without announcement. The disappearing analysts phenomenon should not, however, be considered a sell short signal: when Wall Street analysts forget they have a stock under coverage, worry if you're long, but it's probably too late to short.

The National Education short represents the best kind of financial detective work: clue gathering from financial reports and company announcements followed by an intuitive leap of judgment triggered by a specific event.

Current Nominations For Unreadable Financials

The list of companies with unreadable financials is longer than it should be. Financial statements should be a reflection of the company business. The accounting descriptors should be informative and identifiable with explanatory notes when any further detail is required. If the analyst must struggle to learn what the operating earnings are and what assets and liabilities compose the net worth, the company is not communicating clearly. Two recent examples are Marriott and Green Tree Acceptance.

Marriott Corporation

Marriott is a company that builds hotels, sells the hotels to partnerships for fee income, keeps a percentage of the ownership as general partner, manages the hotels for a percentage of the revenue, and then sells the hotels for the partnership. A readable income statement would break out revenues and expenses along those lines. Revenue might be divided into management fees, fees for partnership origination, interest income from partnerships, and sale of property. Too simple. After all, what are analysts paid for?

Marriott breaks revenues down into three general headings: Lodging, Contract Services, and Restaurants. Lodging is then subdivided into Rooms, Food and Beverage, and Other. Gains on sales of property are jumbled up with recurring revenues. The verbiage in the notes to the financial statements discloses sales of property, but the thoughtful table that the company adds to the end of the 10Q, "Earnings to Fixed Charges," forgets to deduct the capital gains from income from continuing operations. The company's position is probably that sales of property *are* the recurring business of the company. Marriott also capitalizes over half the interest charges on new builds, further muddying the waters of the income statement. From an analyst's point of view, the jumble makes it hard to estimate what earnings and interest coverage might be in a sustained period of overbuilding in the hotel industry or in a general downturn in the economy.

The partnership accounting is even more obtuse for the limited partnership hotels that Marriott manages. The absence of accounting rules on the consolidation of general partnership interests makes anybody's guess reasonable. According to Joe Morris of the Federal Accounting Standards Board, "As far as Marriott is concerned, we're not sure exactly what they're doing. They seem to consolidate the revenues, expenses and working capital of the hotels that are in the partnerships 100%. How they make their books balance we don't know."[11]

To make matters worse, Marriott has agreed to advance funds to cover debt service if necessary on some deals, up to $346 million according to the 1988 Annual, and the company takes back notes for management fees and interest payments on others. So the balance sheet doesn't exactly give a shareholder a clear picture of what's bankable, sellable, or negotiable if the lenders get hostile. And the financial notes just tell eager analysts that the hotel partnerships are losing money, not what the cash flow looks like. What is the total of guarantees to hotels? What are the terms of preferred returns to partners, a shareholder might ask?

So what you get for your money with Marriott is no idea of what you get. The bondholders should be militant: eroding fixed-charge coverage has been coupled with massive share buy-backs. Why should a company use precious cash flow to buy in common stock at above book value when earnings to fixed charges (by the company's calculation) have dropped from 2.4 times in 1986 to 1.6 times in September 1989? The company regrettably failed to include this table in the March 1990 10Q.

In late 1988, Marriott announced a massive restructuring. Sell divisions, management said, mostly restaurants; pay down debt. Good, you say, sensible, comforting. Wrong; don't jump to conclusions. The company will also buy in shares, probably with borrowed funds. The company moved quickly on the last part, buying in six million shares in the first quarter for around $198 million with debt issuance of $318 million and repayment of $36 million. Are they investing with what might be the next interest payment? "Uncle," cried some bondholders. Enough is enough.

Green Tree Acceptance, Inc.

Green Tree Acceptance is the Rubik's Cube of present value freaks. MBA programs could use this for a case in how different assumptions affect the balance sheet and income statement.

Green Tree purchases, pools, resells, and then services pools of mobile home mortgages or manufactured homes. When the company sells a pool, it records finance income at the time of sale and defers service income over the life of the contract or as the service is performed. OK, calculators ready. To derive the amount of finance income booked today, Green Tree gets the future value of the expected stream of revenues, haircuts the future value by prepayments, defaults, deferred service income, and the amount due to investors, then present values that amount back using the coupon rate on the pool for a discount rate. That amount is then shown on the balance sheet as assets, net of reserves except for credit losses. And Green Tree doesn't give anyone a clue about the assumptions they use to derive this magic number. The company changed the discount rate assumption in the 1989 10K from the rate paid investors to the yield to investors. Huh?

Green Tree reminds analysts that it pays to read 10Ks from

previous years simultaneously with the current year: it's the only way to tell if the company discloses more or less. (For example Oracle Systems dropped the disclosure of "unbilled receivables" after analysts asked aggravating questions. The unbilled receivables didn't go away, but the questions did.) Green Tree's 1989 10K discloses slightly more—for example, the company disclosed the outstanding balance on all securitized and private investor sales, $1.975 billion, for the first time.

The net result is that stockholders not only do not know if revenues are real; they don't know how good the accounts receivable are (the repository of all those fees waiting to be collected over time). And this, in a company that's highly leveraged, in a cyclical industry with an unknown amount of off-balance-sheet liabilities (unless, of course, you know the assumptions behind the present value of liabilities calculation on the balance sheet)! Who would buy a stock like this with a grab bag of assets and the next thing to no disclosure? The College Retirement Equity Fund, Loomis-Sayles, and NewSouth Capital Management for three; they each own 5 percent positions according to the 1990 proxy.

The accounting mumbo jumbo stocks should lead a stockholder to conclude: if you own it and can't understand it, sell it. If you don't own it and can't understand it, consider selling it short if you think the obscurity is just the tip of the iceberg.

Notes

1. Thornton O'glove, "1989 Quality of Earnings Report Roundup," *Quality of Earnings Report,* 30, 1 (January 1989): 2.

2. CUC International, Form 10Q, 30 April 1989, n.p.

3. National Education Corporation, Annual Report, 31 December 1988, 28.

4. Arthur Rade, Merrill Lynch Research Report, 17 April 1989, from National Education Corporation Excerpts, 1 August 1989, n.p.

5. Ram Capoor, Morgan Stanley Research Report, 24 May 1989, from National Education Corporation Excerpts, 1 August 1989, n.p.

6. Arthur Rade, Merrill Lynch Research Report, 12 June 1989, from National Education Corporation Excerpts, 1 August 1989, n.p.

7. Fred Anschel, Dean Witter Reynolds Research Report, 13 June

1989, from National Education Corporation Excerpts, 1 August 1989, n.p.

8. Arthur Rade, Merrill Lynch Research Report, 19 July 1989, from National Education Corporation Excerpts, 1 August 1989, n.p.

9. Ram Capoor, Morgan Stanley Research Report, 21 July 1989, from National Education Corporation Excerpts, 1 August 1989, n.p.

10. National Education Corporation, Form 10Q, 30 June 1989, 7.

11. Michael K. Ozanian, "Marriott's Farewell Tour," *Financial World*, 3 October 1989, 28.

6

Money Suckers: Coining Money to Live

During any period of economic expansion, some companies require great gulps of capital to stay alive. When operations fail to prime the pump of free cash flow, financial markets irrigate the basic business. Stock and bond holders presume that asset prices will continue to grow in a reasonable relationship to past appreciation history, so that everything will be OK when management finally decides to sell valuable assets to pay back growing debt. In this environment of easy asset sales and easier financing, some companies build reputations on the future value of assets and revenues: pay for the future now, the investor is urged. Like carnival hawkers, these companies promise that the view from front row center will someday be worth the admission price.

In order to fund the future, money must be obtained continually. Debt, equity, partnerships, private placements—all the financial instruments—are used. Integrated Resources is the best example in recent years. Cable companies are another, as are real estate ventures that don't cover costs with cash flow. In the 1980s, money was easy to get; companies prospered without earnings and without free cash flow. As the banker said about Jiffy Lube, easy money was the problem. When the market appetite for new debt disappeared, so did the companies.

The Nine Lives of Integrated Resources, Inc.

Integrated Resources takes honors as one of the longest term short positions (except perhaps CopyTele). It seemed like a lay-up in 1986, but it took until June 1989 to default on the layers of debt. At least once or twice a year, short sellers would yell, "Timber, there she goes," but the stock would defy gravity and bounce back.

New Tax Law Death Blow to Shelter Companies

When the Tax Reform Act of 1986 was passed, business looked hard for the companies that made money selling tax shelters. When a fundamental change occurs in the business environment, there are two strategies to follow for the short seller: short the marginal company or short the institutional favorite. Both strategies have proponents. The institutional favorite is the quality company with good growth, pretty financials, and a large number of institutional stockholders. Institutional favorites crash more quickly because large numbers of portfolio managers rush to dump the stock when the analysts are finally convinced that the industry has been dealt an irreparable blow. If the company management is astute, they might dig their way out of the cave-in before the institutions exit. The marginal company, on the other hand, has shaky financials, bad management, and a history of aggressive but often poorly executed business strategies. Problems develop more rapidly when no support exists, either financial or managerial. The stockholder base is less sophisticated: they are slower to sell, pay less attention or, even worse, are composed entirely of friends of the company. The price takes forever to reflect the reality of the company condition.

Integrated Resources was the marginal company. Revenues came from three areas: life insurance companies, direct participation investment programs, and money management. Privately offered investment programs (tax shelters) provided the bulk of

FIGURE 6.1

Integrated Resources, Inc.

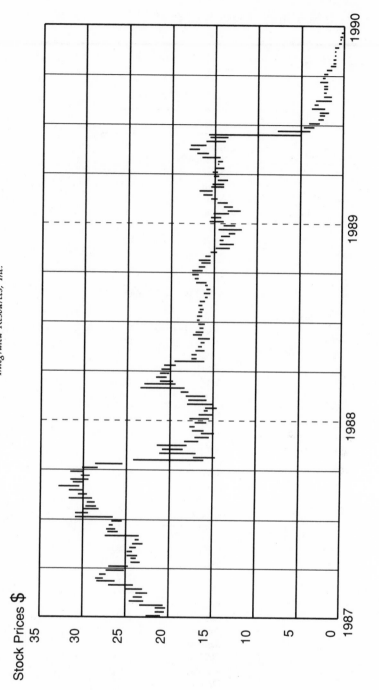

TABLE 6.1

Integrated Resources, Inc.
Short Interest

1987	
January	584,305
February	718,614
March	626,119
April	591,986
May	563,048
June	543,170
July	524,856
August	586,570
September	572,969
October	575,257
November	539,103
December	440,518

1988	
January	325,028
February	347,728
March	408,113
April	441,395
May	447,095
June	482,120
July	497,320
August	504,220
September	490,320
October	453,020
November	455,070
December	489,878

1989	
January	615,760
February	757,701
March	1,057,170
April	1,010,221
May	1,038,495
June	1,365,330
July	2,632,226
August	2,208,990
September	1,925,123
October	1,564,903
November	1,234,121
December	997,833

the revenue and net income: more than 69 percent of investment program revenue in 1982–84, which in turn was 77 percent of pretax income. A change in the tax law should certainly affect net income, unless the company could reposition itself rapidly.

Why was Integrated a marginal company? The 1986 10K and proxy held the clues.

Greedy Management or Valuable Leaders?

First, the Zises brothers—Selig and Jay—and Arthur Goldberg, the executives of Integrated. You could hardly go wrong with the brothers and company. The granddaddies of creative compensation planning, the Zises got paid for just about everything that happened at Integrated: you expected to see a percentage of the pencil purchase order go to the Zises. A few highlights from the proxy:

- Selig owned 6 percent, Jay 5.4 percent of the common; "other family members" owned 3.5 percent, Goldberg 2.3 percent.
- Total salary + bonus + compensation for the five top officers was $5,855,920. The top twenty-one executives as a group earned over $15 million. The company earned $49,812,000.
- That included a minimum of 5.5 percent of pretax profits and a guideline of 10 percent of pretax profits before unusual charges and credits. An additional 5.7 percent went to other executive officers.

The company even paid medical costs not covered by insurance policies for the Zises' father and brother, $22,342 and $16,018 in 1985. Corporate headquarters was a daily family reunion. Everybody got paid and everybody had a job. Father Bernard got $125,000 in consulting fees, $27,500 in bonuses, and $417,000 in allocated partnership losses. Brother Seymour was an insurance agent and registered representative and got a hefty cut. Jay's wife made a paltry $100,000. In 1985, Integrated gave the printing company of the Zises' brother-in-law $922,115 in printing business.

Integrated also had a creative stock bonus incentive plan.

When grantors exercised the stock option, they paid 5 percent in cash and the balance in installments over the vesting period. But each grantor was also entitled to a bonus equal to the installment payment when it was due. The executives, therefore, paid just 5 percent cash money for their stock.

Selig also bought a condominium in Manhattan from the company. Integrated bought it for $1.4 million in 1982 and added $170,000 in improvements. Selig improved it another $275,000. The appraisal in 1986 was $1.825 million, or less than the purchase price plus improvements, so Selig bought it for $1.55 million. Manhattan real estate was apparently flat for four years in the mid 1980s.

Chief executives paid no money management fees to the company's subsidiary money manager, although they had funds under management—waived fees were $49,208 each a year. They had, of course, disability, life insurance, and "additional personal benefits." Officers also purchased interest in limited partnerships, and the company granted bonuses in the amount of the capital contribution. Officers were also allocated $18.2 million in losses from the partnerships before the limited partners were admitted, presumably to shelter their salary/bonus packages.

For the period 1981–85, Integrated paid officers and directors approximately $50 million under compensation, bonus incentive, reimbursement for partnership investments, life insurance, and medical reimbursements. In 1986 a stockholder sued, claiming excessive compensation was paid to executives.

Challenging Financial Statements

The financial statements of the company were as edifying as the executives' perks. The December 31, 1986 10K was a long and enlightening document. First, the balance sheet (table 6.2): equity as a percentage of assets had dropped from over 20 percent to under 10 percent in a year—not a lot of cushion for bad times.

Next, the assets looked a little funny: what was real and bankable? Notes and receivables were 22 percent of assets. Were those due from investors in old partnerships that were no longer attractive? Were they from partnerships with negative cash flow? Were they collectable?

TABLE 6.2

Integrated Resources
Balance Sheet
(Dollars in thousands)

	December 31,	
	1986	**1985**
ASSETS		
CASH	$ 69,473	$ 41,536
INVESTMENTS:		
Held by life insurance subsidiaries	2,178,550	388,992
Short-term investments, at cost (approximates market)	34,230	25,205
Equity securities, at lower of cost or market (1986—cost $28,740, 1985—market $44,256)	26,039	43,830
Other	85,723	67,677
	2,324,542	525,704
NOTES AND RECEIVABLES	1,149,808	935,993
PROPERTY, EQUIPMENT AND IMPROVEMENTS, at cost, net of accumulated depreciation and amortization of $24,773 and $16,029	52,066	40,904
PREPAID ACQUISITION COSTS of life insurance, investment programs and value of acquired insurance in force	445,392	203,068
ASSETS OF SEPARATE ACCOUNTS	948,469	275,395
OTHER ASSETS	62,301	49,775
INTANGIBLE ASSETS, net of accumulated amortization of $5,494 and $4,449	84,617	38,193
TOTAL ASSETS	$5,136,668	$2,110,568
LIABILITIES AND SHAREHOLDERS' EQUITY		
FUTURE POLICY BENEFITS AND CLAIM RESERVES	$2,541,423	$362,227
SHORT-TERM LOANS	200,960	281,585
ACCOUNTS PAYABLE AND OTHER LIABILITIES (Note F)	248,428	207,740
DEFERRED INCOME TAXES	101,873	109,905
LIABILITIES OF SEPARATE ACCOUNTS	948,469	275,395
SENIOR INDEBTEDNESS	111,411	134,743
SUBORDINATED INDEBTEDNESS	478,393	276,607
COMMITMENTS AND CONTINGENCIES		
REDEEMABLE PREFERRED STOCK	—	13,088
SHAREHOLDERS' EQUITY	505,711	449,278
TOTAL LIABILITIES AND SHAREHOLDERS' EQUITY	$5,136,668	$2,110,568

Source: Integrated Resources, Inc., Form 10K, 31 December 1986.

Notes to the financials explained a little. Of the $692,010,000 due from investment programs, $231,409,000 was due from limited partnerships, $131,227,000 from investors in partnerships, and $299,395,000 represented deferred fees and contract rights. Deferred fees? Yes, Integrated booked revenues from future rental proceeds and proceeds realized on sale of property up front when it closed the partnership. If the deals turned sour, not only were receivables and assets inflated, but the company also would have to reverse revenues previously realized.

Keep in mind that shareholders' equity was only $505,711,000 —10 percent of assets. Common stockholders' equity was $145 million—2.8 percent of assets. With that as a base, $299 million of the assets were aggressively booked revenues based on future events. Common equity has an impact on how much money can be raised in hard times—eroding equity capital affects bargaining and credit standing in the markets. The composition of capital was an important trail sign to track Integrated's demise.

Prepaid acquisition costs were $445 million, up from $203 million, a big jump. Notes, again, explained a little. Prepaid acquisition costs on investment programs had gone from $89 million to $193 million. Prepaid acquisition costs, remember, are costs that the company decided to defer expensing until later. They can be commissions paid to salespeople, costs of acquiring the business from another company, or costs of putting a partnership together. Integrated looked like it was attempting to manage earnings by deferring expenses. Not only does that not match cash flow (you pay now, collect later), but it puts future earnings in jeopardy. If revenues should slow (say, because the tax law changed), the company still has expenses to deduct every quarter, even without revenue—an interesting balance sheet structure for a company in flux.

Now, the income statement. Maybe Integrated has already straightened out the basic business questions and the resulting cash flow will strengthen the balance sheet, an optimistic Wall Streeter would infer. Pretax operating income was $39 million, down from $56 million, and $23 million of that (you have to check the notes for this number—table 6.3) comes from realized gains in the life insurance portfolios. It's hard to get cash money out of a life insurance sub: it may look pretty on consolidated income statements, but there are some restrictions on its use and repatriation back to the parent (more on this in chapter 7).

Net income of $18 million (before preferred dividend) looks a little pallid, next to the Zises brothers' income, but it's tough to run a company.

Shifting Focus: 1987

Integrated decided to change the product emphasis to income-producing partnerships, variable annuities, and money management. The company, as it diversified, continued to assure the public that the basic business was intact: the Japanese purchase of Integrated's property, 666 Fifth Avenue, by Sumitomo was widely publicized as a coup for the company, although it wasn't booked as a gain until a subsequent quarter. What followed in 1987 was a year of inventive earnings management.

The first quarter of 1987 was a victory for Integrated as far as the company was concerned, with "advances in revenues and income per share from continuing operations" despite conservative accounting.[1] Well, not exactly. Income from operations was $11.7 million, down from $12.5 million, and cash flow continued to deteriorate.

Let's stop a minute for a lecture on cash flow. Cash flow is

TABLE 6.3

Gains in the Insurance Subsidiaries
(Dollars in thousands)

	1986	1985	1984
Fixed maturities	$ 82,244	$29,759	$17,436
Equity securities	1,384	1,296	424
Mortgage loans on real estate	21,052	1,474	—
Policy loans	7,207	3,577	1,998
Short-term and other investments	12,354	1,998	2,155
	124,241	38,104	22,013
Realized gains	23,169	5,478	1,841
	147,410	43,582	23,854
Investment expenses	1,474	326	280
	$145,936	$43,256	$23,574

Source: Integrated Resources, Inc. Form 10K, 31 December 1986

defined as net income plus depreciation, amortization, and deferred taxes. Cash flow from operations generally takes into account working capital as well. An analyst wants to know how much cash is available to the company for expansion, dividends, stock purchase, or retirement of debt—in other words, what's the financial flexibility of the company? That means making subjective decisions about the business of the company and what cash flows relate directly to that business. For instance, a furniture rental company must continually refurbish rental furniture or revenues slow; so the analyst tempers the depreciation add-back number to take this into account, since depreciation is a direct cost of doing business. When analyzing retailers, adjustments must be made for inventory and receivables because they have to have inventory to sell. When analyzing a cable production company, produced programming is surely a cost of staying in business.

Back to Integrated. The company was in the business of buying property, repackaging it into partnerships, selling partnerships, managing the partnership property, then selling it. So cash flow should be reduced by purchases of property and increased by collections—that's not investing, it's the basic business. The March 31, 1987 10Q cash flow defined in those terms was an outflow of $24 million, compared to an inflow of $31 million in March 1986 (operating cash flow from the Statement of Changes minus the purchase of property and investments plus collections) (table 6.4). And that's without deducting for preferred dividends, which are not a necessity of doing business, although they are a factor in financing.

In the second quarter, management thought the company had turned the corner. Sharply higher results heralded the transition. Integrated had discovered the roll-up. Income from operations of $23 million vs. $13.3 million was backed with solid declines in cash flow. Six month burn was ($190.9 million) vs. ($54 million). Management mentioned in the notes to the 10Q that part of the increases in net income (no disclosure yet on how much) had come from "restructuring public net lease real estate limited partnerships."[2] Integrated folded 13 limited partnerships into New York Stock Exchange depository units and collected a fee one more time on partnerships they had previously packaged, sold, and booked as revenue.

TABLE 6.4

Integrated Resources Statement of Changes
(Unaudited)
(Dollars in thousands)

	Three Months Ended March 31,	
	1987	1986
OPERATING ACTIVITIES:		
Net cash (used in) continuing operating activities	$ (5,406)	$ (5,920)
INVESTING ACTIVITIES:		
Net cash (used in) discontinued operations	—	(2,924)
Purchases of property, equipment, and improvements, net of sales	(1,740)	(5,779)
Purchases of investments, net of sales	(47,482)	(317)
Net collections on notes and receivables	30,611	43,038
Net (increase) in other assets	(4,500)	(6,973)
Net cash (used in) provided from investing activities	(23,111)	27,045
FINANCING ACTIVITIES:		
Shareholders' equity:		
Issuance of capital stock	—	70,998
Redemption of preferred stock	—	(13,088)
Preferred dividends	(7,325)	(9,187)
Debt:		
Increase (decrease) in short-term loans	46,620	(237,001)
Issuance of subordinated indebtedness	—	287,207
Early extinguishment of subordinated indebtedness	—	(118,050)
Payments of indebtedness	(11,618)	(4,268)
Net cash provided from (used in) financing activities	27,677	(23,389)
NET (DECREASE) IN CASH	$ (840)	$ (2,264)

Source: Integrated Resources, Inc. Form 10Q, 31 March 1987.

The stock price returned to health with a move off September 1986 lows of $16.25 to $30 by July 8, 1987. Everybody was happy, especially the Zises (Selig sold a little stock—41,000 shares—in the early fall). *Value Line* commented that Integrated's business was booming; they predicted an earnings growth rate of 30 percent in 1988 after more than tripling in 1987 and rated the stock "2" for timeliness.[3] "A Resourceful Turnaround," *Fortune* announced after panning the stock in June 1986.[4]

The stock price peaked at $32.875 in the fall.

The Drop

The third quarter was another good one, not up sequentially but still $22.5 million in operating earnings vs. $4.5 million. Cash flow was ($244 million) vs. $8.2 million for nine months. The cash burn was ameliorated by new long-term and short-term debt. Shareholders' equity as a percent of assets was now 8.6 percent. Income for the quarter included the gain on the sale of 666 Fifth Avenue.

Wall Street never warmed to Integrated. Drexel, Burnham, the investment banker, was really the only advocate of the stock. Maybe that was because there were too few shares outstanding, or because the company didn't tempt the Street with fees on new issue stock deals. Most firms on the Street sold Integrated's private partnerships in the early 1980s, so it was odd, this lack of interest. It helped the shorts. The stock escaped the notice of the investment community, so a short squeeze never developed, even toward the end when it was a lay-up.

But the stock was something of an institutional favorite. The 1987 10K notes that Templeton Funds owned 15.8 percent of the company, and Equitable had another 14.4 percent. *Value Line* periodically liked the stock. And, of course, the Drexel daisy chain owned paper and bonds and a little stock. First Executive had 6.9 percent of the common, $27 million in bonds (the 10.75 percent of 1996), together with $39 million book value of preferred stock.

The stock chopped along in late 1987 and early 1988—$16–$24 was the range. When the 10K came out around the end of March, equity per share was listed in the 10K as $21.97 and income was $2.98, up from $1.06.

The 10K had a particularly interesting footnote: a change in amortization of prepaid acquisition costs in the fourth quarter added $.97 to earnings. Net for the quarter was $.97 from continuing operations. The change wasn't booked as an extraordinary item.

To recap the earnings for the year: the second quarter growth was from fees for the roll-up; the third quarter was the sale of a building; the fourth quarter was an accounting change. Throw in a gain from termination of a pension plan and fees from previously syndicated programs. Integrated was having a tough time generating recurring operating earnings, even as debt climbed.

Pretax income was down in the first quarter of 1988. The new amortization schedule helped the comparison by $.20, but interest expense was up. The 10Q again stated that the company "will continue to require additional funds from sources other than operations."[5] And accounts payable was up from $270 million to $426 million in just three months. Integrated needed financing. Who would lend to a company with disastrous operating cash flow and deteriorating ratios, down to less than 8 percent equity to assets, in a dismal business climate for new real estate partnerships?

Who, indeed? Drexel announced a senior subordinated note deal in the summer of 1988, just $100 million. Who bought? Insurance companies, primarily, and S & L's.

Integrated itself owned two insurance companies—Integrated Resources Life and Capitol Life. The insurance subs in turn owned a fair amount of Integrated and Integrated affiliate paper— stocks, bonds, notes. The insurance company portfolios turned out to be a problem (more in chapter 7).

Integrated Resources Life's 1988 Convention Statements show $41 million in Integrated and other subsidiary debt, acquired in 1988, and $3.5 million in common stock (including Integrated's American Insured Mortgage Investors Series), plus $6.2 million in book value of Diasonics stock, a company that Integrated senior was trying to acquire. And that's in a life company with total assets of $3.086 billion and a surplus of only $77.3 million (up from $51.1 million after Integrated contributed a note to a surplus of $15 million). Integrated Life also owned $17.8 million in real estate. Of the bond portfolio, 24 percent was classified in the 20 percent reserve category (meaning high-yield junk bonds).

Capitol Life looked worse. It owned $38 million in a promissory note of the parent acquired in 1986 and $2 million in demand notes of Integrated Life. But the real clunker in Capitol was $187.56 million invested in the stock of subsidiaries, mostly Realty Investors, a real estate holding company. Twenty percent of the bond portfolio—$249 million—was in the maximum reserve category, and the company owned an additional $8.5 million in real estate, with a current value of $5.6 million. Capitol had assets of $1.9 billion and a surplus of $61 million after paying the parent an $8 million dividend in 1988, according to the 1988 Convention Statement.

The insurance companies were clearly unhealthy. They were perilously close to running through surplus if the parent floundered. So the entire Integrated empire, not only the parent, looked shaky.

The 1988 June quarter was uneventful, and the stock continued to wallow from $15.50 to $20.75. Operating income was down, $17.2 million versus $23 million, despite revenues of $414.5 million versus $289 million. The comparison of net income wasn't as bad as that of operating income because of tax rate decreases.

The bond deal went off without a hitch in August and the proceeds were used to pay down short-term debt.

The September 1988 earnings announcement showed that the struggle for earnings was losing ground. Pretax was $9.5 million versus $22.5 million. The earnings gains of the previous year were tough to match. Equity as a percentage of assets was down to 7.1 percent. Cash resources were disappearing, and only $7 million was available for dividends from the life companies.

Insiders Stampede to Exit

On December 21, 1988 Integrated was trading around $14 a share. The Zises brothers sold 900,000 shares to ICH Corp., an insurance company, for $21! ICH announced that it would buy another 7.5 million to-be-issued shares to gain control of the company.

Short sellers went wild in greedy anticipation of the certain crash. The big trigger, the clue that the game was up, had been announced by the company. But, one more time, the stock didn't drop to single digits. It was a gift—the fat lady sang loud and clear and wore a "the end is here" sign. Takeover greed appeared to be supporting the price: *Value Line* said avoid, despite potential for near-term price rises if the company fetches another buy-out proposal. The shorts used the disparity to short more.

A little history here: ICH owned 20 percent of First Executive. The company had been involved in several other mergers or buy-outs with Drexel clients that had fallen through. ICH didn't have much credibility as anything but a Zises' bailout vehicle.

The market mulled the proposal and the stock price dipped to

$12. One or more of the convertible preferred holders sold 562,-
000 shares at a low. Rumors continued off and on of a new
suitor—maybe JMB, the real estate company. Lawsuits proliferated against the brothers. It looked like the end.

But nothing ever happens fast on Wall Street. The stock stabilized, ran up to $16 and change, backed off a little, and stalled.
Integrated announced earnings for the year March 22, 1989, and
stockholders might have been reassured. After-tax income from
operations was up dramatically from the paltry September quarter—$20 million versus $15.3 million in the previous year. Earnings per share for the year were $2.42. Former president and new
chief executive officer Goldberg made comforting noises about
limited partnership sales, the executive equivalent of toasting
marshmallows on the embers of Carthage.

Then on May 16 Integrated announced that first-quarter results would be late and a net loss after preferred dividends. (Companies have forty-five days to file 10Qs with the SEC after the
end of the quarter, and ninety after the end of the fiscal year.)

The stock spiked again, up over $17. Buyers said: takeover for
sure at higher prices. Look at book on the stock anyway, the bulls
continued; all that real estate wasn't even valued at market. And
the great retail sales network was peerless, according to advo-
cates. A sure thing. Some financial services company would jump
at the value.

Shorts felt a little like this particular dead dog wouldn't ever
keel over. It had been years—and six months since the death
blow. But it felt like more than a lifetime; who says short sellers
are short-term market players? They already had their list of
bondholders and stockholders and all the concentric circles of
other companies that would be affected when the various Integrated securities dropped in price after the blasted stock finally
bit the dust.

Around June 14, 1989 the company admitted cash was a problem. The stock obligingly dropped to $12, down 3.375. But bulls
thought bankers and investment bankers would help out, swap
money for collateral on new loans, or that the company could sell
some assets.

Then Drexel balked and it was all over. The stock traded to $5.
Finally.

And everyone said, "Oh my, it was so sudden, just out of the

blue." *Value Line* owned Integrated commercial paper in the
money market fund, the fall had been so quick. And the company
was so healthy just yesterday, said Wall Street. Except the short
sellers, who sadly punched into their HP–12C calculators the
present value/future value/years to figure the annualized returns
from being short this dog for years.

The most important lesson from Integrated, one that should
have been obvious (but perhaps not in the 1980s), was that banks
and other short-term lenders (Drexel, in this case) control the
destiny of a company with negative cash flow. The lenders decided to foreclose. Nothing had changed with Integrated; the
spigot was just shut off. Assets may be undervalued on the balance sheet, but if your particular asset (be it a buggy whip or real
estate) is illiquid when you need funds, it doesn't count for much
except as collateral for bonds or bank loans. Leopold Bernstein
can lecture in his *Financial Statement Analysis* that financial structure
and working capital affect the essential flexibility of management
to react to varying economic environments, but until you see a
big one topple you really don't believe how important capital
structure can be. Companies don't cause bankruptcies, banks do.
But the companies build the gory mare's nests of financial statements.

After playing footsy with debt holders for six months, Integrated filed for bankruptcy in early 1990.

Cable Companies: We're Gonna Make a Whole Bunch of Money Real Soon

Cable companies have been big winners on Wall Street for the
last decade. Some observers give them credit for educating bankers and investment bankers on highly leveraged transactions. The
first small cable company must have been owned by one crafty
country boy who set out to sell debt to anybody who would listen
and could loan money.

Cable costs a lot to build, and the revenues come in slowly, at
$20 or $30 a month per customer. So the loan couldn't be justified
on any traditional interest-coverage evaluation based on earn-

ings. Cash flow analysis was born, therefore, or resurrected. Investment bankers bought the technique enthusiastically, because it helped do more deals. Banks didn't want to be left out, so they tagged along. And Wall Street analysts jumped on the bandwagon to educate institutional investors about the new methodology as they salivated with lust over promising corporate finance fees. The cable boys built like crazy and grew fast, and everyone in the world would soon have cable with many add-on channels plus pay-per-view.

The scenario worked just fine when price per subscriber was growing in the resale market, so that companies could trade systems back and forth at ever-increasing prices and show mind-boggling capital gains. But as the price per subscriber rose, nobody noticed that payback stretched and stretched—to as much as ten years and more, with new technologies and regulation threatening.

From a short seller's perspective the marginal companies were entrancing. The financials were snickering material, and Adelphia Communications was a favorite because of its simplicity.

Adelphia Communications Corporation

Adelphia Communications Corporation was incorporated in 1986 "for the purpose of reorganizing five cable companies then principally owned by executive officers."[6] The company got off on the right foot. The new corporation owned "clusters" in New Jersey, New York, Florida, and Pennsylvania. Homes "passed" equaled more than a half a million by 1987.

Wall Street, like any other business, creates its own vocabulary for new industries and its own methods of analysis. The cable industry and the real estate business both felt hampered by Graham and Dodd's conservative methodology, so the analysts (or the companies) created a more compelling method of valuation. Cash flow, the language of the bankers, also became outmoded as the cable debt grew. Book didn't matter. It had no significance when prices of assets were rapidly going to the moon. Both industries felt that valuation models should take these spectacular price launchings into numerical account. Thus ENAV was born, Estimated Net Asset Value. (Rouse, the real estate company, did

FIGURE 6.2

Adelphi Communications

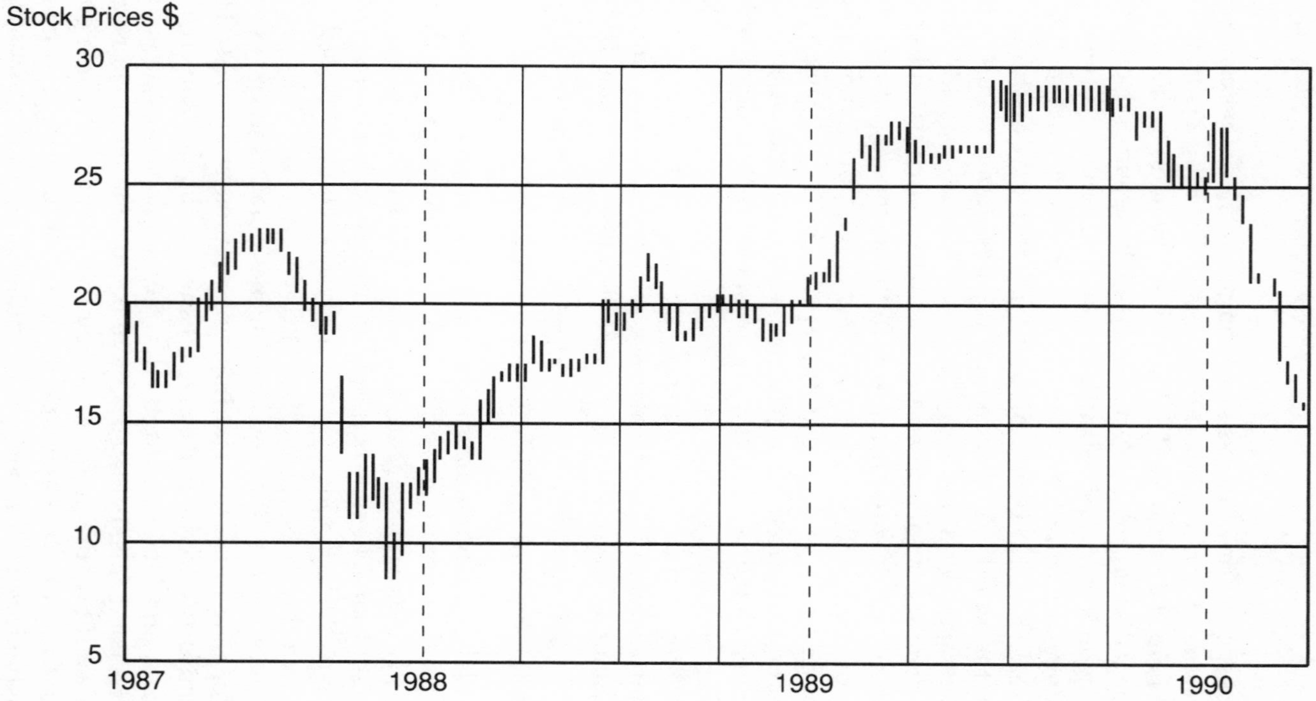

much the same thing with its "current value Shareholders' Equity per share," based on market-value appraisals.) With the new methodology the buyers of the stock and the debt could feel that they were using conservative valuation models to acquire very cheap assets. The ratio of price to ENAV was a popular measure of stock value.

Back to Adelphia. The pertinent point from the short's view was that cash flow, including interest payment less capital expenditures, was growing increasingly negative. The stock or the bonds looked palatable for an investor only if the company sold all its systems at hefty multiples (and prices appeared to have peaked) or if it raised monthly subscriber prices a lot. Congress, meanwhile, seemed to care about quality of service and price increases in this monopoly business.

Here's the way cash flow looked (in thousands) for the fiscal year ending March 31:

	1988	1987	1986
Net loss	(76,840)	(29,354)	(14,914)
Amortization	51,655	20,623	6,093
Depreciation	25,350	15,018	9,558
	165	6,287	737

So the cable aficionados said things were looking better. Additions to property, plant, and equipment were:

	(48,428)	(29,209)	(11,753)
Total outflow	(48,263)	(19,922)	(11,016)

and that doesn't include acquisitions, which were another $317 million in 1988, $329 million in 1987. How much of the capital spending was discretionary and how much was not? You can't tell.

Meanwhile, debt grew, the deficit grew, and Adelphia continued to "provide operating and marketing efficiencies through clustering of systems and the related configuration. . . ."[7] It sounds like insect mating manuals.

The company decided in May 1988 to acquire several systems from the controlling stockholder family, the Rigas, who also ran the company, for a net consideration of $119.5 million in stock and senior promissory notes (11.75 percent due 1993). The company also placed $16 million in Exchangeable Subordinated Notes for a subsidiary, Adelphia Cablevision, privately with an insurance company—twelve-year notes at 10.5 percent. From the comparison of coupon and maturity terms, the insurance companies should have hired the Rigas to negotiate their side, too.

Cash flow for the ensuing fiscal years was:

	1989	1990
Net loss	$(123,645)	$(156,939)
Amortization	78,295	76,912
Depreciation	35,714	45,195
Total	(9,636)	(34,832)
Capital Expenditures	(58,510)	(75,619)
Total outlay	$(68,146)	$(110,451)

As Kidder, Peabody junk analyst Mark Grotevant noted, "many growth-oriented cable companies should not be expected to show significant improvement in cash flow coverages of interest expense. . . . As with many cable companies the primary source of credit quality improvement is through growth in asset values and an increase in the net asset values that represent a support cushion to bondholders."[8] So the increase in prices of cable systems is the credit security the bondholders count on—at least until the music stops.

Cable stocks appear to be waning, and ENAV is not as popular with harder-to-sell junk debt. It will be interesting to see when Adelphia starts printing money for stockholders, too. Until now, shorts have had fearsome battles and a hard row to hoe over cable stocks, but somebody has to give Adelphia money a couple times a year to keep it afloat—and it certainly won't be the short sellers.

The cable wars point firmly to the most prevalent mistake of short sellers: they are often shortsighted about the duration of new industry growth and concomitant asset price increases.

Parabolas can sometimes appear to bend back on themselves, but the rate of return on the short position may look like net income on a cable company in the interim.

Notes

1. Selig A. Zises, Arthur H. Goldberg, and Jay H. Zises, Integrated Resources, Inc., First Quarter Report, 31 March 1987, 2.

2. Integrated Resources, Inc., Form 10Q, 30 March 1987, 10.

3. *Value Line,* 18 September 1987, 2066.

4. "Follow-up," *Fortune,* 28 September 1987, 15.

5. Integrated Resources, Inc., Form 10Q, 31 March 1988, 14.

6. Adelphia Communications Corporation, Form 10K, 31 March 1987, 1.

7. Adelphia Communications Corporation, Form 10Q, 31 December 1989, 11.

8. Mark L. Grotevant, "Adelphia Communications Corporation," Kidder, Peabody High Yield Research, Summer 1989, 12.

7

Check Kiting, Corporate Style

The asset-swapping, check-kiting companies are the most complex financial puzzles and the most fun to discover. The basis of the shell game is to create assets on the balance sheet and to keep liabilities off to give the appearance of financial health. The simplest form is two companies that swap real estate. Both companies take a gain on the income statements, both companies have real estate at higher costs on the balance sheet. Everyone's happy although no economic event has occurred. The S & L's are pros at real estate asset swapping.

Insurance companies are attractive vehicles for pyramiding and hiding assets. The subsidiary companies can swap back and forth to create statutory gains; they buy pieces of each other and hide it all in insurance statements that nobody reads.

But first, an uncomplicated example to introduce the concept of assets from air.

Cheyenne Software: Respectable Ratios by Acquisition

Cheyenne Software neither has headquarters in Wyoming nor receives the majority of its revenues from software, so the corporate name is a bit misleading. The consolidated financials are equally opaque.

If an institutional portfolio manager ran a screen for small cap stocks with revenues over $100 million and losses heading toward breakeven, Cheyenne Software would show up. A quick read of the company's products would suggest that Cheyenne was in a high-growth software area, LAN (local area network) products, and the manager might buy the stock off the computer model without another thought. Not so fast.

A closer look at consolidated financials would reveal that Cheyenne has only $598,000 in revenues for the year ending June 30, 1989 and no earnings over a three-year operating history. The consolidated subsidiary, which is also a publicly traded company, F. A. Computer Technologies, has revenues in excess of $100 million (with its acquisition of Gates in early 1989), was in default of bank covenants by December 1989, and is in a rotten, low-margin, highly competitive commodity business, computer hardware sales and delivery.

Consolidation is the preferred method of combining financials of parent and subsidiaries when the parent owns more than 50 percent of the subsidiary. If, however, the investment drops below 50 percent, the equity method—or one-line consolidation—is generally used. Revenues and assets are not then combined; a single, one-line amount is shown on the income statement and balance sheet for the value of the investment and the quarterly change in that amount.

From a value perspective, the market price deconsolidation is an interesting calculation. In October 1989 the market valued F. A. Computer Technologies at $.625 a share times 33.6 million shares, or $21 million. Cheyenne owned 53 percent, or $11 million worth. Yet the market valued Cheyenne, with its $598,000 in revenues, at $7.25 a share times 9.6 million shares, or $70 million. The $70 million market value minus $10 million for the hardware distributing subsidiary equals $60 million—for $598,000 in revenues, no income, and assets minus F. A. Computer Technologies of under $5 million.

Why the disparity? Computer models, perhaps? Who knows. But the market did it, not the company. The company simply acquired a portion of another company and combined the financials according to the rules; then the buyers of Cheyenne common stock moved it up to the ridiculous stratosphere. The company understands that if F. A. Computer Technologies did a stock offering and diluted the Cheyenne stake, Cheyenne management would have quite a job reeducating stockholders and Wall Street to the new numbers when Cheyenne deconsolidated the financial statements.

So Cheyenne Software is a simple example of the Wall Street maxim, "appearance is reality," which was carried to extreme in the 1960s with consolidations and pooling of interest (read Abraham Briloff's classic exposé articles) and, perhaps, in the 1980s with Drexel daisy chains. Since no one digs behind the numbers, what appears on the financials is gospel. That's the market context for the asset mirage.

The Weasel Launches a Hot Air Balloon

The problem for an analyst is how to detect by reading their public histories which companies are built on worthless and illiquid assets before the market realizes the disparity. Particularly in the financial sector, company portfolios are akin to blind pools. For example, it's difficult to ascertain the quality of loans in a bank portfolio.

Western Savings and Loan Association, or "the Weasel," as it was dubbed, was an Arizona savings and loan that the market priced above any rational valuation. In 1986 the stock traded above $20 despite book value of $6 and a Standard and Poors write-up that alluded to the inflated balance sheet.

The questions about the Weasel's market valuation rested on two concerns:

- What was the equity after adjustment for odd, unpriceable assets: securities, loans, and real estate?
- What were recurring earnings, if any?

It took a couple of years for the market to resolve those issues to satisfaction.

Background

Western had a colorful history. The Driggs family had run the S & L for three generations and son Gary Driggs, who had control in the 1980s, was the architect of the assets. After a downturn in the early 1980s, when significant losses threatened to sink the 20 percent family-owned company, Gary Driggs pulled Western out of a death spiral with an infusion of approved capital in the guise of Western preferred stock (considered capital by regulators), which he swapped for land.[1] In 1983 he helped another S & L improve its capital base when he booked a gain on real estate that Western sold to Broadview Savings and Loan for preferred stock, a note, and cash. The preferred stock quit paying interest quickly—in 1984—but it stayed on in the financials at the original swap price. The Broadview Savings stock became a cornerstone for shorts' asset evaluation.

Gary was famous in Phoenix for his economics sound and light shows. He'd pack the Arizona Biltmore with business people and use multiple projectors and pulsating jazz soundtracks to communicate his ever-bullish view on the economy of Arizona. He put his shareholders' money where his mouth was.

By 1986, when we pick up the story, Gary Driggs had shifted the mission of the S & L in an effort to hedge the vagaries of interest rate swings. He'd been strung out in the early 1980s on a huge interest rate bet with the S & L portfolio. The December 31, 1986 10K chats about his new strategy:

> Western Savings availed itself of these new investment opportunities by aggressively diversifying its operations with investments in real estate and in the securities of other companies in an effort to produce non-interest income. Western Savings believes that the problems experienced by the industry over the last few years as a result of volatile interest rates demonstrate that a strategy of diversification is important for future growth and stability.[2]

Detecting Asset Values: Hide and Go Seek

In practice this meant that the balance sheet changed (table 7.2) —on the asset side, direct investments steadily grew to 16.5 per-

FIGURE 7.1

Western Savings & Loan Association

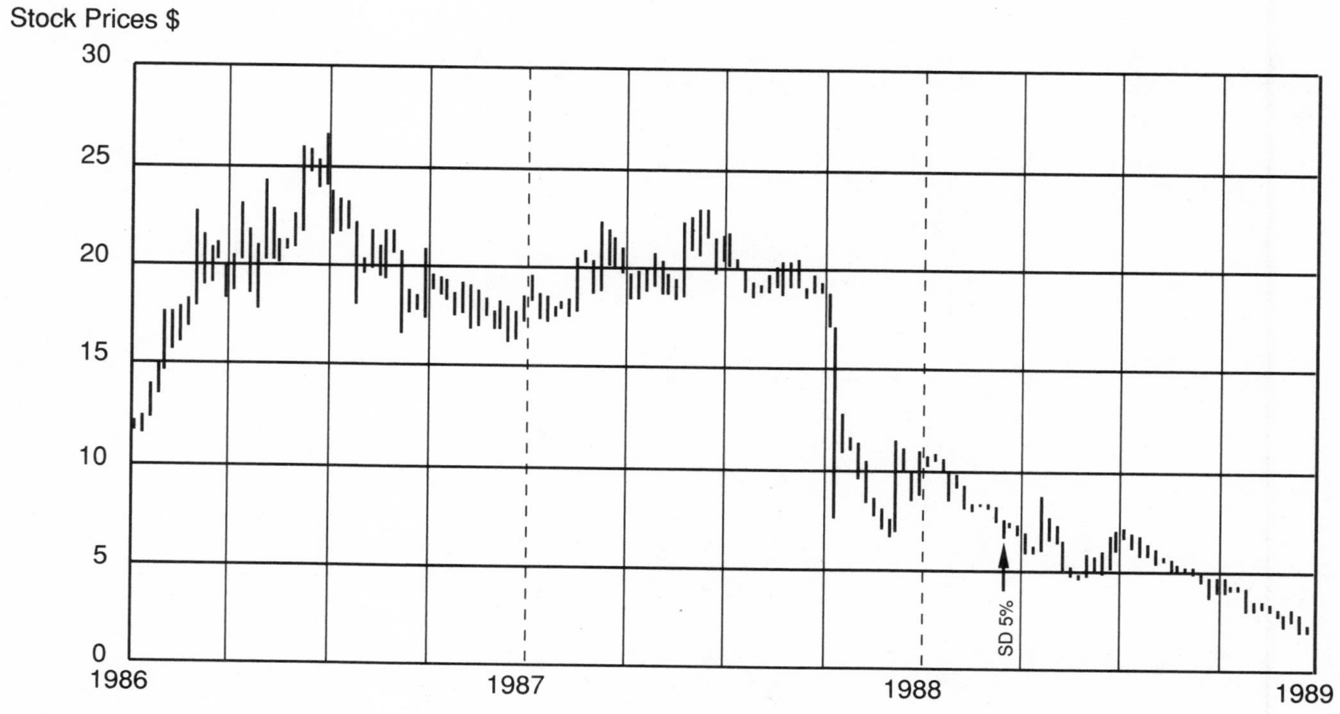

Stock Prices $

TABLE 7.1

*Western Savings and Loan
Association
Short Interest*

1986	
January	151,800
February	135,900
March	79,800
April	72,100
May	53,400
June	65,800
July	277,200
August	263,200
September	267,500
October	268,200
November	255,700
December	289,100

1987	
January	360,600
February	360,600
March	293,700
April	287,045
May	319,000
June	339,010
July	351,506
August	371,545
September	411,446
October	413,216
November	291,803
December	269,994

1988	
January	240,580
February	243,990
March	361,140
April	459,212
May	743,575
June	576,643
July	616,442
August	612,282
September	583,061
October	649,641
November	666,476
December	814,051

TABLE 7.2

Western's Balance Sheet
(Dollars in thousands)

	1986	1985
Assets		
Cash	$ 92,461	$ 54,788
Federal funds sold—At cost, which approximates market	85,000	—
U.S. Government securities—At amortized cost (market value of $698,940 and $466,277, respectively)	707,334	475,304
Mortgage-backed securities (market value of $380,504 and $483,421, respectively)	372,594	484,930
Loans receivable, net	2,995,312	2,686,857
Accrued interest receivable	47,495	44,785
Real estate		
Loans with additional interest provisions, accounted for as joint ventures, net	197,665	186,111
Acquired for development or investment, net	571,601	493,104
Acquired in settlement of loans, net	30,885	23,368
Capital stock of the Federal Home Loan Bank—At cost	26,213	22,500
Investments in affiliates	66,920	51,662
Other investments—At cost	88,786	94,378
Office properties and equipment—At cost, less accumulated depreciation and amortization	173,843	76,873
Goodwill and other intangible—At cost, less accumulated amortization	32,271	33,650
Other assets and deferred charges	58,725	56,287
Total assets	$5,547,105	$4,784,597
Liabilities and Stockholders' Equity		
Deposits	$3,813,475	$3,279,691
Advances from Federal Home Loan Bank	450,000	450,000
Securities sold under agreements to repurchase	836,292	694,518
Notes payable	91,654	39,332
Advances from borrowers for taxes and insurance	10,219	10,910
Accounts payable and accrued expenses	52,621	46,284
Income tax liabilities	43,730	28,883
Subordinated capital notes	121,130	121,904
Total liabilities	5,419,121	4,671,522

TABLE 7.2 *(continued)*

	1986	1985
Contingencies and commitments		
Stockholders' equity		
Preferred stock, $1 par value—Authorized 1,000,000 shares; issued and outstanding: 1986, 460,010 shares; 1985, 460,020 shares (Preference Value: 1986, $55,200; 1985, $58,200)	460	460
Common stock, $1 par value—Authorized, 25,000,000 shares; issued: 1986, 14,387,602 shares; 1985, 14,262,982 shares; outstanding: 1986, 12,087,624 shares; 1985, 12,096,304 shares	14,388	14,263
Additional paid-in capital	52,108	55,060
Retained earnings	73,245	53,032
Treasury stock—At cost: 1986, 2,299,978 shares; 1985, 2,166,678 shares	(12,217)	(9,740)
Total stockholders' equity	127,984	113,075
Total	$5,547,105	$4,784,597

Source: Western Savings and Loan Association, Form 10K, 31 December 1986.

cent of assets, or $915 million of $5.5 billion. It got your attention, from a quality of assets perspective. The Federal Home Loan Bank Board (FHLBB) had exhibited interest in the "direct investment" category as a percentage of regulatory net worth when it issued its first regulation on the subject in 1985. Western had stockholders' equity of $128 million on December 31, 1986, including preferred with liquidation value of $55.2 million and common equity, then, of $72.7 million.

What were these assets? First, Western had $571.6 million in real estate development projects in six states. The bank also stated that it "expected to expend up to $975 million toward the development of such projects, excluding capitalized interest, over a period of 10 to 20 years."[3] So that's OK; real estate always goes up, thoughtful investors must have said.

Investment securities were the next category. Right out of the 10K (table 7.3): Western had invested $155.7 million carrying value of assets in a grab bag of companies worth how much? The Weasel's estimated market value, Column 4, appears to be all footnotes and no numbers. Footnote 5c of the Consolidated Financial Statement says, "Many of the investments held by the

Association are not publicly traded; accordingly, market value is not readily determinable. In the opinion of management, the estimated aggregate market value of the above investments approximated cost at December 31, 1986 and 1985."[4] Of these investments, John Driggs was a director of America West Airlines, Inc., and Gary was a director of Newell Co. and Thousand Trails.

So start at the top of the investment security list to try to cipher a reasonable value—Thousand Trails, first. Trails was a notorious campground with memberships that sometimes forgot to pay after the initial sign-up fee. Negative cash flow had pushed the common stock price from the $20s to $2.9375 by December 31, 1986. After earning $1.8 million in 1985, Thousand Trails lost $50.4 million in 1986 and was in talks with lenders to restructure debt. Western's exposure to Trails was $22 million in common stock and $30.1 million face value in subordinated debt with a carrying cost of $15 million. The footnote says that the values of the securities are "substantially higher than the quoted market value."[5] The number of common shares owned was 2.4 million, or less than $7.2 million at current market, certainly "substantially" less than the $22 million carrying value. Notes to the financials also mention that Western had committed up to $50 million on two credit lines to Thousand Trails, $48.4 outstanding at year end, collateralized by real estate operating properties and receivables—no doubt the famous uncollectible ones. The total hook on Weasel's books was $85.4 million for the Trails investment.

Newell Co., in contrast, was a home run for Western, having almost doubled from the original cost of $29.9 million. Western owned 1.73 million shares worth $27 each on December 31, 1986, or close to $46.7 million, for a profit of $16.8 million. The securities were held for sale as soon as the details of transfer could be worked out.

Broadview Financial Corporation, however, was in arrears by $12.6 million on the preferred dividend and below capital requirements, with asset writedowns from construction lending mounting. Broadview common stock traded in November 1986 around $2 a share. Clearly, Broadview stock was worth something less than the $1 million for the common and $35 million on the cumulative preferred carrying value.

TABLE 7.3

Western's Odd Assets
(Dollars in thousands)

	December 31, 1985		December 31, 1986	
	Carrying Value	Estimated Market Value[1]	Carrying Value	Estimated Market Value[1]
Common Stock:				
Thousand Trails, Inc.[2]	$24,438	$19,861	$22,000	6
Newell Co.[2]	27,224	38,276	29,876	$46,710
Broadview Financial Corporation[3]	1,030	404	1,030	$350
Charter Federal Savings and Loan Association	696	1,087	0	—
Other	4,243	4,397	5,347	$5,332
Total	$57,631	$64,025	$58,253	
Cumulative Preferred Stock:				
Del E. Webb Corporation	$11,465	4	$11,465	4
Broadview Savings and Loan Company (with warrants)[5]	35,000	4	35,000	4
Convertible Preferred Stock:				
America West Airlines, Inc. 9.75% convertible[7]	6,000	4	0	—
America West Airlines, Inc. 10.5% convertible	14,820	4	14,820	4
Subordinated Debt:				
Del E. Webb Corporation, variable rate	2,866	4	2,866	4
Finalco, Inc., variable rate	10,413	4	10,413	4
Thousand Trails, Inc., 14⅝%	0	—	15,044	6
Public Utility Bonds	7,845	$6,723	7,845	$7,344
Total	$88,409		$97,453	

1. Market values reflect the last reported sales price of the security on the date set forth and may not be indicative of the current market value of these investments.
2. At December 31, 1986, these investments are being held for sale; however, there are certain restrictions which must be met in order to transfer ownership. See Note 5 of the Consolidated Financial Statements at Item 8.
3. The Association is holding these shares for investment.
4. No active public trading market exists for these securities.
5. Broadview Savings has declared but has not paid six semi-annual dividends aggregating $12.6 million as of December 31, 1986. Western Savings believes that it is unlikely that Broadview Savings and Loan Company will pay dividends of $2.1 million due June 30, 1987 and December 31, 1987 and is unable to predict whether Broadview Savings and Loan Company will pay dividends thereafter. See Note 5b of the Consolidated Financial Statements at Item 8.
6. In the opinion of management, the combined value of Thousand Trails, Inc. common stock and subordinated debentures approximated $37,044,000 at December 31, 1986. Management relied upon the advice of an investment banker and market quotations in determining such value, which is substantially higher than the quoted market value.

TABLE 7.3 *(continued)*

7. In April 1986, America West, Inc., redeemed all of the shares of the 9.75% convertible preferred stock held by the Association at a premium of $468,000.

The value of the Association's investments in other companies will fluctuate as a result of changes in the economy in general, the stock market and the business of the companies in which the investments are made and as a result of other factors outside the control of Western Savings. In addition, securities for which there is no active trading market or the transferability of which is otherwise restricted by contractual provisions or applicable securities laws are not liquid investments and thus Western Savings may not be able to dispose of them at the most opportune time to minimize losses or maximize gains.

Source: Western Savings and Loan Association Form 10K, 31 December 1986.

Del E. Webb, American Air West, and Finalco were all in business and the securities were unpriceable.

So adjusting for Trails, Broadview, and Newell and giving the others the benefit of management's valuation skills:

- $7.2 million for Trails common
- $45 million for Newell
- $0 for Broadview common and preferred
- $7 million for the Trails bond
- $52.8 for other securities

The total of priceable securities equals $112 million, for a loss of $43.7 million on the portfolio. And that's without considering the Trails receivables.

In addition to high direct real estate exposure and the investments in unpriceable securities, Western also had, of course, large exposure to real estate and construction loans ($347 million) and mobile home and property improvement loans ($801 million). Equity was $128 million, net worth $248.3, with regulators requiring a minimum net worth of $154.1 million. Western was close to jeopardy on required levels of capital, if the portfolio were carried at more realistic values.

Income Statement and Insiders: Part 2

What about earnings? No doubt all those real estate and securities profits resulted in regular increases; the added risk of the portfolio must have yielded abnormally high returns. Not the case: earnings per share were $1.80 for 1986 versus $2.32 in 1985, with net income of $30 million versus $36 million. "Other income," including gain on sale of loans and investments and income from real estate, was $127 million versus $109 million. Western also capitalized large amounts of interest, $35 million in 1986, $29 million in 1985.

Meanwhile, the Driggs family wasn't doing too badly with the company. John and Gary (chairman of the board and president–chief executive officer, respectively) made $414,016 each in 1986. Net realized value of stock options was $366,393 for John and $1,574,100 for Gary. Mortgage loans from Western to John totaled $500,000 at 9.5 percent and to Gary, $602,119 at rates from 6 to 11.75 percent. Sister Lois Cannon had a PR job in Laguna Beach with the company's West Coast arm.

To summarize, the 1986 10K showed an interested investor that stated book was probably too high and earnings were not necessarily recurring. With a price-to-book ratio of over three times and price-to-tangible-book of six times, Western Savings was trading on hope for either earnings growth, real estate appreciation, or, perhaps, a takeover (unlikely, according to family comments).

Why Write it Down?

Western Savings had a better year in 1987. It included a very peculiar financial transaction—an asset swap that was impossible for an outsider to value. Western took a loss of only $1.3 million on the whole Thousand Trails package of assets, the $50 million receivable loan plus the securities. Western traded it to Southmark for a package of securities that included: a $35.5 million Southmark subordinated convertible debenture, $10.9 million in preferred Southmark stock, $23.2 million in Visa participation rights, a $21.5 million participation in two collateralized real estate loans, and $9.5 million of Thousand Trails' campground memberships. Whew. What could they do with the campground memberships? Recreational vehicle (RV) hookups were no trouble at all when a major capital-eroding loss disappeared into the air.

A check of the footnotes showed that Broadview preferred was still carried at cost with no writedown in sight. Newell Co. had been sold for a gain.

Net income was up nicely, $33 million vs. $30 million from 1986 with $161 million contributed from other income—$78.9 million from real estate. But stockholders' equity declined from $128 million to $116 million. Western had bought in common stock—1.8 million shares that cost close to $30 million.

The asset shuffle continued in 1988 when Gary announced with the second quarter earnings a prospective sale of branches for a $26 million gain and continued sale of real estate, loans, and investments for profits. For the quarter, earnings were down versus the previous year and, more telling, real estate acquired in settlement of loans had more than doubled to $219 million. The real estate environment in Arizona was adding to the pressure on Gary's asset strategy. Earnings appeared to be hard to come by, even with swaps and sales. Management declared a dividend, then reneged, and offered stock in its place.

In May 1988 *Forbes* noticed the disparity between stock price and asset value in a lovely article by Allan Sloan. He elucidated the shuffles and swaps and alluded to capital in "increasingly short supply."[6]

Western Savings and Loan Association is no more, taken over by regulators, finally, and the auditors' hands were slapped for their whimsical accounting treatment. Gary and family resigned in December 1988 with the stock selling around $3 per share after the wheels continued to fall off. The $6.2 billion thrift is reported to be the probable third largest thrift bailout, with a taxpayer price tag of $1.7 billion and repossessed real estate of $637 million, with an additional $295 million in speculative loans and $46 million in junk bonds. The Broadview Savings preferred may be written down by now and the economic sound and light show quiet this year at the Biltmore.

The Western exercise should teach a prospective buyer or seller to read the footnotes and try to price the securities and assets on the balance sheet—or, at least, to read an S&P sheet on a company that issues a lot of probably convertible–preferred–privately issued–no-market securities that sit on the balance sheet like a hippo thinly disguised as equity.

Insurance Companies: Who's on First?

Any asset that doesn't have a ready market is fair game for asset shuffling. Junk bonds, real estate, mortgage pools, funny preferred stocks, convertibles and notes all work just fine when a company is bent on optimistic valuations. Insurance companies, like banks and thrifts, are grounded on portfolios. All business, especially in life companies, is irreparably linked to the underlying assets: payment of benefits, ability to write new business, and solvency are all functions of the stocks and bonds held by the company.

"Insurance Company Insolvencies," a February 1990 report by the Subcommittee on Oversight and Investigations of the U.S. House of Representatives, comes down hard on the insurance industry for this skill, among others. John Dingell, representative from Michigan and chairman, makes the point that insurance abuses have skyrocketing insolvencies and parallel the early stages of the S & L crisis. One of the main weaknesses that the committee noted was unreliable information:

> Much of the information used to measure solvency by state regulators, industry participants, and ratings services is simply unreliable as a basis for accurately determining an insurance company's financial condition. Most such information is provided by insurance companies themselves, with no verification by regulators, independent auditors, or qualified actuaries. Information may also be outdated and based on "guesstimates," omissions, creative accounting, and even bold-faced lies.[7]

If the committee is right, insurance company games will be attention getters in the 1990s, so let's run through a couple of basics about tracking one area of abuse in insurance companies, including an example from Integrated.

How to Glue Your Attention to Tiny Print

First, and most important, everybody but Joseph Belth (a one-person vigilante on abusive insurance company practices) hates to read insurance companies' financials.[8] Rumor has it that some investment bankers working on acquisitions of insurance companies don't even look at the Schedule D of potential targets. And that's point number two. The few people who do understand insurance companies speak in unknown tongues (like saying Schedule D, when they really mean the portfolio) so nobody else can understand. It creates a massive market inefficiency.

Insurance companies are regulated almost exclusively by individual states. The state insurance commissioners have responsibility for overseeing the financial stability of the companies licensed to do business in their state. A voluntary association, the National Association of Insurance Commissioners (NAIC), creates uniform standards for examination and is the acknowledged authority on financial standards. It is the most important source for valuation of securities and other assets and is a quasi-legal body because of its widespread acceptance by state authorities.

The following are the most important points about insurance company financial statements (skip this section if you bore easily).

First, all insurance companies are required to file annual financial statements, which are available for public inspection with the state insurance department. Called annual statements—blue books for life companies, yellow for property and casualty—the financials are on standard forms dubbed "blanks." You can get copies of the statements at the state insurance department in the capitol if the insurance company of your choice won't send them. They're filed the first of March.

Second, these statements require different accounting practices (called statutory accounting), so they won't match with 10Ks and 10Qs and annuals (GAAP—generally accepted accounting principles—accounting). The driving force of statutory accounting is liquidity: for example, acquisition costs are expensed immediately, not over several years. The spirit of the rule is the determination of solvency or of claims-paying ability—which makes it easier for a financial detective to analyze. Statutory is quasi-cash accounting, close to tax accounting. Here's a quick road map to life companies (remember that the forms, page numbers, and line numbers are standard):

- Page 2 tells you the assets: bonds, stocks, real estate, and policy loans.

- Page 3 tells you the liabilities and surplus: the mandatory securities valuation reserve on line 24.1 (more later) and the surplus, line 36.
- Page 4 is the income statement with net income (line 33), realized capital gains and losses (line 32), and unrealized capital gains and losses (line 36).
- Page 4A is cash flow.
- Page 8 is the detail of income and gains and losses by type of security.
- Notes to Financial Statements a couple of pages later tell all the dirt: who owns the company, what dividends were paid to the owner, prohibitions on dividends paid, and information about transactions between parent and subs.
- Schedule A is real estate—Part 1 owned, Part 2 sold.
- Schedule B is mortgages, Part I owned, Line 13 and 14 foreclosed and transferred to real estate, and acquired by deed in lieu of foreclosure. Schedule B, I, 2 is mortgages by state. Schedule B, II, 3 is mortgages in process of foreclosure.
- Schedule BA, Part I shows other long-term investments, such as real estate joint ventures and partnerships.
- Next comes the "Form for calculating the Mandatory Securities Valuation."
- And, then, Schedule D—the details of the investment portfolio. Schedule D, Part 1 lists the bonds held with the book value, cost, market, interest collected, and NAIC designation as of December 31.
- Schedule D, Part 2, Section 1 lists the preferred stocks, and Schedule D, Part 2, Section 2 gives the common stocks.
- Schedule D, Part 3 shows all the stocks and bonds acquired for the year and from whom. Part 4 is stocks and bonds sold or redeemed with gain or loss, and Part 5 gives those acquired and disposed of in the same year.

Finally, all of this fits together in one number called surplus. Surplus = Assets − (Liabilities + Capital). In other words, surplus equals retained earnings. In the words of the Life Management Institute accounting textbook by Paul Zucconi, "The proper valuation of assets and liabilities is most important to the accuracy of the surplus total."[9] Surplus provides the cushion for surprises and it provides funds for expansion. It's the heart. It also determines how much the owner can take out and whether the regulators take over.

As you can see, the insurance commission makes the companies publish everything an analyst needs to know. But it requires patience to read all those tiny numbers and try to track reality.

As an analyst, you want to know the possibility that problems in the portfolio will eat through surplus (that's like eating through the net worth). Clair and Joseph Galloway in their blockbuster insurance accounting textbook, *Handbook of Accounting for Insurance Companies,* say that policyholders' surplus is not meant to imply value of the company, but is "intended to measure the strength of the company for regulatory purposes. . . . Because of conservative statutory accounting practices, including the exclusion of nonadmitted assets, the policyholders' surplus does provide an estimate of minimum financial strength of the company available for policyholders."[10]

The NAIC suggests that life companies reserve for possible problems and cushion for capital gains and losses in the investment portfolio by establishing a liability account that reduces surplus, much like banks must have reserves for loan losses. Like banks, there is a direct relationship between problem assets and reserves. The NAIC does this with the mandatory securities valuation reserve (MSVR), which is a liability of the company—that means an increase in MSVR causes a decrease in surplus; in fact, changes in MSVR are charged directly to surplus, and capital losses are charged to MSVR.

The MSVR requirements concerning portfolio reserves follow. Stocks are automatic 20 percent reserves, preferreds, 5 and 20 percent. Bonds currently have four categories: 2 percent reserves ("Yes" designation for good assets on Schedule D, comparable to AAA/Aaa to B/B), 10 percent reserves ("No*" is the designation for BB, B), 20 percent reserves ("No**" for CCC and lower not in default), and 20 percent maximum reserve class ("No" usually for bonds in or near default). The NAIC adopted new categories for bonds that rely more heavily on rating services, and some insurance companies are a little nervous about the impact on surplus if the change is approved. The new categories are:

NAIC Designation	Rating Agency	Maximum Accumulation
(1)	AAA/Aaa, AA/Aa, A/A	1%
(2)	BBB/Baa	2%
(3)	BB/Ba	5%
(4)	B/B	10%
(5)	CCC/Caa and lower	20%
(6)	In or near default	20%

Insurance companies don't have to write down defaulted bonds by more than 20 percent until bankruptcy is declared unless the investment officer is of conservative bent. So the burden of reality for risky assets rests on either the regulating arm or conservative management, whichever comes first.

Armed with all this tedious information, let's look at some examples.

Capitol Life: An Integrated Resources Hazardous Waste Holding Tank

The point is to determine from the financials the likelihood that problem assets can eat up surplus. A simplistic, but useful, approach is to add up illiquid, risky assets to get a problem asset total. Then add back accumulated MSVR for the assets you've spotted to surplus. Finally, divide the adjusted surplus by the perceived problem asset number to see what the coverage is before the regulators' hornet's nest is stirred or a capital infusion is necessary.

Capitol Life's capital structure as of December 31, 1988 was:

Assets	$1,900,327,685
Liabilities	$1,834,267,556
including MSVR of	$46,447,775
Surplus	$61,560,309

So the surplus is the cushion.

The next step is to go over Schedules A through D and make

subjective decisions about which assets are potential problems—
in other words, to critique the NAIC's valuations.

- Schedule A shows $8.5 million in real estate, of which $3.9 million represents mortgages foreclosed on from Schedule B.
- Schedule BA has $30 million in real estate partnerships.
- Schedule D has $249 million in 20 percent reserve CCC or in default bonds, so add back $49.8 million to surplus.
- Schedule D also has $43.5 million in notes and bonds of subsidiaries and parents, including a $38 million note from its parent, Integrated, designated "Yes," 2 percent. The NAIC designation No** is on only $1.5 million of the total, so add back $1.14 million to surplus.
- Common stock shows $137.2 million in stock of affiliates, including $123.2 million in Realty Investors. Add back $27.4 to surplus for the necessary 20 percent MSVR for common stocks.

Problem Asset		MSVR Addback
Real estate	$ 8.5 million	—
Venture capital	$ 30 million	—
Bonds, rated CCC or in default	$ 249 million	$ 49.8 million
Subsidiary notes/bonds	$ 43.5 million	$ 1.14 million
Stock in affiliates	$ 137.2 million	$ 27.4 million
Total	$ 468.20 million	$ 78.34 million

The total is $468.20 million for potential problem illiquid assets. Add back the accumulated MSVR of $46.5 million since the full $78.34 has not yet reduced surplus to avoid double deducting. Adjusted surplus is $108 million, so coverage is one-fourth. That is, if one-fourth of the problems materialize, Capitol Life is in trouble. MSVR is $46.5 million, or one-tenth, and therefore provides some small protection.

This exercise reveals to an analyst the pulse of the company. If Integrated and Realty Investors get in trouble, there's no room in surplus and certainly little already anticipated in MSVR. The bugbear is clearly the securities of parent and affiliates, so a pessimist needs to watch Integrated and Realty, not just the insurance company. The NAIC, meanwhile, thought Integrated Resources looked good enough to give it a "Yes," 2 percent reserve necessary, and that says loud and clear, DO YOUR OWN WORK.

Insurance companies have a lot of leeway on the carrying value of securities, particularly when the stocks or bonds don't have a public market value. As a critical bystander, all you have to do is cast doubt on the quality of some of those assets to avoid owning the parent stock. If you question a significant number of assets relative to surplus, short the parent.

More Rules of the Insurance Game

According to GAAP rules, no gain or loss is realized when controlling or controlled entities swap securities. The security must be sold to a third party in order to take realized gains. Statutory reporting (remember, that's the conservative, cash-based accounting that figures surplus) is more lenient in this regard: the transferring company can recognize a gain or loss, which will affect surplus of the company selling the security, which in turn affects how much cash money the parent can take home.

Most states also have limitations about how much money can be pulled out of a company by the parent. A typical restriction reads that all of the net income (sometimes, operating profits) or 10 percent of surplus may be paid out to the parent. This limitation is always spelled out in the Convention Statement in "Notes to Financial Statements." Companies can, however, pay out interest to the parent on surplus debentures (a capital infusion that is neither cat nor dog, debt nor equity) as long as adequate surplus exists and the state regulators are happy.

All that means is that it's harder to repatriate money to the parent than it seems, and it's also harder to generate accounting gains by swapping securities between subsidiaries.

Unrelated companies can certainly help out in tough times by owning each other's securities. And, in the event of problems with the issuer, they can also neglect to write down those securities—as in the case of First Executive with its holdings in terminal companies, Integrated Resources and Southmark.

After the junk bond debacle works its way through the arteries of insurance companies, attention will no doubt focus on mortgages with their huge potential for abuse. Mortgages are hard to get market data on, difficult to price consistently, and they are owned in quantity by insurance companies. Joseph Belth reports that the total of delinquent and foreclosed mortgages in the 2,020-company NAIC database was $7.4 billion, not an insignificant number.[11]

New games appear in the insurance industry as fast as analysts learn to track the old ones. Reading Convention Statements, however, significantly lowers the chance of being broadsided by fast-swapping mavens.

The conclusion from studying insurance companies is that the tough stocks to analyze are usually the most lucrative because they are generally the most overvalued (or undervalued, but definitely mispriced).

Notes

1. Allan Sloan, "Phoenix' Wild West Show," *Forbes,* 30 May 1988, 38.
2. Western Savings and Loan Association, Form 10K, 31 December 1986, 39.
3. Ibid., 15.
4. Ibid., 59.
5. Ibid., 16.
6. Sloan, "Phoenix' Wild West Show," 38.
7. U.S. House of Representatives, Committee on Energy and Commerce, Subcommittee on Oversight and Investigations, *Failed Promises: Insurance Company Insolvencies* (Washington, D.C.: Government Printing Office, 1990), 4.
8. Belth writes a wonderful newsletter for insurance company nuts called *The Insurance Forum,* P.O. Box 245, Ellettsville, Ind., 47429.
9. Paul J. Zucconi, *Accounting in Life and Health Insurance Companies* (Atlanta: LOMA, 1987), 210.
10. Clair J. and Joseph M. Galloway, *Handbook of Accounting for Insurance Companies* (New York: McGraw Hill, 1986), 255.
11. Joseph M. Belth, *The Insurance Forum,* 17:4, 102.

8

If You Can't Fix It, Sell It

During a period of recurring buy-outs and mergers, any company can see an immediate rise in share price by announcing that the company seeks to sell part or all of its assets. During a time of prosperity and economic expansion, the companies that can't earn a respectable living are left no recourse but to sell out or restructure if the level of the stock price aggravates shareholders or if a raider notes the underlying assets. Three kinds of opportunities appeared in this environment in the late 1980s: the restructured and heavily indebted company close to a stumble, the "for sale" but not sold company or partial company, and the corporate acquirer who bought too dear and with no regard for long-range strategy.

The restructured companies, or stub stocks, were easy shorts: Harcourt Brace Jovanovich is a prime example. Close attention to the quarterly financial statements told the story over time. Texas Air, by virtue of its leverage, was a stub of sorts with perennial assets for sale.

In the second category, the short sellers, as sharp-eyed asset evaluators, were among the first on Wall Street to question the subsequent stock price surge and to benefit from "for sale" signs. Corporate finance departments in search of fees continue to break trails for shorts looking for absurd prices. Assets, however, are hard to value in a greater fool environment—before a stock is shorted, the maximum buy-out value must be lower than the stock price. In the 1980s LBO artists were always around to state publicly that they could pay a zillion times cash flow for any pig's ear. Cooper Companies, Agency-Rent-a-Car, and Kay Jewelers were examples of companies for sale.

Acquirers looking for growth or for protection from a raider were easy pickings as well. Service Corporation and Tonka were two companies that apparently bought without regard for the health of the parent.

Harcourt Brace Jovanovich Escapes Maxwell's Money

Harcourt Brace Jovanovich, Inc., went through a number of changes in financial structure from 1987 to 1989. With each twist in the tale, short sellers were confident that the disparity between the capital structure and the earnings power of the business would drive the price of the recapitalized stub stock lower.

In 1987 Harcourt Brace Jovanovich recapitalized in a massive effort to escape the clutches of lusting acquirer Robert Maxwell. The cash flow requirements of the new debt were ponderous, and short sellers decided after copious pro formas that the company couldn't support the new structure even after slashes to expenses. Jim Grant commented in the October 5, 1987 *Grant's Interest Rate Observer* that the new HBJ seemed sensitive to interest rates and small economic slowdowns—in fact, to any adverse breeze that created revenue dips. He used HBJ as a paradigm for the highly leveraged corporate phenomenon, the antithesis of Graham and Dodd's safety and value.[1]

In November 1988, the company again modified its capital structure under yet another refinancing that included extending debt maturities, loosening restrictive covenants, and issuing 10.5 million new shares of common stock. The stock deal was ragged, but First Boston moved the product at $9.50.

Although the new interest burden seemed heavy, the company and Wall Street appeared to be cheerful about prospects for the three divisions. "Will not sell assets," management announced unconditionally, despite previous rumors to the contrary.[2] Common wisdom was that the parks group would supply the growth,

FIGURE 8.1

Harcourt Brace Jovanovich

Stock Prices $

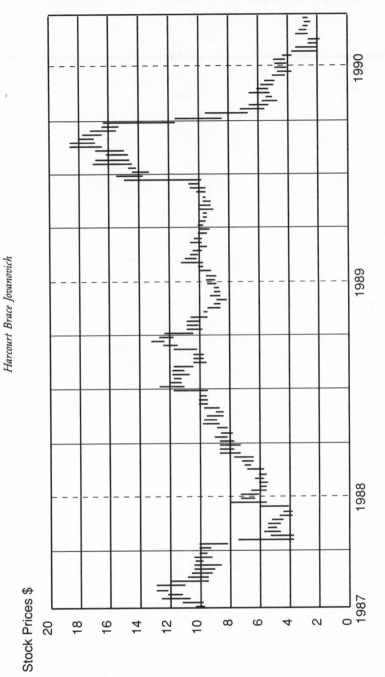

TABLE 8.1

Harcourt Brace Jovanovich
Short Interest

1988	
January	688,933
February	650,842
March	1,066,889
April	1,378,761
May	1,329,648
June	338,490
July	668,316
August	691,875
September	720,553
October	843,996
November	885,535
December	970,507

1989	
January	1,011,275
February	833,838
March	867,495
April	1,250,723
May	1,191,152
June	1,105,775
July	2,084,067
August	2,553,254
September	2,715,213
October	3,145,210
November	3,044,787
December	4,005,125

publishing would coin money, and the insurance company provide a safety if the company needed to sell something.

In September 1988, Oppenheimer & Company, Inc. analyst Joseph C. Frazzano projected cash flow of $550 million in 1989 with asset value of $28–$32. After the deal, he adjusted his cash flow down to $510 million for 1989. Asset value was projected confidently at $26–$28 a share. The stock price was around $9. "Very attractive," he said, and pointed to the operating efficiencies of 1988.[3] That was at the end of 1988.

Short sellers disagreed. They calculated cash flow for each division, gave it a multiple, and came up with a negative value for the company after debt and preferred stock were subtracted. Parks, they felt, was a problem, eating money even after substantial capital improvements in recent years. Attendance was rumored to be dropping, ticket prices were escalating, and cost reductions might hurt comparisons with competition if acreage started looking seedy. Publishing, with the textbook division, might see the same level of shrinkage that the school-age population saw, at best GNP level growth with not much more room for margin improvement after the initial round of cost cutting.

It was a stalemate. Wall Street pounded the table, particularly Gabelli & Company, Inc.'s Elizabeth Bramwell and Oppenheimer's Frazzano. The shorts snarled and pointed to the debt.

Then first-quarter 1989 earnings came out. HBJ had elected to take a hit in the publishing division. Sampling and marketing costs for new editions were high, and college returns of unsold textbooks were a month early, counting in the first quarter, not the second. Publishing revenues in elementary and secondary declined as well. No problem. Sea World had higher attendance and higher per capita spending. Bulls gulped and regrouped; shorts said, "I told you so and the book margins are shot, too." And things went along again.

One point that made HBJ different in short sale annals was that the big float, 72-plus million shares outstanding, the institutional following and the Wall Street participation all combined to make it an easy stock to have an opinion on. So the shorts were outspoken, playful, haranguing and the longs were assured and hyperbolic. HBJ, all in all, was pretty good fun in a boring market.

HBJ Sells Shamu

The real drama came when HBJ announced in June 1989 that, after all, the company would sell Parks, including Sea World and Shamu. Shorts shrieked with glee that HBJ had come to this, and so quickly. The only source of growth was going on the block. To their collective amazement and disbelief, the longs ballyhooed too. Billions, they said. Many, many billions. Huh?

So the two camps settled down to name calling, spitting, and cursing. The argument revolved around what multiple of cash flow Parks would sell for and what that would subsequently do for the balance sheet and cash flow statement of the parent. The admirable disclosure of HBJ made the numbers easy to come by. Depreciation and amortization for Parks was $37 million in 1988, and net income was $62 million from continuing operations, for a total of $99 million in cash flow. Recent sales of parks suggested twelve to thirteen was a realistic, possibly optimistic, multiple for cash flow, said shorts, so call it $1.3 billion for the sticker price. Longs said, you're outta your mind, $1.75 billion. Then they figured out that wasn't quite enough and raised the number once, twice until some optimistic soul actually mentioned $3 billion, thirty times cash flow. Only, said the shorts, if they sell Shamu for sushi. Disney will buy, said one analyst with assurance. The Japanese, definitely, said another. A bunch of old fish, countered shorts.

Both camps then retreated behind closed doors to pro forma cash flow on their computers. The crux, of course, was what the sale would do for the company's post-sale cash flow and thus HBJ's ability to pay PIKS (which converted to cash interest in the early 1990s).

If HBJ sold Parks for $1.3 billion and paid taxes on the gain (the assets were on the books at around $470 million), it could pay down 12 percent bank debt of $900 million (not the high-coupon, noncallable-until-1990 debt), thereby reducing interest payments by $110 million. If free cash flow from Parks was supposed to be $120 million next year, the transaction was a push. It meant that the company was desperate. If, on the other hand, Parks sold for $3 billion, reducing debt by $2 billion and interest by $240 million, with only $100 million in projected cash flow, the sale was a win. The assumptions made all the difference.

Somewhere in the middle of all this, earnings for the second quarter were announced. Publishing didn't look any better (increases were due to sales shifting from third quarter to second), and Parks was down in revenues—lower attendance due to competition—but margins improved because of more cost cutting. Disney doesn't have to cut costs, shorts taunted.

With every round of rumors, the stock lurched higher, accompanied by the stomachs of tapped-out shorts. Maybe there was someone dumb enough to pay thirty times cash flow; stranger things had happened in recent years. Texas Air, another big cap short favorite, was also running to new highs, with stories about many planes sold for very high prices indeed. So the shorts were morose. They lost their taunt and settled down to a bunker mentality—or more appropriately, they emulated American Brigadier General Anthony C. McAuliffe's attitude in Bastogne when surrounded by Germans requesting an unconditional surrender. "Nuts," he is reputed to have said and hunkered down to wait for George Patton.

On August 14, 1989, *New York Times* reporter Thomas Hayes announced that "people close to the company" said an agreement would be signed soon: "Disney, MCA, and Anheuser-Busch each have the financial muscle to pay $1.5 billion or more."[4] Short shock treatment, it seemed at the time. With every announcement the stock lurched higher.

And then the announcement came in September: $1.1 billion to Anheuser-Busch. Cash interest would be reduced by $115 million. The stock dropped $4.125 within 24 hours to $12.125. The shorts cheered and hung on for more. The stock settled around $9 and change.

The next salvo came in October, when the company hinted that cash flow estimates were still a little high on the Street. Company officials were said to have guided Frazzano to a lower number. Analysts backpedaled, sweated, made furious phone calls. Everyone speculated on soon-to-be-announced earnings. The company was unavailable for comment. Shorts shorted more, gleefully. The stock kept going down.

Frazzano started to get worried with the stock at $5 plus. His October 26, 1989 report mentions that the stock might take three to six months to recover. His 1989 cash flow number was now around $260 million (down from $510), with 1990 at $300 million. Asset value was $22 with the target price of the stock $15–$16, "considerably undervalued," he still said.

Third-quarter earnings came out. Publishing was pallid. Margins had continued to decrease. Sales were a mite disappointing. Operating income from publishing, even without write-offs, was $50 million less than the previous year.

And the shorts smiled and stayed short. "There was never anything there," they said. "Where do those guys get those silly numbers, anyway?"

HBJ still flurries from its $3 base. One recent rumor had Canadians buying part of the publishing division for a whole lot of money; then talks were terminated. Short interest has doubled—again. The debt still looks too high for remaining income, and HBJ is running out of assets to sell.

Texas Air: Flying with Frank

One can't very well talk about HBJ without mentioning Texas Air Corporation, since that was the other stock that made shorts bone weary in the summer of 1989. Texas Air never went up for sale, but Wall Street decided it had takeover sizzle.

Texas Air, like HBJ, was a stock that was worth more as parts than as an operating company. In other words, analysts added up all the prices of bits and pieces, subtracted the elephant-sized debt, and got numbers far in excess of the stock price. Texas Air was worth $26 plus, they said. The stock initially traded around $9 and shot up to the $20s about the same time that HBJ was at $18.

The bull side rested on several points: airlines were hot (all the airline takeovers were flying), slots and planes were worth a lot, and as soon as Frank Lorenzo could get rid of that nasty union or sell Eastern, operating profits would look a whole lot better. The bull side was espoused by Ken Heebner of Loomis and Sayles, Michael Steinhardt, Drexel Burnham, and many brokerage houses on the Street.

The bear case was spearheaded by Jim Chanos. Shorts felt, first, that you couldn't go wrong with a record like Frank Lorenzo's: several bankruptcies and a personality that unions appeared to dislike. Second, they believed that the liquidation value was lower than bulls anticipated and that the cash burn in a shaky airline could be mammoth. By the end of 1988 Texas Air's consolidated balance sheet had negative equity and loss per share of $18.88 in 1988 and $12.58 in 1987 with positive cash flow dependent on new debt and property sales.

Long before the battle of summer 1989 raged, bulls on the stock had calculated the net asset value (NAV) of Eastern and the subsequent stock price of Texas Air should they manage to re-

FIGURE 8.2

Texas Air Corp.

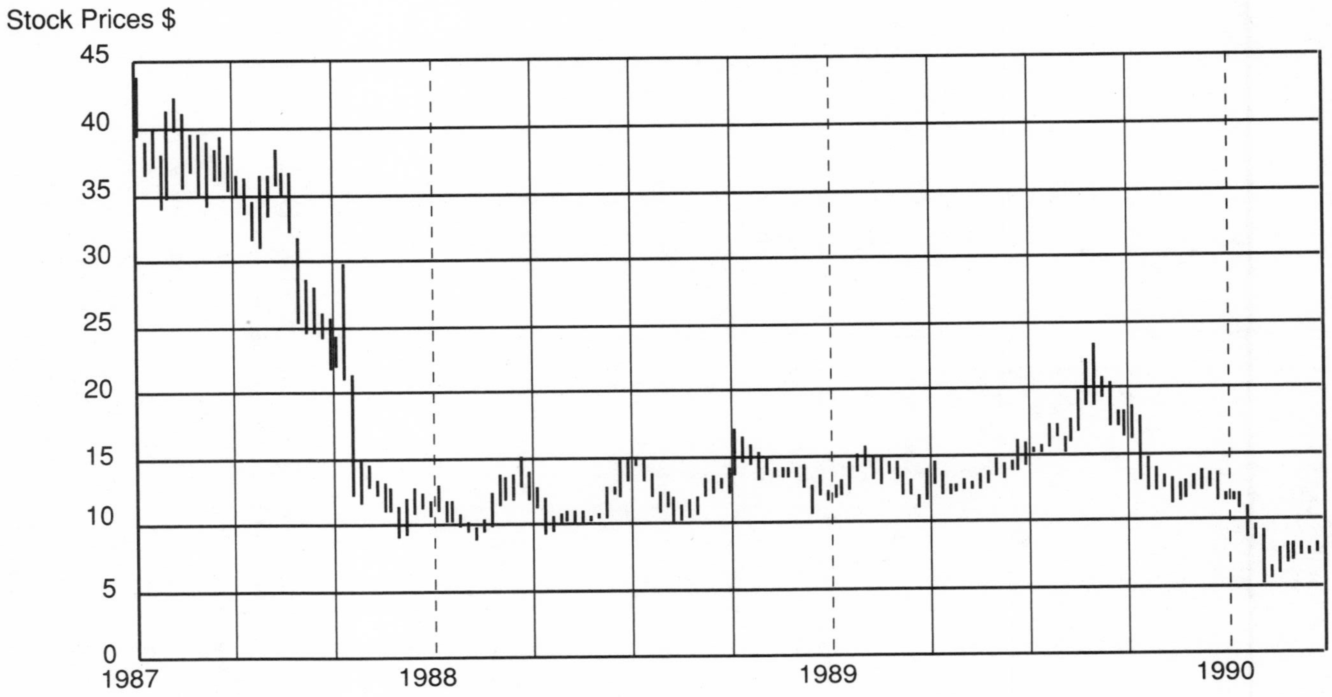

TABLE 8.2

Texas Air Corp.
Short Interest

1988	
January	627,645
February	695,973
March	612,330
April	572,436
May	527,873
June	627,086
July	792,736
August	695,136
September	978,091
October	1,024,032
November	997,267
December	1,177,390

1989	
January	1,088,449
February	1,570,924
March	2,726,953
April	4,069,267
May	3,535,667
June	3,459,665
July	3,679,215
August	3,673,092
September	3,363,949
October	3,820,634
November	6,229,967
December	6,872,002

move the troublesome child. Michael Derchin of Drexel Burnham added up the assets of Eastern (planes, shuttle, South American routes, the Caribbean, Atlanta and Miami hubs, etc.), subtracted the debt, assumed net operating losses (NOL's) and investment tax credits (ITC's) would shelter the gain, and Texas Air would net from $16 to $38 per share plus Continental and System One, of course.[5] So Texas Air indeed looked cheap to the bulls with the stock trading around $12.

Events moved along through the end of 1988. Never a dull moment with Frank Lorenzo. SAS announced an alliance with Texas Air in October, leading the bulls to speculate that they might combine with the union to buy Eastern out. Donald Trump offered $365 million for the shuttle, but the purchase was held up in court. Texas Air quit paying dividends on four preferreds, but not a cash bind, said analysts; just a small problem with debt covenants, negative net worth, and all that.

The new year came. SAS announced that it owned 6.3 percent of Texas, and union negotiations with the machinists were expected to be a mite testy. Derchin lowered his Eastern NAV to $16–$24 but thought discounted normal earnings for Continental/System One (minus that nasty Eastern) were $5–$7 per share.[6] The stock price was $15 at the end of January.

Easy Money Isn't

The short sellers were short Texas Air before the Eastern strike, and when the machinists went out in March 1989 shorts were pleased but not surprised. When the pilots and the flight attendants joined in sympathy, they sat back to wait for a quick conclusion. The stock, however, baffled them—it didn't drop.

Floyd Norris's *New York Times* column on March 9, 1989 recapped the struggle. Michael Steinhardt said that Texas Air was "worth more dead than alive." Norris quoted one bull estimate of the Eastern sale at $1 billion (equivalent to $27), but Jim Chanos disagreed. He pointed out that only two years were left on the lease of the Miami repair facility, and he noted that Eastern's planes were old.

Lorenzo responded with the confidence of practice; he declared bankruptcy for Eastern on March 9, 1989, but the move didn't work quite as well as it had with Continental. Times had changed. But the investing public wasn't yet aware and the stock moved up.

Things deteriorated for the shorts; they wouldn't have another confident high like the strike for months. First Peter Ueberroth decided to buy Eastern, then reneged after hostile encounters with creditors and disagreements about interim control. Analysts were highly confident that Lorenzo could sell off the odd pieces and rebuild the core. The Trump shuttle sale was completed. South American routes were sold and then not sold.

The noteworthy part of the Texas Air episode was the speed,

or momentum, of the ascent as more and more buyers jumped on the bandwagon. There was nothing rational about it: it was a greed frenzy. The psychology of the summer of 1989 was that many managers felt left out by the takeover rage. They wanted badly to believe. Analysts like Drexel's Derchin came out with nice rows of numbers that added up to a lot. So the institutions bought, and then bought more. The valuation numbers went higher as the stock price went up, just like earnings estimates on a rising growth stock.

The shorts were flabbergasted, but unwavering. As Kynikos Associates analyst Scott Bessent said, "What made Texas Air a wonderful short was that even if you believed some of the absurd valuations, our model showed that the company was going to lose $18–$20 per share before the end of the year, so even if the bulls were right in August, the stock would be at least 50 percent lower by December."[7]

Part of the final price frenzy and unrelenting volume surge in a stock like Texas Air is that toward the end of the parabolic price run, weak shorts get scared and cover, and strong shorts run out of shorting room. The positions dwarf the usually well-diversified short portfolios, and managers short in smaller size, if at all. So there's unabated buying, with none of the balance or hesitation of the first part of the advance: white knuckle stuff. The shorts' conclusion was: Parkinson's Law of Short Selling should be, "The stock price expands to fill the available short capacity and last iota of patience, particularly when it's a no-brainer."

After the demise of the United Air Lines deal in October 1989, airline assets were not quite as valuable to stock buyers. So in the fall, Texas Air declined from its summer hysteria and floundered as Eastern beat its planned numbers for planes and revenues, then didn't. Robert McAdoo of Oppenheimer castigated sellers in his October 16, 1989 report: "The doubters continue to promote the idea that Texas Air is a great short sale idea. . . . Our target for Texas Air is still $25–$30 per share by the spring of 1990 based on the realization in the market that Texas Air will have succeeded in fixing its problems by that time."[8] He reported what Texas Air would earn if they made one-third, one-half, and 100 percent of American Airlines' margins—as if Frank could turn Texas Air into American Airlines by spring.

In January 1990 Ken Heebner of Loomis unloaded his 5-million-share position and clipped the stock back to $6. Astronomical losses continue to mount. McAdoo missed his price target in the spring of 1990. Lorenzo finally got ousted from Eastern in April 1990, and the shorts have made a little money for a whole lot of pain. Most are convinced that Texas Air isn't over yet: it's still a high-priced stock with a lot of debt in a cyclical business.

Kay Jewelers Sells Out (or Tries to) at the Annual Sale

Kay Jewelers was a growth retailer with well-known problems. In the *Wall Street Journal* "Heard on the Street" column on January 4, 1990, Roger Lowenstein pointed out that same-store sales were down, inventories were up, and receivables were deteriorating. Apparently, Kay had offered credit too leniently in order to promote sales. While receivables were factored to NCNB, they were recourse back to Kay for defaults, so that Kay carried the liability for problems. A problem with receivables meant losses, but more important, it also meant a subsequent tighter credit policy and lower revenues.

Meanwhile, consumers had been on a spree for years, and fad jewelry had held a spot in the purchasing pocket of middle-mall America. Kay already had locations in malls, but that position could deteriorate, particularly with mall anchors dropping like flies with department store bankruptcies.

The shorts were interested in Kay and aware that a buy-out was a possibility, as Lowenstein had mentioned. A sell-out by the company was sensible, except for one problem: debt. Kay was already leveraged. It had been the recipient of acquisition rumors before—in July 1989—and the stock had moved up to $23 from $16. That was after a $6 million write-off in the spring of 1989 for bad debts and an optimistic assessment by company officials for a strong Christmas bailout. Some short sellers sold stock in January 1990.

Then on February 1, 1990 Kay suspended the dividend and announced a weak quarter. Toward the end of the month, Kay

FIGURE 8.3

Kay Jewelers, Inc.

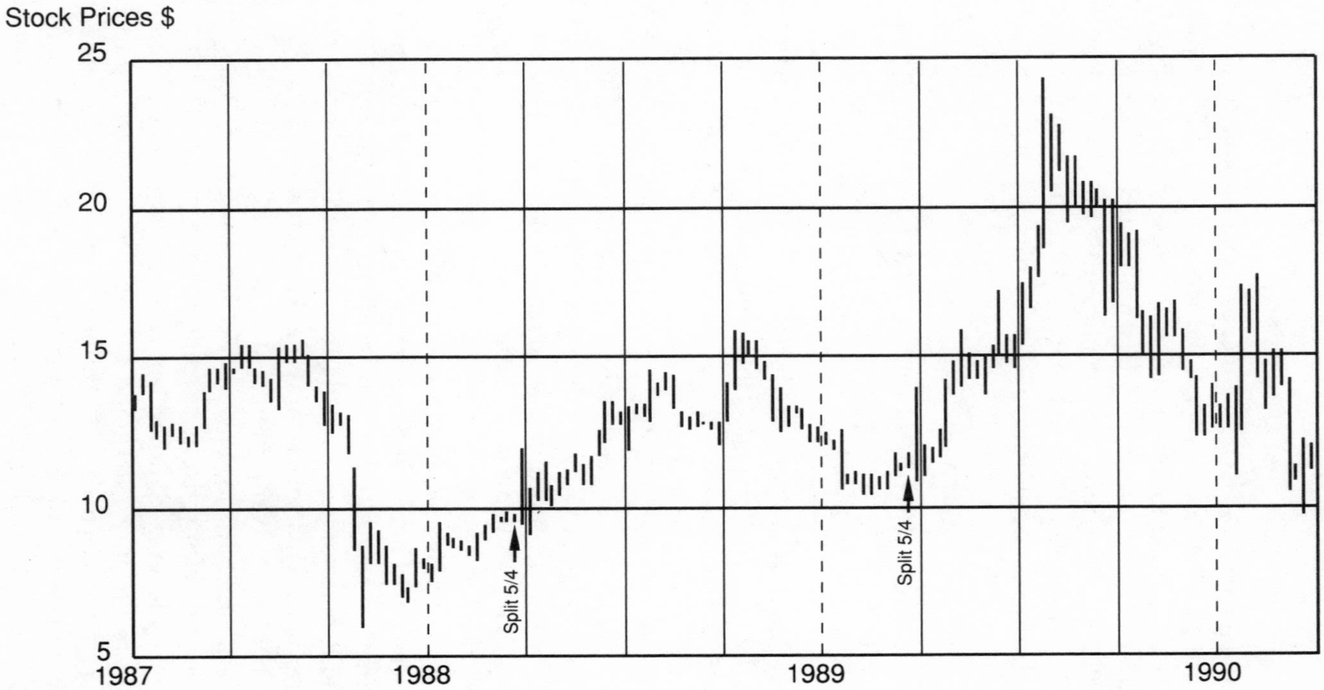

Stock Prices $

TABLE 8.3

Kay Jewelers, Inc.
Short Interest

1989	
October	42,244
November	228,943
December	366,868

1990	
January	1,340,903
February	2,013,435
March	1,856,247
April	1,908,418
May	1,894,047
June	1,852,564

announced that it had hired First Boston to shop the company. The stock spiked with eager buy-out groupies running the price to $17. The shorts acted so fast that all available stock to borrow for shorting was gone in a heartbeat, so the options took the brunt of short interest with puts immediately overvalued. The Swiss shareholders were said to be particularly interested in doing something, buying or selling, but a denouement of some sort was desired.

The shorts felt that a sale price of 50 percent of revenues was a benchmark, since Kay's highest earnings were only $.88 per share and cash flow (negative) and book (irrelevant for retail) weren't important. That put the buy-out at $17, so the stock was a short around that level.

In March, year-end earnings came out—down 98 percent from the previous year with revenues up only 2 percent. "Bloated inventories and cash short," said the *Wall Street Journal.* [9] The stock languished, a victim of a dead takeover market.

A denouement of sorts was reached July 2, 1990 when Ratners Group, a British jewelry chain, made an offer—to buy Kay for stock worth $17 a share to Kay holders if the bondholders agreed to revised terms. The speculators who bought at the top for a quick profit ended up breaking even if they held their shares, and the shorts who stayed short bought at $14.50 after the announcement, so they made a little. The shorts concluded from the buy-out announcement frenzy that short speculation on "for sale" candidates was a less risky business than risk arbitrage—particularly if you could stand the news announcements and upward lurches.

Service Corporation: Short the Acquirer

Service Corp. illustrates an important point about takeovers. If a company pays an outrageous price for another company that appears to be already overpriced (and one that may be a short position), there may be cracks in the foundation of the acquirer, too.

In August 1986 William M. Alpert wrote an article on funeral accounting for *Barron's* focusing on Morlan.[10] The gist was that aggressive accounting hit Morlan's revenues in two places: burial services (pre-need openings and closings—or reloads, as the industry calls them) and cemetery property sales.

Generally with cemetery property sales, the purchaser puts money down and then pays installments over time. The revenue can be booked many different ways, and so can the expenses. The cash arrives over a multi-year period, so the situation is analogous to campground memberships for Thousand Trails or tax shelter sales with Integrated. The most aggressive accounting treatment is to book the revenues now and the expenses over time. If sales slow, the expenses stay constant and earnings drop. Morlan booked the sales at the front end, Service Corp. after 20 percent was paid.

Reloads were more dramatic. Usually people buy plots in advance but pay for the funeral service at time of death. Morlan aggressively marketed advance burial sales, on the installment plan. And they booked the sales immediately and paid out commissions; other expenses, of course, would be unknown for decades. Service Corp. booked after the funeral service was performed.

So Morlan was in a bit of a cash bind, with insiders selling,

FIGURE 8.4

Service Corporation International

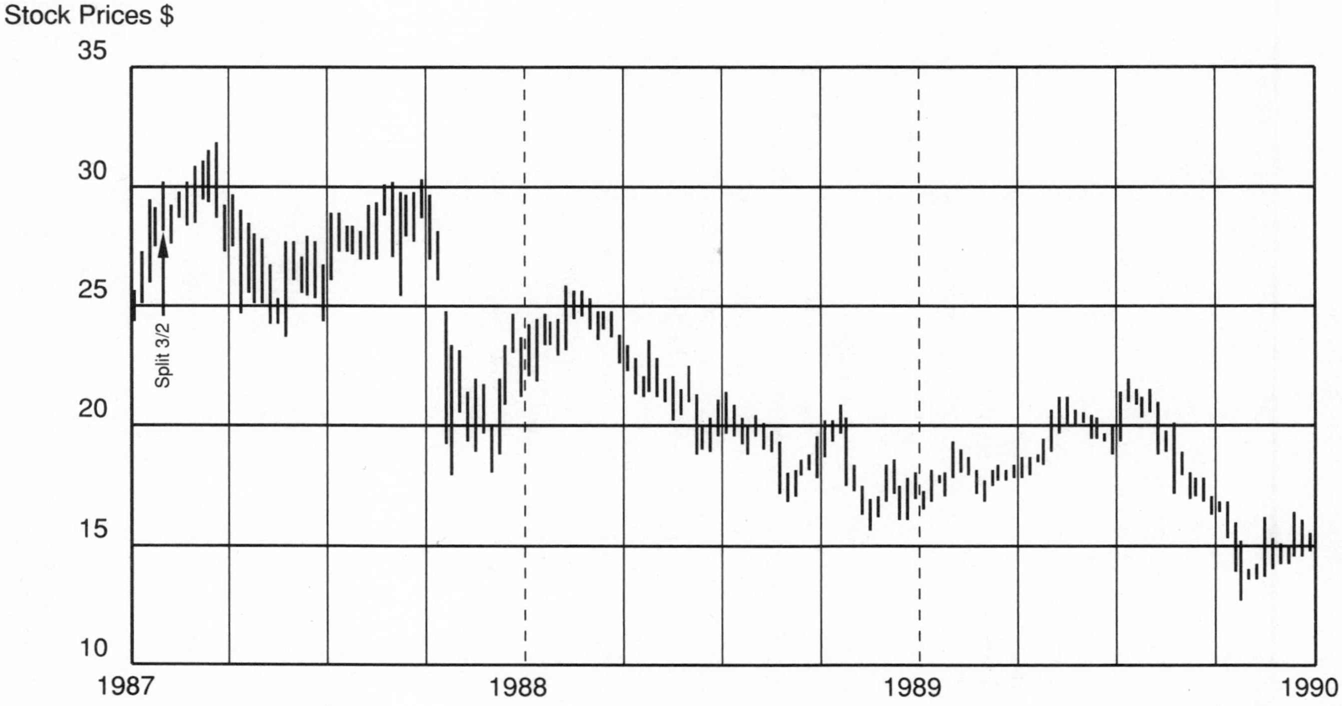

dubious revenues and, probably, understated expenses: a perfect short.

Service Corp. was quoted throughout the *Barron's* article as being dismayed by the leniency in the revenue policy of their competitor. When Service announced in July 1987 that it planned to acquire the perpetrator, it was a surprise. Fortunately for short sellers, it was a stock swap. Service traded from $27 to $30 all summer and early fall.

Service Corp. (or Service Corpse, as it was fondly known) was a fashionable demographics growth stock. The aging of America was difficult to play as a pure equity bet. Service Corp. fit the bill, since the bulge was expected to exit graveside after buying one of Service's "pre-need packages," and the Street loved it. Everybody failed to notice, however, that death is not a growth industry (even if Wall Street says it is): there's only one per person no matter how you count it, and cremations cut into margins.

So the Morlan acquisition focused attention on the financials of Service Corp., and what the financials showed was interesting and somewhat unexpected. Growth had slowed. Earnings increases came from things like insurance company portfolio capital gains and a change in the accounting for sales commissions (deferred marketing costs). Service badly needed to buy growth to keep the stock inflated at its current multiple so they could continue to acquire mom-and-pops with stock. Insiders were selling a fair amount of stock, it was institutionally owned (56 percent in the summer of 1987), and it had a growth multiple on earnings (twenty times). It was a good stock to stay short after the merger.

Shearson, Lehman and Goldman Sachs were two of the big bulls on the stock. "18% growth rate," said Shearson's Laurie Goldberger. "Stock is currently trading at an historically low relative valuation—a 10% premium to the market multiple."[11] Goldman's Paul Farrell had a twelve-month target of $36–$38. One analyst at Karp Financial Group, after the October market adjustment, said there were two things you could count on— death and food—so buy Service Corp.[12] He was wrong.

When the October 31, 1987 10Q came out, pretax income was $47 million versus $34 million for the six months. The additional deferral of marketing costs added $9.3 million in 1987 and $2.4

million in 1986. Funeral service volume for facilities owned in both years was up just .2 percent, and price increases, acquisitions, and bigger ticket purchases accounted for the rest. Service Corp. was filing a note deal. Cash flow looked a little ragged if you took cash from operations minus deferred commissions and sales expenses and increased receivables, additions to property (but not acquisitions), and dividends.

Vertical Integration Goes Only So Far

Earnings continued to be disappointing; the Street noticed and inched down their estimates, a nickel here, a dime there. Somewhere about this time Wall Street started talking about additional use of all that precious real estate. Service would bail out earnings and realize shareholder value with undervalued cemetery land. The Japanese were mentioned. Someone even said that the company was considering a par-three golf course on adjacent land. One wag responded, "so yuppies could chip off the old block." It got sillier.

Shorts covered in fall 1988 at $16. The stock wallowed around at that level after the company divested several divisions. Funeral supply, purchased in 1986 for $131 million in stock, was sold for $55 million in cash and $7.5 million in notes in 1990. Rival funeral home operators wouldn't buy coffins from a competitor, they discovered, even with case discounts. The insurance companies were also on the block; pre-need insurance was too expensive to sell, with all those small policies. Earnings expectations for 1989 were $1 with growth estimates reduced to a 10–20 percent range.

Acquisitions can add as many problems as solutions. The stumble seems to come a year after the fact, when revenue euphoria fades and "synergy" dissipates into in-fighting and back-stabbing as cost-cutting measures address not "their" jobs, but your job.

Notes

1. James Grant, "The Annotated Harcourt," *Grant's Interest Rate Observer*, 5 October 1987, 5–10.

2. Greg Johnson, *Los Angeles Times,* 30 September 1988, 2.

3. Joseph C. Frazzano, "Weekly Research Review," Oppenheimer and Co., Inc., 6 December 1988, 6.

4. Thomas Hayes, *New York Times,* 14 August 1989.

5. Michael W. Derchin, Drexel Burnham, Lambert, Research Abstracts, 23 August 1988, 8054.

6. Ibid., 16 February 1989, 2077.

7. Personal Communication, June 28, 1990.

8. Robert McAdoo, "Daily Action Notes," Oppenheimer, October 1989, 3.

9. Vindu P. Goel, *Wall Street Journal,* 19 March 1990.

10. William M. Alpert, "Morlan Cashes in on Funeral Business," *Barron's,* 25 August 1986, 16, 27, 29.

11. Laurie Goldberger, Shearson, Lehman Brothers, Inc., Equity Comments, 13 July 1987, 14.

12. Abraham Karp, "The Apprehensive Market," Karp Financial Group, 27 October 1987, 1.

9

Industry Obsolescence: Theme Stocks

When a major, industry-wrenching change occurs, money can be made by taking a position in a group of stocks clustered around a theme. Massive industry change can be triggered by macroeconomic events, a specific product revolution, or the death of a fad.

When oil prices plummeted, any company associated with Texas wealth was ripe for selling. The Texas banks, in particular, were worthy candidates that reflected optimistic economic scenarios and pricing for months. The Arizona real estate decline and the under-regulated S & L abuses represented two other opportunities to short an industry-wide phenomenon.

Industry obsolescence can also be the flip side of Wall Street's concept stock, when a product change sinks a group of companies. For example, when a tech toy becomes passé—like CB radios—or when the oil price rise sent RV's into a fishtail, any stock associated with those products is fair game for a collapse. Use a shotgun, not a rifle, for a sector bet.

Donald Trump's saga is an example of both phenomena. The real estate environment changed and the perception of Atlantic City as a high-growth gambling environment faded, so that bankers became concerned about a cash flow that had always been negative. A shotgun short of any of Trump's bonds would have yielded a reasonable return.

All it takes is an eye for trends, because Wall Street turns like

the *Queen Elizabeth II:* there's a whole lot of time to get firmly
positioned before the first wave of downdraft, followed by the
tell-me-it-ain't-so bounce, sinks the stocks. Wall Street is much
quicker to hype a new fad than to discard the old.

The Arizona Land Race

Sometime in early 1988 visitors to Arizona started coming back
with odd tales. It looked overbuilt. The crane count was still
spectacularly high, despite the growing vacancy rate and slowing
growth. The absence of zoning restrictions meant that every fast-
buck developer in the United States was in there pouring con-
crete—and getting construction bank loans.

Since the Texas debacle was recent enough for even Wall
Street's memory, the shorts salivated. In Texas the inevitable bust
had followed the not-so-eternal boom, and real estate collapses
compounded oil price collapses to sink all the banks that had lent
cheerfully and aggressively to anyone with a hankering to build.

Texas taught investors that when a region and its economy is
built on growth, a slowing rate of change in the growth engine
can pull the whole structure to the ground. A dropping real estate
market takes the economy with it, including commercial loans
and basic bank business. Even sacred single-family mortgage default rates can escalate. It's not just construction lending that
creates cannon fodder for bank regulators.

When a sector is isolated as a potential war zone, the first step is
to find lists of associated stocks. In the Arizona case, a local newspaper could provide lists of regional stocks—banks and S & L's
were easy to spot. Local gossip can be particularly useful, since
in-town developers usually know who's the aggressive lender in
the area, whether balloon payments are common, and who's got
the least conservative appraisal practices. A first-hand look at
construction billboards lauding lender and developer alike can be
another quick source of names. Western Savings (chapter 7) was
already well known, so sellers started looking under rocks for
similar real estate plays. Three showed up: American Continental
and Sun State Savings were S & L's, Valley National was a commercial bank.

American Continental: What's All the Ruckus About?

American Continental (AMCC), the big holding company for both Lincoln Savings and a land development company, had financial statements that made fine reading, even before Charles Keating started spending more time in Washington at hearings. If you're betting on a real estate downturn, short the companies with big real estate exposure. AMCC was almost all real estate and not much equity by the end of 1987.

Short sellers were confused by the ruckus in 1990 over Charles Keating and his S & L, Lincoln Savings; anybody could have seen in 1988, even without an X ray, what the skeleton looked like, plus or minus a few tumors. The short sellers' perspective on American Continental should be reassuring to investors who felt that the SEC left stockholders without a blanket in a blizzard. The 10K and Annual for the year ended December 31, 1987 were the documents that short sellers read first. The facts were clear, although some of the details would be missing for years. Perhaps the disclosure wasn't all-encompassing, but the numbers gave a good clue.

A Real Estate Company or an S & L?

American Continental was a Phoenix-based holding company that had been principally engaged in real estate until the acquisition of Lincoln Savings for $51 million in 1984. Prior to its acquisition, Lincoln's main activity was single-family mortgage lending; American realigned Lincoln's policy to emphasize mortgage loans exceeding $1 million. After the acquisition, American phased out its own home building activities but still worked in the areas of land development, syndication, sale, and management. In 1987 86 percent of pretax income came from financial services, most of which was Lincoln.

Since Lincoln was a hefty percentage of revenues and assets for AMCC, the short sellers first needed to determine how much of the income came from basic S & L business and how much from nonrecurring real estate–related business.

Parent AMCC had consolidated earnings before preferred divi-

FIGURE 9.1

American Continental Corp.

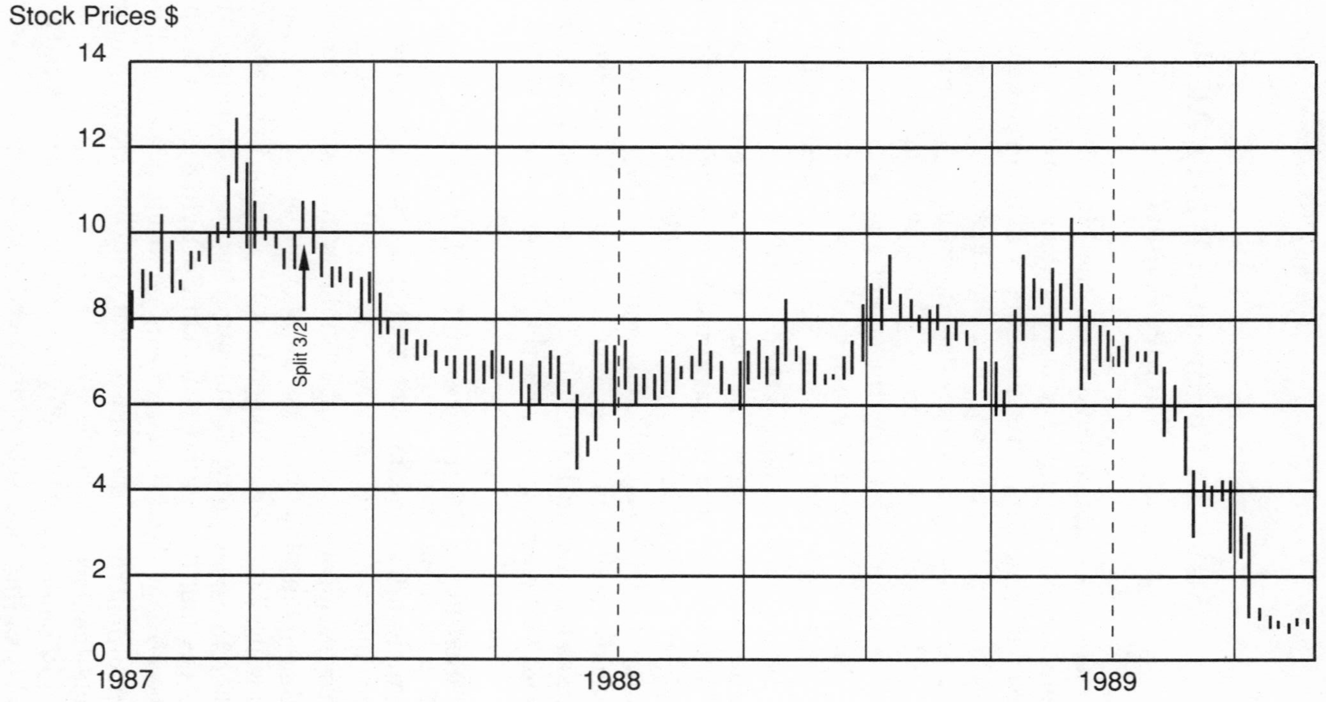

TABLE 9.1

American Continental Corp.
Short Interest

1988	
July	635,554
August	677,242
September	730,614
October	922,225
November	1,073,273
December	874,049
1989	
January	888,459
February	827,776
March	832,189
April	867,920
May	831,429
June	not published

dends of $19.3 million in 1987. Lincoln's net earnings were $41 million in 1987, so the parent was certainly dependent on the child for sustenance.

Lincoln's summary of operations (table 9.2) showed net interest income, the major component of old-style S & L earnings, of $16.1 million. The notes mentioned that this was after capitalization of $65 million in interest expense, but including $14 million of additional interest related to loan profit participations. The 10K went on to explain that "at December 31, 1987, Lincoln Savings' interest bearing liabilities exceeded its interest earning assets by $1,086,000,000."[1] Lincoln Savings also owned $622 million in corporate bonds, "substantially all of which securities are rated less than investment grade," that added dramatically to interest income.[2] So net interest income didn't come from the traditional spread between deposits for CDs and lending to single-family mortgagees.

Where did the bulk of earnings come from? Net gains on sale of securities, loans, mortgage-backed certificates, and distributions from unconsolidated affiliates were $89.6 million. Other income (including real estate gains of $78.7 million) was $92.6

TABLE 9.2

Lincoln Savings' Income Summary
(Dollars in thousands)

	Year Ended December 31,		
	1987	1986	1985
Interest income	$292,113	$269,356	$235,103
Interest expense	275,979	268,838	231,964
Net interest income	16,134	518	3,139
Net gains on sale of investment securities, loans and mortgage-backed certificates and distributions from unconsolidated affiliates	89,657	131,407	120,129
Other income, net[1]	92,569	79,689	55,977
General, administrative, and other expenses	135,210	129,925	78,895
Earnings before income taxes and cumulative effect of a change in accounting for income taxes	63,150	81,689	100,350
Income taxes	25,205	32,731	20,500
Earnings before cumulative effect of a change in accounting for income taxes	37,945	48,958	79,850
Cumulative effect of a change in accounting for income taxes	3,075	—	—
Net earnings	$41,020	$48,958	$79,850

1. "Other income" includes real estate gains of $78,708,000, $73,924,000 and $47,567,000 for the periods ended, December 31 1987, 1986, and 1985, respectively. See "Business—Real Estate Activities." Source: American Continental Corporation, Form 10K, 31 December 1987.

million. And 1987 was not an aberration; in fact, net interest income was higher as a percentage of net income than in previous years. American Continental, therefore, was not a mom-and-pop lender.

The next look was at the balance sheet of Lincoln (total assets of the consolidated parent were $5 billion with shareholder equity, including preferred, of $137 million) to see how stable and liquid the assets were in the event of the expected real estate crash (table 9.3). Stockholders' equity was $221 million. Goodwill was $106 million, real estate was $827, and other assets were $531 million (including $60 million in investments in unconsolidated subs). So deduct intangibles, haircut real estate by 10 percent, arbitrarily scratch out the subs, and you get negative $28 million. A winner—and that's without increases in nonperforming assets or without deducting for the problems in the $622 million junk bond portfolio. Regulators weren't as fond of negative net worth as LBO impresarios, even back in 1988.

For a little more detail, short sellers went to the loan portfolio to see how much was loaned for construction: $225.8 million for construction in 1987, up from $138 million in 1986. Acquisition and development lending was a monumental $760.6 million, up from $482.7 million. Conventional mortgages were a piddling $179 million versus $250.5 million in 1986: no plain, ordinary, single-family lender here, just like they said in the 10K.

AMCC's other line of business was real estate, which contributed $221 million in revenues and $3.6 million in pretax earnings in 1987. The Phoenician, a glitzy luxury resort hotel, was under construction and rumored to be running over budget. The ratio of earnings to fixed charges, including all noncash charges and

TABLE 9.3

Lincoln Savings' Balance Sheet
(Dollars in thousands)

	As of December 31,		
	1987	1986	1985
Cash and cash equivalents	$242,612	$358,681	$843,607
Investment securities-equity	157,699	96,249	90,879
Investment securities-debt	1,298,190	1,193,453	426,750
Loans receivable and mortgage-backed securities[1]	1,585,820	902,021	929,519
Real estate	827,272	777,165	553,696
Other assets[2]	530,622	466,974	258,653
Excess of cost over net assets acquired	106,252	109,184	108,654
Total assets	$4,748,467	$3,903,727	$3,211,758
Savings deposits	$3,374,531	$2,821,375	$2,406,958
Borrowings	813,784	629,890	570,173
Other liabilities	338,775	259,438	89,047
Stockholder's equity	221,377	193,024	145,580
Total liabilities and stockholder's equity	$4,748,467	$3,903,727	$3,211,758

1. "Loans receivable and mortgage-backed securities" include mortgage-backed securities of $472,-461,000, $67,135,000 and $58,364,000 for the years ended December 31, 1987, 1986 and 1985, respectively.
2. "Other assets" include $60,525,000 in 1987, $69,996,000 in 1986 and $105,895,000 in 1985 of investments in unconsolidated affiliates, representing the Company's interests in certain companies accounted for under the cost and equity methods. See Note (A) to the Consolidated Financial Statements.
Source: American Continental Corporation, Form 10K, 31 December 1987.

capitalized interest (another $65 million), was 1.18 coverage for 1987. So the parent was equally exposed to real estate.

Insiders Sell Stock—to AMCC

The related-party transactions in the back of the 10K gave a flavor for management. The company and the Employee Stock Ownership Plan (ESOP) purchased 1,141,878 and 1,014,561 shares from 1985 to 1987 from Chairman Keating and from the directors, officers, and others for an aggregate of $10,742,000 and $8,000,000: beats paying commissions. In May 1986 the chairman purchased from a subsidiary a limited partnership interest for $3.45 million. The list of purchases and sales of partnership interests went on from there. Corporate salaries were spectacular: Keating made $1,954,914 in 1987 plus use of the aircraft and other facilities. His son and three sons-in-law worked for him. Charles, the son, earned $863,494 and Robert Wurzelbacher (a son-in-law), $647,129.

In spring 1988 Lincoln did the famous $200 million bond deal that supposedly flipped CD holders into veritably worthless American Continental paper that had no recourse to Lincoln. Shorts chuckled over the offering document, amazed that it had a market. The bond prospectus recapped in lurid detail the short case: low interest rate spread, no recourse to subs, big junk bond portfolio, profitability dependent on nonrecurring earnings, risky real estate loans, real estate operations, substantially all activities conducted through the subs (to which there was no recourse), ongoing FHLBB and SEC investigations, and no market for the new securities. How could anyone buy with a document like that?

So it required only an hour to read American Continental's financial documents and reach a judgment on the condition of the company and short it the first half of 1988. That was the easy part.

Short Squeeze

The hard part was staying short the stock in the supposed soon-to-be frontal attack by Keating to squeeze short sellers silly.

Rumors flew about buy-ins and harassment of stock lenders by American Continental to stop lending stock. On December 26, 1988 *Forbes* detailed the tactics of the squeeze: Keating had a two-pronged program.[3] First, the bank would lend to the stock's owners to take them off margin at their brokerage houses so the stock couldn't be loaned to short sellers by the brokers. Second, they requested delivery of 1.5 million shares housed at two brokerage offices, thereby reducing the float to around 2 million shares with a short position of 1 million. In addition, they hired a proxy-soliciting firm to ask shareholders to have stock delivered out of margin accounts. AMCC's stated purpose was to convince the marketplace that trading was illiquid.

As early as September 1987, *National Mortgage News* came out with the first story on the Keating Five, and in the fall of 1988, the regulatory concerns came to the fore again. Squeeze or no, Keating was being circled.

Remaining short sellers were rewarded for tenacity with a classic warning bell, as the 8K announced a change in corporate accountants. Arthur Young had quit because of disagreements on timing of capital gains and declined to be associated with any financial statements after December 31, 1987: an admirable showing during a time when accountants appeared to be somnolent. But a lot of good it did short sellers—the stock failed to drop.

Losses mounted, equity declined, and Charles Keating kept on blaming the regulators for his problems. Cash deficit for the first nine months of 1988 was $100 million. The SEC was investigating AMCC's accounting.

In December, *Barron's* article "Phoenix Descending" came out, with its detailed work on the real estate market and the related lenders.[4] Naturally, American Continental was featured, along with Sun State, Western, and Valley.

The price of American Continental didn't really break until February 1989, and by the first of March it was around $3. A proposed savior for Lincoln fell through, and the Justice Department was investigating a couple of the officers for fraud. In late April the stock was trading in fractions. By then the regulators had seized the bank, reported to be one of the two most costly bail-outs, and Charles Keating was just starting his long saga in Washington.

Sun State Savings Acquired on Margin

"Phoenix Descending," to borrow *Barron's* headline, was a nice combination of levity and brevity for the short sellers. Sun State was classic stuff, and anybody who could borrow it had fun.

Sun State Savings and Loan Association (SSSL) commenced operations in 1980. By December 1987 it was a full-blown real estate lending and developing S & L in the best Arizona tradition. Stockholders' equity was $7.90 a share with 5.85 million shares outstanding and earnings per share of $1.10 for the year.

The financial statements were a little gamey. Acquisition, development, and unimproved land loans totaled 33 percent of the loan portfolio at $218 million. Construction loans were another $89 million. Nonaccruing loans were $17 million, with allowances for loan loss reserves of $2.4 million. Investments in real estate were $29 million and in joint ventures, $50 million. The joint venture program put up all the capital on undeveloped land and bore all the losses, while the partner provided expertise in planning, zoning, and developing to offer to a third-party developer. And that was with equity of $42.8 million and foreclosures climbing from $7.4 million in 1986 to $28.4 million in 1987. Sun State looked poised to go off the high board into a waterless pool.

Buy-Out on Margin

But that was before the amazing Maniatis or, to be more precise, after his first 13D filing but before he decided to buy the whole thing. David Maniatis and family filed a 13D on April 14, 1987 on 19.27 percent of common stock. On January 21, 1988 Sun State filed a complaint against the Maniatis Group alleging misleading information. SSSL said Maniatis had been denied the right to purchase more than 15 percent by the superintendent of Arizona banks, that this wasn't disclosed, and besides, the position wasn't just for investment, as the 13D said.

So Maniatis filed an amendment attaching the denial by the superintendent dated October 20, 1987. The superintendent's letter made some provocative points. It said that "the financial condition of the applicant is such as may jeopardize the financial stability of the Association," and that the "overall moral charac-

FIGURE 9.2

Sun State Savings & Loan

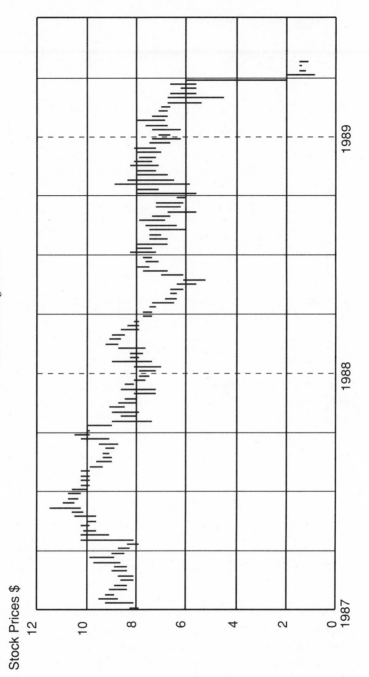

TABLE 9.4

Sun State Savings & Loan
Short Interest

1988	
July	171,662
August	188,372
September	101,910
October	315,359
November	916,638
December	912,561

1989	
January	952,268
February	1,030,137
March	1,182,150
April	934,277
May	664,630
June	not published

ter or integrity of David P. Maniatis indicates it would not be in the interest of the depositors, beneficiaries, creditors or shareholders . . . to permit [him] to control the Association."[5] Harsh. And this from Charles Keating's own state.

The action escalated in the fall, which is when the shorts got intrigued. SSSL received an unsolicited acquisition proposal from Maniatis at $11 a share on October 21, 1988. His group owned 1.4 million shares that they had bought on 50 percent margin through their broker, Blunt, Ellis & Loewi.

Earnings Continue to Drop, But Not the Buy-Out Bid

On October 25, 1988 SSSL announced the quarter's loss, bringing the total loss for nine months to $2.6 million. Nonperformers and those joint ventures appeared to hurt earnings. The head guy said no problem. He added that the big lenders in town had cut back on loans because of area real estate problems. SSSL had taken advantage of their departure by increasing its loan originations by 30 percent![6]

SSSL turned down the Maniatis offer as too vague, despite

Blunt, Ellis & Loewi's letter that they could finance it. A spokesperson also said in *The Business Journal* on November 7, 1988 that Maniatis's margin purchase of Sun State stock at an average price of $9 was the reason he made the offer, an attempt to move the price up. Maniatis responded that "his margin calls were irrelevant."[7]

Indefatigable Maniatis came back in December 1988 with another alternative transaction, accompanied by "an unusually qualified highly confident letter from Blunt and Ellis."[8] Unusual, it seems, because it contained no details for financing—maybe they planned more margin calls.

On January 20, 1989 SSSL announced a problem quarter, with an aftertax loss from $6 million to $16 million. The accountants weren't able to be precise yet. The Federal Home Loan Bank Board had, in fact, sent them a letter telling them to restrict growth and reduce the risk profile. Maniatis mulled another offer. Is this, you ask, a Monty Python skit? Why is this man bidding repeatedly for disappearing assets?

The stock traded from $6 to $7 in the first quarter, presumably supported by the offer on the table. And then, in the second half of March, it rolled over to $2. Around March 31, 1989 the company became more explicit about the issues that concerned the auditors: real estate appraisals, accounting matters involving below-market interest rates, loan loss reserves. It seemed clear, said the company, that "we will fall short of meeting the current 3 percent minimum regulatory capital requirement."[9] So the board decided to meet with Maniatis. Perhaps the superintendent no longer had moral and financial problems in the face of the growing avalanche. To no avail.

The loan problems continued until capital was decimated, and on June 16, 1989 both Western Savings and Loan and Sun State Savings were seized by the regulators.

Valley National: Uncharacteristic Wall Street Battle

The big commercial bank in the Phoenix area was Valley National Corporation, something of a Wall Street darling. Unlike the other sector bets in Arizona, it had broad institutional ownership and an analyst at almost every house on the Street. The shorts barged in without thinking too much about supply and demand, the effect on the stock price, and the duration of the position. Short interaction with professional analysts had been minimal in the years prior to 1988 (before HBJ and Texas Air). The bank analysts on the Street, meanwhile, weren't aware that a few short sellers were independently foaming at the mouth over Arizona. So Valley was unique.

First, the financials. The year-end 1987 Annual showed stockholders' equity of $580 million. Total nonperforming assets were $294.7, with total loans past due ninety days and accruing interest of $34.3 million. The bulk of nonperformers were real estate—no surprise there. Allowance for credit losses was $195 million. The Valley picture, then, didn't look great, but it didn't look like American Continental and Western, either.

The number that engrossed the short sellers was loans for construction and development—$1.264 billion out of a domestic loan portfolio of around $8 billion. If Phoenix was really blowing up, nonperformers would explode as well. That was spring 1988, with the stock around $24.

A Little Media Attention Sparks Discussion

Grant's Interest Rate Observer chronicled the Valley story in the April 15, 1988 issue, noting that its ratio of total real estate to equity was in the top twenty-five in a ragged real estate environment.[10]

Forbes wrote up Valley in May 30, 1988, a blurb that commented on the real estate problems and the price perspective—lower, was the conclusion.[11] The stock price, however, failed to recognize the rising voices and pointed fingers.

The battle escalated from there, since that was the first clue Wall Street had that there was a marked difference of opinion on the value of Valley. Several analysts shifted estimates and ratings and reassessed the Phoenix economy. It was rare in 1988 for bank analysts to consider the real estate environment in a particular geographical area in their view of a bank's loan portfolio. Remember, real estate prices had moved only up since 1974 (except in Texas, and that was a fluke). They mostly looked at the num-

FIGURE 9.3

Valley National Corp.

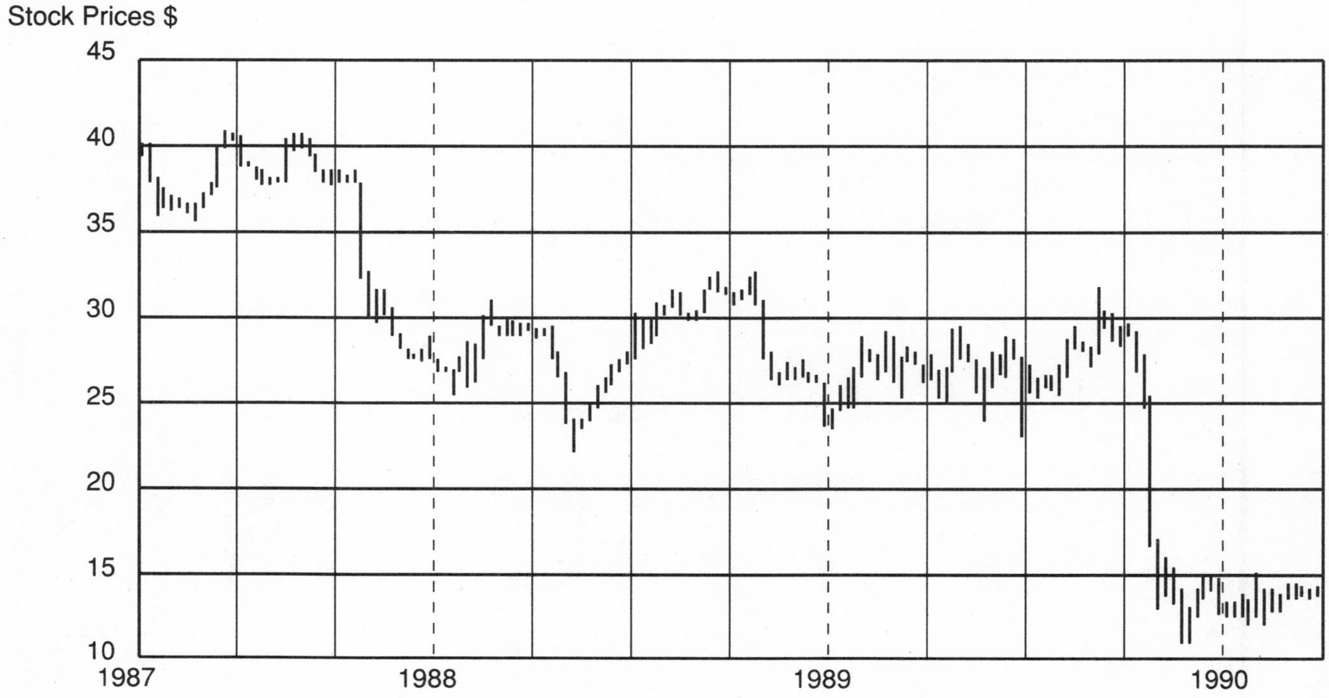

TABLE 9.5

Valley National Corporation
Short Interest

1988	
January	2,535
February	33,811
March	not published
April	24,673
May	118,616
June	148,727
July	218,514
August	153,080
September	202,519
October	247,378
November	595,548
December	1,114,252

1989	
January	1,922,930
February	2,148,008
March	1,890,543
April	2,088,248
May	2,584,052
June	3,445,731
July	3,689,062
August	3,562,404
September	3,682,334
October	3,671,649
November	3,648,937
December	4,713,386

bers and listened to the bank officials. Arizona was a good warm-up for New England.

Charles Peabody at Kidder, Peabody was the first big-name bank analyst to depart from group-think with a resounding sell in October 1988. He went from a two to a four rating (from buy to sell), in itself unusual for Wall Street, since everything is always half-steps and slow motion to avoid conflict. Management, he said, was not dealing with the problem, and he felt that instead of taking a proactive restructuring stance, they nibbled and hedged. His conclusion was sell.

Management came to town the end of October for a dog and pony show at the New York Society of Security Analysts. They made the Street a bit more nervous, since they didn't address the real estate debacle until the question and answer session, when they reassured the audience that reserves were adequate. They did talk about cutting costs and margin improvements, but everyone naturally wanted to know the details of the life-threatening injury, not just the cosmetic work.

So late winter 1988–89 turned into a bit of a shoving match between analysts: "Are reserved enough." "Aren't." "Stock's cheap." "Not either." Everyone pulled out a battery of statistics and devised various ways of looking at deterioration and turns in real estate. They calculated different formulas for the effect on earnings and the appropriate level of reserves, if reserves were appropriate. As nonperformers climbed, half the analysts lost their nerve and went to "hold" until a trend was discernable.

The short sellers sat back and watched. Real estate always takes a while to work out, because it's not marked to market every day. The stock moved up; the stock moved down.

Turmoil Intensifies

And then around January 1989, things started to get bad. The short sellers had been chatty among themselves on Valley, contrary to their usual restraint and paranoia. The chatter snowballed. Inexperienced nouveau short sellers shorted Valley, and that did two things. First, the supply of stock evaporated, so buy-ins started occurring randomly, and no stock was available to borrow to short on run-ups. Next, the nouveau shorts didn't have conviction or experience, so every time the stock flurried they panicked and ran it up some more by buying. A rabid short-hater couldn't have strategized more effectively.

Tom Brown at Smith, Barney had just come off a huge score the year before on BankAmerica. He was (and is) acknowledged by institutions to be one of the top bank analysts. He had had Valley rated a buy since June 1988, but come January he picked it as his stock of the year. Phoenix, he thought was old news. The *Barron's* article was late to the party, he argued; 1986 was the right year for the Arizona crash, and the environment was improving now. "I believe," he said, that "Valley's real estate related non-performing assets will peak here in the fourth quarter and decline throughout 1989, and there will be no need for a special loan loss provision to boost the reserve."[12] He continued to say that the short sellers "have driven the stock down and they're the ones that are going to help drive it higher in 1989."[13] And the stock responded by moving to $27 from $24.

Charles Peabody answered his rival's recommendation and commented on Valley's fourth-quarter earnings announcement on January 18, 1989. Real estate nonperforming assets (NPA's) were up from $292.7 million to $319.1 million, with loan loss reserve declining from $187.3 million to $178.8 million. The ratio of total reserves to NPA's went from 47.3 to 39.7 percent. A four rating was justified, he concluded. "Unattractive," agreed Paine Webber's Sandra Flannigan.[14]

"Excellent investment opportunity," said Tom Brown. "Fourth quarter EPS on target."[15]

So Valley acted like it was possessed by poltergeists. Price action had no connection to announcements, or to any discernable reality. On one preholiday afternoon, the company reannounced a previously announced asset sale, and the stock spiked a couple of points. Nobody was around to tell anybody what to think or do, so the few nonanalytical sorts staring at the Quotrons spooked the action. The options took on a life of their own, with trading shifting to puts which exhibited a high implied volatility for the far out cycles. It was nuts. And it reminded old, grizzled, short veterans why they never talked to anyone: all those incompetent shorts got involved and jerked the price around.

The Effect of Real Estate on Banks

The argument on Valley, which seemed to last for years, centered around one very big point. How much damage can a wretched real estate environment do to a bank? Most of the young analysts couldn't remember the 1974 real estate downturn and subsequent bank collapse, so they had no benchmark. The real estate pros knew that when it came, it lasted—three to four years minimum to clear out the overhang, with banks trading as low as 40 percent of book. And furthermore, no one rang a bell at the bottom. The stocks just started sneaking back up, but it took more than a quarter's earnings to prod the prices off the lows.

So the shorts felt comfortable that all the Wall Street spread-sheets on banks reserves, core earnings, and rate of change on nonperformers wouldn't—couldn't—condense mayhem into one quick number. They just watched.

They knew that buying a bank or an S & L stock was like buying a blind pool. You never knew what you had, so the macro environment had better be right. This point was reinforced repeatedly in the Valley debate. For example, one analyst of large repute said, "Valley has no strip shopping center loans." Another equally renowned prognosticator said, "Valley has 9% of total loans in strip shopping centers." The shorts said, "Who cares? It ain't the point, guys."

A fair number of analysts decided after a year of bad quarters that things had to get better soon. So they marshalled their courage and re-recommended the stock. And the push-pull would start all over again. First Boston joined Smith, Barney; both thought the stock price fully reflected the difficulties. Charles Peabody continued to recommend short sale of the stock. The *Wall Street Journal*'s "Heard on the Street" column and the *New York Times* recapped the conflict on February 21, 1989. Roger Lowenstein at the *Journal* quoted Brown and Peabody, who threw the special language of banks around like mantras. Peabody repeated that the domestic loan-loss reserve ratio to nonperforming loans was only 47 percent, compared to an industry average of 80 percent with more traumas on the way. Brown said nonperformers would come down and the reserves would look adequate. Valley backed Brown; Eliot Rosen, investor relations for Valley, said, "Tom Brown has been out here to kick the tires three times in the past year. He has done his homework. Charles Peabody's report isn't very insightful. It's the type of thing you could do from press releases."[16]

Valley officials finally took off their gloves and punched back after a round of what they felt was specific misinformation in late April 1989. Peabody said that Valley was exposed to Maniatis (of SSSL margin fame) with a $14.5 million loan on one of his real estate partnerships, and he linked Valley to American Continental, as well. Valley officials demanded a retraction, stating, "The information is absolutely wrong."[17] "Remember," they should have said, "it's a blind pool." The company executives reminded analysts one more time to keep their honest opinions to themselves. Dummy up and take notes was the message. Come out and visit, and we'll give you the right story.

The second quarter was a loss of $90 million to clean up everything and was somewhat uneventful.

Earnings Announcement Clears Controversy

Everyone got surprised in October 1989, and no one more surprised than Tom Brown. The company announced yet another big loss of $72.2 million for the third quarter and suspended the dividend. Nonperformers were $523.2 million. The stock dropped, or more accurately, plunged to $13.50 and then wallowed for months.

Rumors continued to drift. In the silliest sequence (but not uncommon), the Dow tape showed first-quarter 1990 earnings at $.62 versus $.62 late on Maundy Thursday afternoon. The stock moved up a couple of points in euphoria. Few had noted that they were the wrong earnings—those for Valley of New Jersey. The stock moved down the next Tuesday when the real numbers came through at $.03 versus $.96.

By that time, bank analysts also had New England and the East Coast to think about. Phoenix had been overshadowed by more current controversies. When no one really cares anymore, it will probably be time to buy long or at least to cover shorts. Now the shorts swarm after the examiners as they rap knuckles across the country in the liquidity purge of the 1990s.

Banks, with their arcane and specialized terminology, are boring to analyze, much like insurance companies. As a group, they are perceived as sacred, inviolate, protected by the government and the many insurance programs. They are, in fact, highly leveraged corporations. When equity is only 5 percent of assets, it doesn't take much to nibble through the base. So banks can be profitable and predictable on both sides, particularly if stockholders or stock sellers count cranes in their own backyards to determine how frenetic the pace of real estate expansion really is relative to the perceived economic growth in town.

Notes

1. American Continental Corporation, Form 10K, 31 December 1987, 4.

2. Ibid., 13.

3. Allan Sloan and John H. Taylor, "Mr. Keating, Meet Mr. Short," *Forbes,* 26 December 1988, 35–36.

4. Jonathan R. Laing, "Phoenix Descending," *Barron's,* 19 December 1988, 8.

5. Letter of the superintendent dated 20 October 1987, attached to Maniatis Group Amendment no. 13 to the Schedule 13D, Sun State Savings and Loan Association, Form 10K, 31 December 1987, 39.

6. Sun State Savings and Loan Association, press release, 25 October 1988.

7. Pat O'Brien, "Maniatis Determined to Gain Control of Sun State Saving," *The Business Journal,* 7 November 1988.

8. Sun State Savings and Loan Association, press release, 8 December 1988.

9. Ibid., 31 March 1989.

10. "Real Estate Lenders," *Grant's Interest Rate Observer,* 15 April 1988, 9.

11. "Down in the Valley," *Forbes,* 30 May 1988, 330.

12. Tom Brown, Smith Barney, 3 January 1989, n.p.

13. Ibid.

14. Sandra Flannigan, Paine Webber, 18 January 1989, n.p.

15. Tom Brown, "Valley National Corporation," Smith Barney Research, 30 January 1989, 2.

16. Eliot Rosen in Roger Lowenstein, "Heard on the Street," *Wall Street Journal,* 21 February 1989, C2.

17. Valley National Corporation, press release, 26 April 1989.

10

All of the Above: Crazy Eddie

Sophisticated bubbles, Wall Street icons, and greed bring the strains of previous chapters together in a short for the all-star list—Crazy Eddie, Inc. First, the financials were a dream, with debt and inventories increasing steadily. Next, Wall Street hype pushed the bubble higher and higher. Finally, the level of obvious sleaze and greed was particularly gratifying to short sellers when the bubble burst. And all of it was there for the reading in the June 1986 convertible prospectus, long before the precipitous decline in the stock price began in October 1986. And not a short squeeze or buy-in in the whole saga.

An Identifiable Story Stock

In June 1986 Crazy Eddie owned twenty-four retail consumer electronics stores in the New York metropolitan area. The television advertisements made the company visible to every analyst and portfolio manager in the area: even if you hadn't been in the store, you knew Crazy Eddie the store because of Crazy Eddie, the actor, hawking the merchandise and prices on TV. Name recognition also helped the stock price: it moved from $4.50 in the second half of 1984 to $37.50 in the second quarter of 1986. By then, fifteen analysts covered the stock and it was 41 percent institutionally owned.

FIGURE 10.1
Crazy Eddie, Inc.

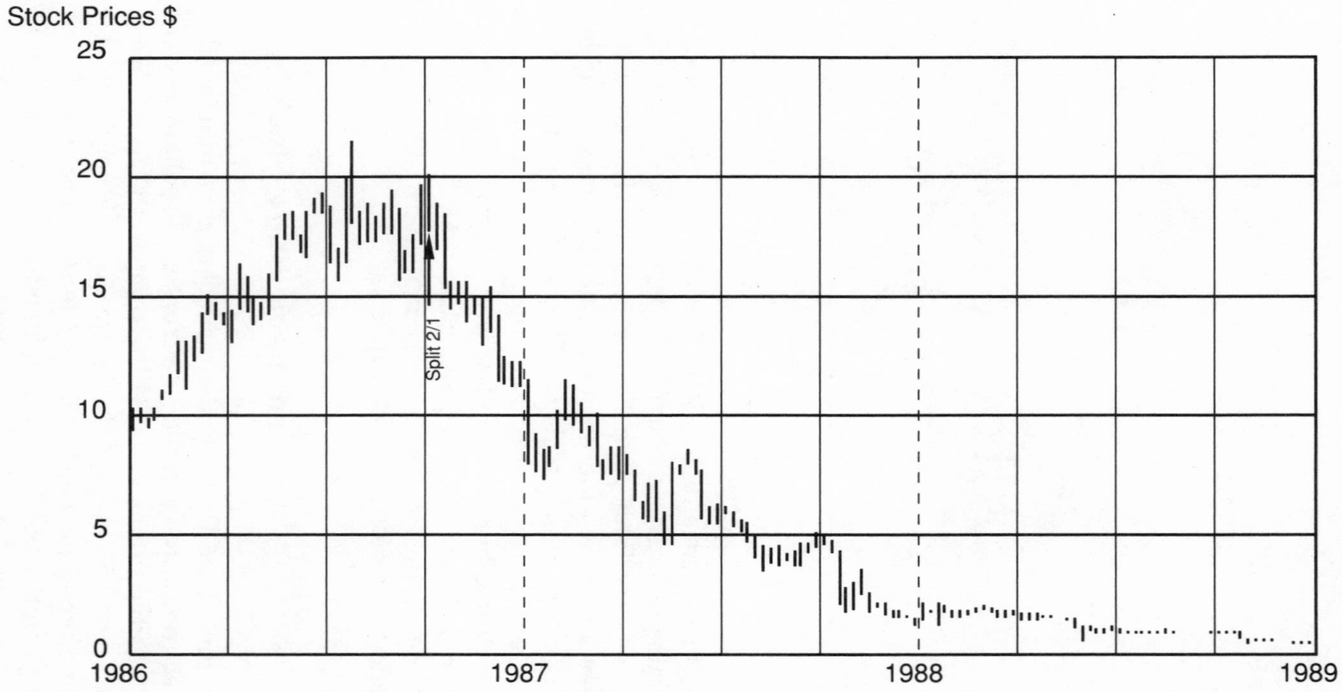

The company caught the attention of the shorts primarily because of valuation. Crazy Eddie earned $.96 for March 2, 1986 year end, so the stock was trading at thirty-nine times earnings. With approximately 15.5 million shares outstanding, the capitalization was $580 million, or $24 million per store (that's around two times revenues). Crazy Eddie rented the stores, so no underlying real estate inflated the valuation. Each store averaged $13 million a year in sales with after-tax net of 5 percent. And this for a company selling a highly competitive commodity product in the most competitive market in the United States. To put this in perspective, Kentucky Fried Chicken sold their stores about the same time for around $700,000 per store and 1.4 times revenues.

So the stock seemed a little overpriced, but so did many stocks in the summer of 1986. Clearly, the Street analysts were counting on growth. And that's when the prospectus began to fill in the blanks where the valuation exercise left off. First, it showed same-store sales growth of 10 percent for the quarter ended June 1, 1986. Not spectacular, which meant the growth had to be coming from new stores. The financials supported the feeling that top-line revenue growth was the key to the company. Then, the reader's eye drifted to the character of the men who would direct the ambitious store-opening program.

A Private Family Bank or an Electronics Chain?

The real pith to the Crazy story was the insiders. The prospectus was particularly rich with detail; nobody could make this one up. Where to start?

The organizational chart was made up solidly of Antars or Antars-in-law. Crazy Eddie Antar himself (yes, there was a real person named Eddie) was at the helm: 38 years old and another Sam Walton, according to his fans. Cousin Sam E. Antar was controller and soon to become chief financial officer at 29. Brother Mitchell was executive vice-president of marketing. Uncle Eddy was treasurer. Cousin Mort Gindi was vice-president of store development. Another cousin, Solomon Antar, was senior vice-president and general counsel. Two members of top management, however, were not Antars.

Next, Sam and Eddie Antar had sold stock worth approximately $71.5 million by the June 1986 convertible prospectus date. Cumulative six-year net income for the company was only $24.2 million. The Antars believed in being compensated for their genius; stockholders could wait for price appreciation.

The prospectus repeatedly referred to new employment contract terms for chairman of the board, president, and chief operating officer Eddie Antar to be decided at the annual meeting. He was currently paid $300,000, and an increase had been postponed until then.

The stock option plan appeared to be generous, but again, a new plan with options for a total of one million shares might be approved at the upcoming annual meeting.

Crazy Eddie had a Stock Appreciation Right (SAR) plan initiated in July 1986 in keeping with the family-directed largesse in the prospectus. The company gave the recipients cash, large amounts of it, periodically if the stock price appreciated. For example, the insiders had SAR's for 264,200 options at an average price of $8.29. The stock sold for around $40. The plan gave the options holder $31.71 in cash. The market for the stock didn't have to take the hit, and SEC Form 144 wasn't filed. At one point there were 605,000 options outstanding at an option price of $34; for every $1 in stock appreciation, the shareholders were billed for $605,000 in additional payment to their executives in a hit to the next quarter's earnings. A total of 2 million shares were reserved for issuance in the 1987 Annual.

The Money Purchase Pension plan also contributed 25 percent of W–2 compensation for each eligible participant. This unusual fringe allowed Eddie to extricate an additional $267,001 from the company.

Does A Medical School Count as Vertical Integration?

The "Certain Transactions" section was particularly entertaining, less complex than Jiffy Lube but with a reckless abandon rarely found in a Wall Street darling. First, the company leased a couple of stores from family members. Not too bad. Next, Benel Distributors, a corporation owned by a brother-in-law and sister, had numerous odd dealings back and forth with Crazy, including inventory sales, leases, and joint advertising expenses.

The best section by an ample magnitude, however, was "Transactions with other related companies." Prior to the initial public offering, Crazy did business with or made loans to a number of family-owned entities, including Acousti-phase, which manufactured speakers, Disc-O-Mat, which sold pre-recorded cassettes, S&M Discount, which sold unnamed home entertainment, and—the most compelling—the University of St. Lucia School of Medicine, Ltd., and Educators International. The Antar family operated its own Caribbean island medical school and a medical school recruiting company, Educators. Right out of *Doonesbury*. How could you not short a retail electronics company that operates a medical school?

In addition, prior to the May 1984 initial public offering, the company made interest-free loans to Eddie, Sam, and other family members; the company was unable to determine the exact amount. The company also guaranteed borrowings by Shoe Time, another Sam company, which filed for bankruptcy. Crazy Eddie had all the trappings of a personal bank for the Antar family—or, perhaps, personal mint.

Wall Street Hysteria and Home Shopping

So, you say, why did Wall Street embrace this company with slobbering euphoria? Analysts liked the industry. It looked good. It had momentum. Videocassette recorder (VCR) sales had accelerated in 1984 and 1985, up 86 and 56 percent. TV and video were 53 percent of Crazy's sales. Wall Street straightline projected VCR growth with their collective spreadsheets. Popular wisdom said that every VCR owner would trade up; every home would own many. And replace them frequently. Weird. Compact disk (CD) players were just hitting the stores, and clearly people would buy a lot of them at high prices. No competition, just blissfully high margins forever.

Analysts particularly liked the company's way of doing business, the company strategy. Prices for electronics in Crazy Eddie stores weren't actually that low, comparatively. Customers were supposed to bargain, to argue, to negotiate a cheap price, and Crazy Eddie would comply. But most people don't like to haggle for hard goods, so Crazy Eddie stores had a reputation for low prices without the financial burden of consistent price competitiveness. Analysts liked the feel of pulling the wool over the consumer's eyes—ironic, as events turned out, since Eddie Antar was ultimately more successful at conning smart Wall Street analysts than street-smart New Yorkers.

Drexel, Salomon, Morgan Stanley, First Manhattan, and Wertheim loved the stock. Wertheim was a particularly rabid promoter. The reports read like a Crazy Eddie TV advertisement: "We judge the results no less than outstanding, especially given the company's known conservative accounting practices. . . . Eddie Antar relishes beating earnings estimates, and we see no reason to deny him this pleasure if the company continues to perform exceptionally well."[1] Is this a stock or a fetish, you ask?

The Drexel analyst was equally ebullient: "By 1990, we believe Crazy Eddie can achieve $1 billion in sales and be the dominant consumer electronics retailer on the Northeastern Seaboard . . . a better buying opportunity, in our view, may not appear in the future."[2] By the summer his January report was badly outdated: he had projected annual increase of shares outstanding at 8 percent, and the company had already surpassed his five-year 1990 number with the new shares issued plus the convertible and stock options. He kept raising his earnings per share estimate nonetheless.

The financials became more interesting over the summer. Since Crazy Eddie was in a commodity business and aftertax margins were only 5 percent, it needed to turn inventory quickly to generate a high enough rate of return to support the stock price. However, inventory turns were dropping. Inventory was building. And, the inventory accounting system was manual. Amazing. Clerks wrote tickets by hand at night and the company figured out what the stores had, what had been sold, and what to order in a couple of days. Eddie made a point of saying computer systems can't run a retail business. The Street analysts applauded his gutsy retail acumen.

The Plot Develops

Eddie Antar wasn't content with a thirty-nine multiple—he went for the brass ring.

Placid shorts sat with their positions like pigs in mud and waited for the stock to work back down. One Friday afternoon in late July, they were shocked off their collective Quotrons by a cattle prod; the stock started moving fast and big, the kind of move that shrieks of buy-out or cure for cancer, up five points to $40. Many phone calls and many calculator punches later (times revenue, times cash flow, times earnings), the cause was identified. Crazy Eddie Antar was going in for home shopping. He bought a transponder, whatever that is, and announced at an Atlanta trade show the wave of the electronic retail future. "Icing on the cake," the bull analysts yelped. "Gained a jump on competitors," they cried. The shorts sighed and settled in for the second home shopping siege of the summer.

Analysts were quick to evaluate the impact of the new shopping service euphorically. The Drexel analyst, Barry Bryant, had a comment out by Monday with a long report soon after that moved the price target from $50 to $55, following that old analysts' adage that if the price moves, change the target and earnings estimate accordingly. He said home shopping would contribute $.20 to earnings in 1987. He arrived at this number after serious thought: he assumed that Crazy would do "half the sales volume at half the profitability achieved by Home Shopping Network in its first six months of national broadcasting."[3] He also mentioned in his report that Crazy said the main market for the new show was 1.5 million satellite dish owners. He neglected to point out, however, that each and every dish owner would have to buy $43.33 of merchandise a year to hit his $65 million revenue target.

The Goldman Sachs analyst Gary Balter was insightful enough to comment that the home shopping announcement would primarily affect the stock price and multiple (and not the earnings) because of Wall Street's current assessment of home shopping stocks. He didn't recommend sale, however.[4]

Salomon analyst Bruce Missett pounded the table: "high-demand product line, powerful buying organization, strong balance sheet."[5] He got the number of shares wrong, too, and planned for well-controlled expenses, apparently not giving credence to Eddie's lust for personal wealth or the family appetite for salaries and stock options.

In September 1986 senior Wall Street retail analyst Walter Loeb at Morgan Stanley jumped on the bandwagon with a rousing purchase recommendation: "I strongly recommend purchase . . . satellite-television home-shopping network planned for introduction later this year could catapult the Firm into national prominence."[6] New products, he continued, a bunch of new electronic products would propel sales up 35 percent a year for five years. Jewelry, too, he said; they're test marketing jewelry.

Crazy was relatively quiet through the early fall. The stock split and earnings were announced in October for the second quarter. The press release said same-store sales were up 15 percent for the second quarter and net income was up 57 percent on a net sales increase of 41 percent. The stock traded down, although the number was on track. Analysts explained that stockholders were used to earnings above Street consensus and that the target number was below the unusually high expectations of some owners. That was the beginning.

In the middle of October 1986, Eddie Antar told institutional investors that the third quarter might be slightly lower than some Street estimates. The stock dropped 15 percent to a post–two-for-one split price of $15.25. Analysts compliantly followed the leader and lowered estimates "slightly," $.02 for the quarter, none for the year for Barry Bryant. (Mysteriously Barry's new home shopping–induced price target of $27.50 was back down to $25.) Nobody was too concerned, except perhaps the stockholders. Analysts collectively said: expense increases result from developing a major new business, competition in New York creates price erosion, slowing same store sales due to already extraordinary volume in stores. No problem. Buy now. Stock price is the opportunity of a lifetime. The shorts nodded and loaded up.

The 10Q for the second quarter, when it came out in October, showed that inventories were up 147 percent, with sales up 42 percent. General expenses were up. Interest expense was up. More important, but nobody noticed, incentive stock options and nonqualified options for 735,360 shares had been issued to management in August 1986. More shares means lower earnings per share, but nobody cared. Another odd point: the press release said "identical store sales increased 15% for the second quarter and 13% for the first half," but the 10Q said "5% comparable store increase" for the three-month period and 12.8 percent for the first half. Strange disparity. Analysts apparently read press material, not financials.

A word here about the Crazy Eddie press agent, Ed Colloton of the Colloton Group. He was the best: smooth, enthusiastic, helpful. He knew all the analysts on the Street and was always available with the latest word from Eddie Antar. He made it easy to be an analyst. Wall Street analysts just wrote down what Ed Colloton told them and didn't bother with all that messy financial stuff. Then they could revel in the sales charm of Eddie Antar himself and feel comfortable that everything was OK.

Meanwhile, Bloomingdale's left the electronics market in New York—too much competition. Lafayette Radio had exited in March. Trader Horn was up for sale. "Opportunity for savvy specialists, such as Crazy Eddie," said First Manhattan.[7]

The dissonant clues continued. In November 1986 Crazy Eddie Antar sold 1.5 million shares. For tax reasons. At $13.875. In December he gave 500,000 shares away, reducing his position to 2.9 million shares.

On December 23, 1986 Crazy Eddie, the company, announced the repurchase of 3 million shares. "Reflects the board's confidence that the stock is undervalued," said Walter Loeb at Morgan Stanley.[8] He made, however, no comment on key executive Eddie's opinion of the stock's valuation when he put his feet solidly behind his company outlook with the early December stock sale.

The Big Break

On January 5, 1987 the stock dropped $1.375 on big volume, 1.3 million shares, to $9.875. Crazy Eddie announced after the close that same-store sales decreased 9 percent during December 1986. On January 9 the company announced that Eddie Antar had resigned, effective immediately, for personal reasons. Rumors had been circulating since December that he was terminally ill. Same-store sales for the quarter were up 5 percent, and the company would repurchase an additional 2 million shares. Earnings of $.12, up from $.09, were also released.

A call to helpful Ed Colloton yielded the information that he was no longer working for Crazy Eddie. Crazy Eddie was now without key player Eddie Antar and street mouthpiece Ed Colloton. Wall Street was a little concerned, but not panicky. "Hold," said Morgan Stanley. "We expect these very capable executives (Mitchell, 30, and Sam, 29, Antar) to follow diligently in the chief executive's footsteps and continue the Company's expansion."[9]

Here's where shorts made their first big mistake. Some of them covered positions: short interest went from 460,686 in December 1986 to 227,720 in January 1987. Eddie had quit and sold. The 10Q was due out any day with more puzzle pieces. Evidence was mounting that the Crazy Eddie situation was much worse than previously imagined, and $20 to $10 is only half a collapse.

The 10Q came out in the middle of January. 10Qs are probably a short seller's favorite document. The document tells whether the short is right or wrong, whether to cover, hold, or short more. The Crazy 10Q was a nice example. First, one of the main clues for the initial position, inventories: up 134 percent year over year (to take out seasonality) with sales for the nine months up 42 percent. To say it another way, inventory turns continued to drop—from 4.3 times last year to 2.9 times. The situation looked worse. Total debt was $178 million with equity of $92 million. The proposed share buyback, up to 5 million shares authorized, would increase the debt further. Gross margins were down 1.6 percent from the previous quarter. The company also continued in its role as employee banker with new loans of $275,000 to employee Edmond Levy. Despite short-term investments of $100 million, $22.7 million in commercial paper (used for working capital) was outstanding, suggesting restrictions on the cash balances. Short more, the financials screamed.

Business didn't get better. On March 10, 1987 the new management lineup announced that same-store sales were down 19 percent for the quarter with sales up 22 percent—a far cry from analysts' aspirations for 50 percent-plus growth. Management offered solutions: Crazy would now sell appliances, like refrigerators, and jewelry, but best of all, Crazy would install operating systems, including point-of-sale systems. In other words, Crazy was getting a computer to track sales and inventories.

Earnings for the fourth quarter were announced on April 28, 1987—$.02 versus $.26 with gross margins down again, from 25.9 to 22.8 percent in a year, in a business with slim aftertax margins. The stock price continued to edge down.

In May, Eddie came back to save the day. He made a $7-a-share bid for the company, only to be topped by Elias Zinn of Entertainment Marketing with an $8 offer. Both bids were subject to a definitive agreement and other contingencies. The stock popped up over $8 on takeover talk.

In June the SEC announced an inquiry. The 10K revealed that Chemical Bank had cut off its $52 million line of credit. The 10K also had five pages of legal proceedings including an action filed by the New York State attorney general for selling air conditioners that didn't meet state standards. It also noted that Sam the elder had resigned from the board on March 17, 1987. The company loaned Sam the younger $100,000 in May. The old family lending practices proved habit-forming.

The 1987 10K continued the encouraging trends that the shorts had uncovered in the previous year's prospectus. Eddie's salary had been doubled in September 1986 to $600,000, and he had continued to collect it, despite his resignation in January. Shareholder suits proliferated. Benel Distributors, the brother-in-law's tape distribution company that Crazy had considered buying, filed for bankruptcy.

Then in August, Eddie dropped his takeover bid after suggesting that his group might have trouble financing it. The stock traded down to $3.50 and Eddie was rumored, again, to be a recluse, seriously ill. Wall Street didn't offer opinions or jump in to buy cheap stock.

In November 1987 the shorts got moral satisfaction; escalating inventories of the previous year were finally explained. New management said that they were missing $45 million in inventory. Elias Zinn, with his winning bid, took over the first of November and closed the stores to count inventory: his audit showed $75 million rather than $126.7 million in goods. The loss grew to a $65 million shortfall, and Peat, Marwick, the auditors, were named in a complaint. (How do accountants really count inventories?)

As the financial puzzle continued to clear, the company charged that Eddie had falsified inventory and profit reports, created phantom inventory, and destroyed the records in a cover-up in order "to artificially inflate the net worth of the company" and the value of the stock. So that's why they didn't have a computer system, you say. Eddie also inflated same-store sales figures by including wholesale sales with lower margins in revenue figures.

Eddie looted the company, sold stock on insider information (someone had to know about those bogus inventories), and took Wall Street for one big-time joy ride.

The company finally filed for bankruptcy in June 1989. Eddie was on the lam with many unhappy ex-participants trying to repatriate his winnings (alleged $60 million) from miscellaneous foreign caches. He surrendered to U.S. marshals in February 1990.

Crazy Eddie Antar taught us that sleaze is sleaze, and doesn't change. If you read the proxy and the "certain transactions" section of the 10K or the prospectus and follow the insider sales, a irrefutable profile appears. It wasn't necessary to meet the man in order to understand his priorities.

Notes

1. Robert J. Schweich, "Specialty Retailing Notes," Wertheim & Co., Inc., 9 July 1986, 1.

2. Barry Bryant, "Crazy Eddie," Drexel, Burnham, Lambert, 24 January 1986, 1.

3. Barry Bryant, "Crazy Eddie" Research Abstracts, Drexel, Burnham, Lambert, 29 July 1986, 5466.

4. Gary Balter, "Crazy Eddie," Goldman Sachs Research, 28 July 28 1986, n.p.

5. Bruce M. Missett, "Crazy Eddie, Inc.—New Venture Adds to Company Prospects," Salomon Brothers, Inc., 5 August 1986, 1.

6. Walter F. Loeb, "Crazy Eddie," Retail Purchase Recommendation, Morgan Stanley, 18 September 1986, 1.

7. Cathleen W. Mackey, "Crazy Eddie," First Manhattan Co. Research, 24 October 1986, 3.

8. Walter F. Loeb, "Crazy Eddie" Research Comment, Morgan Stanley, 12 January 1987, 28.

9. Ibid.

PART 3

HISTORY AND GENERAL LESSONS

11

Shortcomings

Short sellers are a little different from most institutional managers because they spend a fair amount of time and energy analyzing their mistakes—probably because errors are terrifying and costly, or because their egos make it particularly tough to admit defeat. Hindsight by definition is valuable when trying to understand mistakes. The short seller's post–price run-up exercise is to determine where the clues failed, why the price levitated, why a normally accurate trail sign was misleading.

Three Short Sins

Sloth

The biggest reason for failure in stock selection on either the short or the long side is too little work. Particularly treacherous on the short side, the absence of a carefully reasoned case can have painful consequences. Since short sellers, by their nature, can't blame mistakes on analysts or friends or, even, assistants, analytical sloth is cause for the short equivalent of a hair shirt and mental flagellation.

Usually, sloth is prompted by shorting someone else's idea. If in moments of greed for new ideas, short sellers short stocks without the normal painstaking file-building, spreadsheet-accumulating, brain-crunching work, the stocks will *always* go up quickly and scare hell out of chastised short sellers. But they can't admit, then, that they didn't do the work, that they shorted without cause (an extreme violation of short principles, making them no better than longs). So they cover. As one hedge fund manager says, "shorting's easy. You short a stock, watch it double, cover in panic, then wait for the inevitable bankruptcy." Like being short Texas Air or HBJ and covering when they spiked, if you hadn't done the work yourself.

Pride

The second major sin is hubris. Shorts have prima donna problems, like the rest of megabuck-earning Wall Street. But with investment bankers and mutual fund managers, it's other people's money. When shorts get the big head, their own pocketbooks and pride get clipped resoundingly. Short sellers normally revel in two-sided arguments; they like to be disagreed with and they generally listen. When they don't, the lapse is noteworthy. Success, of course, is the cause of the glitch. Always being right hurts in the long run.

Hubris is manifest in two primary analytical errors: the sudden use of rigid formulas and the short sale of good companies. The rigid formula problem arises when short sellers start acting like Wall Street analysts and apply the same formula or spreadsheet or valuation methodology to a group of stocks without thinking. If you've seen six S & L's go under with the same profile, it's easy to short the seventh without worry. And that's the one that will bite you. Because something may have changed, like the real estate environment or the government, but you quit paying attention because the formula worked. Merabank, Pinnacle West's S & L, was a disaster, as ugly as any in Arizona. The shorts shorted Pinnacle West but underestimated the marginal stupidity of the government and its propensity to bail out anything that looked like it had anything to do with taxpayers or a regulated industry. The shorts started thinking things were rational, and Pinnacle lost them money on the positions, then made them pay again out of their taxpaying pocket. The irony was not lost.

The second hubris error is the good company mistake. Most professionals have this one branded in fire someplace on their body; most amateurs don't realize it's why they don't like to short stocks anymore. Both Julian Robertson and Jim Chanos identified this phenomenon as the major short error. Shorting a good company is always risky. A good company is a company with smart management who pay attention to business trends and customers and who have financial statements reflecting that unlikely blend. If the stock is sold short simply because of valuation, the market immediately shows how high the earnings multiple can go. Buy index puts, instead; a valuation short is no different than a market bet. If you short the stock because of perceived temporary problems and because of excessive valuation, good management can fix a problem fast.

Jim Chanos talks about shorting Federal Express. He says Federal Express was overvalued relative to earnings expectations. The company had temporary problems with both Zapmail and new competitors that were causing operating margin problems. The company told him these were solvable. "I don't know whether it was overconfidence, hubris or what but I didn't believe them," he commented.[1] When they reported the quarter, it was a turnaround, and the stock ran up 40 percent.

Most exceptional short sellers are investors, not short-term traders. On occasion they may make profitable trades based on temporary imbalances in the financial statements. But on the whole, even if they know the company cold, it's impossible to be prescient about the timing. When they make those bets, they do it with the knowledge that they are departing from fundamental wisdom, and if the bet doesn't work quickly, it's smart to exit. Novices, fools, and retail brokers sell short for quick trades.

Timing

Timing is an error of judgment for which short sellers have no solution; it's what turns a profitable and monumental bankruptcy into a 2 percent annualized return because the seller was too visionary. The timing error is another one that scares novices into permanent T-bills. Since professional short sellers earn interest on short balances, they get paid to wait; most individuals don't have the luxury. The timing problem is the single biggest argument against individuals' selling short—it throws off the risk/

return relationships and suggests that individuals should use the discipline for selling or not owning stocks rather than for selling short.

The first reason for bad timing is underestimating the insanity of the public. Optimism in the face of defeat is a custom of the country, as short sellers of Harrier, Crazy Eddie, and numerous other companies will attest. Investor ebullience can keep a stock price up for years in spite of no earnings, even no product. Copy-Tele is generally acknowledged to be the Rasputin of stocks. Despite the lack of product (a purported flat computer screen) and its faithful promise of appearance at every annual meeting, the stock trades routinely from $9 to $12 and back again. New drug companies never decline in price: who knows what the outlook is, but it might be fantastic.

The second reason for the timing problem is the ability of investment bankers to sell another round of financing despite a seriously flawed corporate business plan. Continued flows of financing can keep a dead company on a respirator for years. Integrated Resources certainly outlived its corporate mission; the untimely survival was promoted by bankers and investors who bought the paper without reading the financials.

Unfortunately, in some instances the lag time between the discovery of the fatal flaw and the demise of the company results in a change in the macro environment that bails out the troubled short sale candidate. McBear mentioned Capital Cities and Fannie Mae as examples. The interest rate turn saved Fannie Mae from bad operating results. With Capital Cities, some of the companies' other lines of revenue strengthened and saved the basic business, which was losing money.

In the same vein, some short sales fail because the seller underestimated the ability of a leveraged company to grow its way out of the problem—to grow top line faster than the debt capitalization, for example. In the 1980s when short sellers were first titillated by the LBO balance sheet, they failed to realize how long debt takes to sink a company when the business environment is good. Most feel that the jury is still out on the stocks. The ones they covered in dismay can still make them money in the 1990s.

Short sellers respond to the problem in several ways. Michael Murphy, a short seller and newsletter writer, covers automatically after a 25 percent price run-up and waits to short again. He feels that if the price moves that far, something is wrong, either the timing or the analysis, and that short sellers err the same way longs do—they cut the profits and let the losses run. Other managers wait until a stock cracks to short initially, after the first drop when the earnings and price momentum have slowed. Joe DiMenna never shorts a stock with great relative strength, such as Home Shopping on the rise.

Almost every short position lasts too long for sellers. Once they solve the puzzle, they feel that everyone should. Another prescriptive to the timing error is to add to short positions fearlessly when the crack finally comes. If conviction keeps you in the stocks when they spike in the face of rumors, conviction should require additional investment when HBJ sells Shamu for too little money, or when Eddie Antar sells his stock.

And a Multitude of Small Follies

Commodity Cycles

Trade cocoa if you want to, but don't double the risk unintentionally. If a stock you're thinking of shorting is affected by commodity prices, track the underlying commodity price. If you're short a chicken stock, make sure you understand the chicken cycle, the impact of a drought or an ice storm, and corn prices. It's easier to find fundamental balance sheet flaws than to trade grain prices unless you work on the Chicago Board of Trade.

Sometimes, however, the presence of a large inventory of a commodity on a balance sheet can be a good clue that the company is either speculating rather than attending to business or has lost control of inventories. Jan Bell Marketing was a hot Wall Street pick at Christmas 1989: the First Boston analyst picked it as growth stock of the year and Goldman, Sachs brought it public earlier. Inventories, including raw materials inventories, rose 152 percent with sales up only 40 percent for the first nine months. The company management implied that the increases were due to smart buying on diamonds and gold, and the Street applauded.

A month later Jan Bell surprised Wall Street with lost contracts and lower-than-expected sales and earnings. The business of the company was selling gold jewelry, not speculating on gold prices (with the cost of carry eating into very competitive margins). Banks that speculate on securities, stocks, or junk bonds are another example, as are utilities with real estate development. But make sure the bet is on the company, not the commodity.

Technology Stocks

Many shorts avoid them like the plague because the normal trail signs don't usually apply. Normal inventory change ratios don't work: technology inventories rise when a new product is in the works. Insiders own volumes of stock and sell often and without apparent regard for company condition. Receivables are strange beasts, with so many payment terms that the occasional swells don't consistently tell of collection problems. Margins can contract and expand with product cycles and the pricing curve. The anomaly of technology is certainly consistent on the long side, since few analysts have consistent credibility on the stocks.

Squeezes

Short squeezes could be considered a market phenomenon rather than a short error, but they are, in fact, a self-inflicted wound. The float of a stock is of paramount importance for a short position. As in the case of American Continental, sometimes the return is worth the risk.

To review from chapter 1, brokerage houses can lend out stock that is in margin accounts or available for lending from institutions who charge a fee to the brokerage house for the loan. Each short sale must be backed by the loan of stock from one of these places. If the stock is no longer available to lend, a buy-in can occur. (As Joe Feshbach says, "If you want to whine and complain about buy-ins, you're in the wrong business.")

If a company gets hostile or aggressive toward short sellers, it can do two things: write stockholders and ask them to take stock out of margin accounts and either put it into cash accounts or have it sent to them; or ask major institutional owners not to lend their stock. Indirectly, the company can also reduce the float by buying in stock for the company or the company retirement accounts, or by placing large blocks in friendly hands. Some companies also use diversionary tactics like odd cash dividends and strange new shares of preferred or Class Z stock. Or the company can employ the most vicious defense—improve revenues and earnings.

Short-slamming tactics don't work well for a company with a large float and a heavy Wall Street following. They are, however, effective for small companies. The equation for the short seller is simply risk and return. If the stock has good potential for disappearing forever, short sellers can withstand the vagaries of squeeze problems for the possibility of a high return. If the company has significant but not fatal problems, most sophisticated sellers won't stay short the stock; therefore, a concerted effort to purge shorts works for those companies.

Total Systems is a good example. The company launched a short attack on June 29, 1988 when they sent a letter to shareholders describing abuses of naked short selling, (selling a stock without borrowing it) and the consequences to the stock price. The company management thought naked short selling could be squashed if shareholders ordered out their shares:

> . . . if there are traders holding substantial naked short positions in TSYS stock for their own account, they are interested in keeping the price of your stock down rather than allowing it to rise. It is also certain that the shareholders of TSYS by acting together can put a stop to this practice. If all TSYS shareholders will simply call their broker and "order out" their shares. . . . [2]

The float was small, and the institutional and large individual holders were friends of the company. Total Systems had a product, earnings, and revenues. So short sellers quietly departed on dips, despite the erroneous information in management's letter. (Naked short sellers by definition don't borrow stock, so ordering out stock doesn't have any effect.)

General Development was said to have attempted the same strategy in February 1990. It was a race that short sellers won by a couple of lengths when bankruptcy courts embraced General Development before the executives could squeeze the opposition.

Any history of squeezes in the 1980s includes Chase Medical as a cornerstone. The Chase started with Alan Abelson in a December 12, 1988 *Barron's* column panning the stock.[3] The company had 2.6 million shares outstanding with less than a 1.3 million–share float. The stock price was $10 and the short interest went up to 137,852 shares in December versus 25,319 for the prior month. A corner ensued that would have thrilled Jay Gould, classic turn-of-the-century stuff.

The stock price had doubled on huge volume since August, despite declining company prospects. Then, right before the New Year's holiday, the AMEX stopped the stock, announced that a brokerage firm had accumulated much of the float, and reopened the stock after 1 P.M. with the price down $2 on the day. The shorts who whined about stock manipulation were pleased that trading was finally going in their favor, although it was too small a stock to spark much serious short interest.

Next, the brokerage firm Moore & Shley, Cameron & Co. announced that they had in fact acquired more than 10 percent of shares outstanding to satisfy Reg T calls and that firm and customers combined owned 1.5 million shares. But, of the 2.6 million outstanding, insiders owned 1.2 million (subsequently changed to 1.3). Soon people noticed that 1.5 plus 1.2 equals more than 2.6.

Moore & Shley had, in effect, cornered the available supply of the stock and more. Short sellers couldn't all have stock to borrow, so some had to cover, and the only owners were Moore & Shley and insiders who could, and presumably would, charge any price for Chase stock. Short Squeeze. The stock was duly stopped again, at $13 this time, by the AMEX and the SEC, pending an investigation.

Time passed. Months, in fact. Earnings came out, showing revenues of $400,000 for the quarter after a writedown with a loss of $1.47 million. The AMEX delisted the stock.

And then on August 10, 1989 the stock started trading in the pink sheets from $4 to $6.50, and the shorts were pleased to get out alive although roughed up pretty badly. "Imagine a mugging in progress," said Floyd Norris in his September 8, 1989 column in the *New York Times.* "Just as the mugger is about to get away with the victim's wallet, the cops arrive and arrest the mugger. Then, as the victim is thinking how wonderful the police are, they hand some of the money in the wallet to the next person to walk down the street."[4] That's a short squeeze.

Buy-Outs

Buy-outs were the scourge of the 1980s short market. All short sellers, no matter how sophisticated, have felt the cattle prod of stopped-stock-with-takeover-pending announcements in their portfolios. At the beginning of the LBO cyclone, sober shorts didn't understand the ridiculous multiple that investment bankers would pay for an acquisition. By the middle, most understood the analysis better than the bankers—HBJ, Kay Jewelry, and other wins are testimony to their acumen.

The jury is still out on stocks like Holly Farms and American City Business Journal. Most shorts feel these losses weren't caused by mistakes, but by deal-crazed bankers paying outrageous prices for cyclical companies with dubious earnings or assets. The process certainly tightened up methodology: LBO's were responsible for sharpened pencils on asset value and real cash flow.

Raw Fear

Short selling is the proper province of roller coaster aficionados. It works best for people who thrive on raw fear or masochism. Among lesser human beings, all short sellers panic at some point and cover a well-thought-out, rational position in terror—everybody bolts sometime. Generally, it's a market phenomenon. In the late summers of 1987 and 1989, most shorts had lost hope that the market would ever be rational again. It went on forever. They just sat and waited for bankruptcies (in the summer of 1987 at least several occurred; not so in 1989).

When you can't stand the pain anymore, buy something. It might make you feel better in the very short run. Or even better, short more; if it scares you to death, it's probably the right move. The pain always continues for much longer than the pleasure. That's what makes short sellers different, and that's why the oldest living all-short professional seller is only 47 years old. The rest of them retired rich when they couldn't stand the thought of one more cycle of screaming enthusiasm and irrational, always optimistic security pricing.

Pigheadedness

If something changes, cover. It's not you against them: it's you against you.

Complexity

Many short sellers fall in love with their own analysis, particularly if it's extremely complex. If you can convince yourself that no one else understands a stock, you've closed your mind. Or if you've spent a zillion hours on a company, you feel you must have an opinion and buy or sell the stock. It's a little like reading Proust; after you've finished the last volume, you have to like it.

Crowds

Crowds in a stock are a new phenomenon. Too many nouveau shorts are the bane of the pros' positions. Inexperience makes a stock volatile, and it scares potential buyers away when the short seller is trying to initiate a position. A bunch of scared short sellers can create more pain and aggravation for the pros than the game is worth. Like having horses in a burning barn, it's easier to deal with the crisis without all the stamping and whinnying. And it's gonna get worse.

And Last of All

Direct from Joe Feshbach, *"The* mistake is always shorting the company that's not that bad."[5] He used the examples of New England Critical Care, Systems Software Associates, and L. A. Gear. The analyst has to be convinced that the core business will be overwhelmed by the problem and not just hiccup. "The biggest mistakes we've made are where we've seen a company that is overstating earnings but where the internal engine of the business is still strong."

Companies can manage earnings in many ways—by reducing the reserves for doubtful accounts, by booking earnings aggressively and expenses slowly, by not writing off bad assets. All these signs are easy for a trained analyst to detect. But if the revenues grow by quantum leaps, the manipulation will continue to be only an intellectual point of interest, not a trigger for shorting. You can hide disgusting accounting practices with growth for a very long time.

Notes

1. James Chanos in an interview, 4 May 1990.
2. James H. Blanchard and Richard W. Ussery, Letter to Shareholders of Total System Service, Inc., 29 June 1988, 2.
3. Alan Abelson, "Up and Down Wall Street," *Barron's,* 12 December 1988, 68:39.
4. Floyd Norris, "Market Place," *New York Times,* 8 September 1989, D6.
5. Joseph Feshbach in an interview, 1 June 1990.

12

History and Controversy

History

Short selling is as old as the commodity markets. Whenever a centralized market for goods has existed, business people have hedged their risk and speculated on prices. Short sellers usually go unnoticed until a financial disaster occurs. Then, historically, they have become newsworthy as ruined investors look for a scapegoat for their misery.

Holland

Short sales became common in the earliest organized markets—the Amsterdam exchanges. Around 1610 joint stock companies were created to fund new ventures, such as the Dutch East India Company, for exploration and trade in the New World. A speculative frenzy arose in the shares of that company and others like it on the Amsterdam Bourse in an early version of the South Sea Bubble. As the bubble of the market excess burst, the securities of the Dutch East India Company fell, and the directors of the company launched attacks on short sellers for causing the declines. In response to this drop in the stock price, they wrote a memorandum to the government in 1610, stating that "bear attacks, which generally assume the form of short selling, have caused and continue to cause immeasurable damage to innocent stockholders, among whom one will find many widows and orphans."[1]

The agents of the Amsterdam Bourse responded, "The decline in the price of the corporation's shares has been caused by unsatisfactory business conditions, and even prevailing levels appear too high, as a careful analysis will doubtless reveal. Furthermore, *many highly reputable stockholders would gladly surrender their shares to the directors if they could be assured of a reasonable return on their investment. If speculation were prohibited, prices would be much lower.* . . ." (emphasis mine)[2] In February 1610 the Bourse passed a law prohibiting short selling, which was subsequently disregarded and later repealed.

The Dutch failed to learn the lesson of manias, and shortly after the incident on the Bourse, Tulipmania swept the country. The Tulip Bubble from 1634 to 1637 in Holland was a frenzy of buying and selling of future delivery of tulip bulbs. The furor gained momentum until many more bulbs were traded than existed. When the bubble burst, the courts and magistrates declared some contracts void and attempted to get buyers and sellers to negotiate their differences, since no one, short or long, seemed to want to take or give delivery of the bulbs.

A tax was levied on profits from short sales in January 1689 in response to another speculative cycle. It was later repealed, but the author of the law was accused of knowing more about the corpus juris than commerce.[3]

Great Britain

The South Sea Bubble in Great Britain in 1720 saw the same phenomenon repeated. South Seas Company shares surged from 325 to 1,200 pounds sterling as eager purchasers fought for the right to own a piece of the monopoly of trade in the South Seas. The shares finally fell to 86 pounds sterling, and a political scandal followed. Short sellers were again among the many scapegoats. Sir John Barnard, a political figure and opponent of Robert Walpole, introduced a bill enacted in 1734 that voided sales where the securities where not possessed by the seller. The courts, however, said the prohibition didn't apply to foreign shares or shares in companies, only to British public stocks, so the law had no teeth at the outset. It was finally repealed in 1860, although during its tenure it was ignored as harmful and unenforceable.[4]

A wave of speculation in securities in the London market from 1863 to 1866 resulted in a bank stock panic in Great Britain in 1866, with the failure of the discount house Overend, Gurney. Several banks also failed during the panic, and the result was universal caution and credit shrinkage.[5] The collapse was attributed initially to short sellers, since it was thought short selling bank stock and the ensuing drop in stock price caused a drop in confidence and a run on deposits. Overend, Gurney had been converted from a partnership to a corporation, and short selling of the new security was also thought to have led to a run on that institution. Leeman's Act, to prohibit short sales of bank stocks, was passed by Parliament in 1867 and was soon disregarded by both businessmen and the courts.[6] Testimony in the Royal Commission in 1878 showed that the collapse was attributable to unsound banking practices and poor asset quality, rather than to short sales.

France

France's predecessor mishap to the South Sea Bubble, the Mississippi Bubble, under the leadership of Scotsman John Law, brought criticism of short selling after the crash. A royal decree in 1724 limited transactions to exchanges where the securities were in the possession of the seller.

In the last days of the monarchy as well as during the beginning of the Revolution, the securities markets in France were chaotic. "The readiest scapegoat, as usual, was 'speculation' and the 'short seller.' "[7] The politicians demanded regulation on the erroneous assumption that changing the rules of the market would provide economic stability. When the Paris Bourse was reestablished, it forbade short selling.

Napoleon shared the prejudice against short selling because he felt it dropped the prices of government securities and therefore interfered with the financing of his plans for expansion. He argued with his minister of finance, Mollien, that the practice was treasonous because short sellers wished government securities to collapse.

Restrictions were lightened in 1856, and after the French Panic of 1882 they were lifted at the recommendation of a special commission appointed by the government to study term dealings and short sales after a curb market (the Coulisse, where futures transactions were permitted) was formed to compete with the Bourse.

United States: Pre–Twentieth Century

In 1812 in the United States, the New York legislature prohibited short selling after heavy speculation in paper money and bank shares during the outbreak of war with England. The stock exchange at that time was only a curb market with the primary securities bank and insurance company stock. The volume was small, the impact of the prohibition minuscule. Panics and speculation occurred frequently, particularly in canal and railroad stocks. During the 1857–59 depression, the short selling prohibition was repealed.

The American government also attempted to restrict short selling in the Gold Speculation Act of 1864. It was repealed fifteen days later after aggravating the condition it was created to fix: gold rose from $200 to nearly $300 in two weeks when the law was in effect.

Until the Securities and Exchange Commission was appointed watchdog and the laws were changed after the 1929 Crash, lock-ups, stock manipulation, short squeezes, and corners were frequent features of the securities markets despite the vigilant eye of stock exchange officials. Before 1900 stock corners were routine, particularly in railroad stocks, since the resources of the players frequently dwarfed the capitalization of the stocks. A corner was defined as a case where short sellers were no longer able to borrow stock and were, therefore, compelled to buy it from the creator of the corner, who owned all available stock. Overextended short interest may result in a short squeeze and a subsequent rise in stock price; a short squeeze is not a corner, however, unless the available supply is held solely by one or two entities.

In 1868, Jay Gould and Jim Fisk raised capital for the Erie Railroad with a masterful "lock-up" of currency and the manipulation of Erie Railroad stock, skills that would later assist them in the Gold Ring manoeuvre of 1869. Kenneth Ackerman's history, *The Gold Ring,* relates how the two men flooded the market with new-issue stock, ballooning the capitalization from $34 million to $57 million (after previously issuing a $20 million convertible in England without telling the public, their directors, or stockholders). Then they started selling short massive amounts of stock. They simultaneously withdrew millions of dollars from the New York banking system, already seasonally low in funds in autumn because of the outflow of money for the grain harvest in the West, to create an artificial depression and liquidity crisis. Word leaked in the press that speculators had locked up currency; interest rates moved sharply higher, and markets were chaotic, with stocks dropping until Washington stepped in to release funds. Gould and Fisk covered their Erie shorts and led a bull charge to short squeeze Daniel Drew, a compatriot who reneged on their joint pact and eventually lost $1 million on his short position. Erie moved up 50 percent in twenty-four hours, and the two Erie executives got authorization to buy back shares for the company at $50 from their own personal holdings, which they had bought at $35 after covering their shorts.

Their attempt to squeeze gold shorts a year later was met with abysmal defeat when President Ulysses S. Grant stepped in to flood the market and drop prices.[8]

The New York Stock Exchange policy on listing small companies reduced the occurrence of corners in the twentieth century. Only one corner was reported after 1900—the Stutz Motor corner of 1920. Allan Ryan cornered the supply of Stutz on the NYSE, supposedly to protect the company from short sellers. The NYSE Governing Committee asked him to rectify the situation and provide an open market on the issue. He refused, the stock was delisted, and Ryan was expelled from the exchange amid accusations that the exchange was protecting short sellers.[9]

Germany

The German experience with short selling in 1896 was one of the more telling historical examples. The Germans attempted to abolish speculative trading, and particularly short selling, in both the stock and the commodity markets during a business depression.

In 1888, a corner in coffee occurred in Hamburg, followed by an abysmal drop in sugar prices in 1889 and a break in grain prices in 1891. The failure of several Berlin banks that had been speculating with deposits was the final straw, and politicians rallied for legislation to prohibit speculation.

A commission was formed to study the excesses. It recommended regulation, rather than prohibition, of speculation. Brokerage houses that failed after speculating were to be criminally prosecuted, for example. The commission's somewhat temperate recommendations failed to pacify the agrarian party, which had been battered by plummeting prices.

The Reichstag responded to the outcry by passing a law, effective January 1, 1897, that prohibited the purchase and sale of grain and flour futures, mandated a public register of all "speculators," and prohibited term dealings for mining and industrial shares.

The law was an immediate disaster. The agrarians thought that a prohibition against short sales would cause the price of grain to rise. In fact, the market was thrown into chaos when the traders physically moved from the Bourse so they could continue to carry on the futures business. No central mechanism for pricing existed, so prices were lower and less stable. Similar problems arose in the securities markets, with markets moving to the larger exchanges in London and Amsterdam, thus draining German capital flows.

The law was finally repealed in 1909 for securities and in 1911 for commodities. The German exchange was weakened as a result of the prohibition of free trade, with securities transactions moving to the Berlin banks, which have retained the power in the subsequent century.[10]

United States: Twentieth Century

The twentieth-century history of short selling in the United States is more a history of people and companies than of government intervention. Several legendary investors are rumored to have accumulated fortunes through astute short selling. Jesse Livermore, Bernard Baruch, "Sell 'Em" Ben Smith, and Joseph Kennedy were a few of the active practitioners in the early twentieth century.

Jesse Livermore

Jesse Livermore got his start shorting stocks in the early twentieth century and became known as the "King of the Bears" on Wall Street. In 1906 he is reported to have made a killing shorting Union Pacific the day before the earthquake hit San Francisco. In 1907 he sold short without mercy in a market crash until J. P. Morgan asked him to quit or accept the consequences for a market collapse. His biographer reports that Livermore stopped selling only because he knew he wouldn't realize his profits if brokerage houses folded. He emerged with $3 million, his national reputation made.[11] He was bankrupt by 1915 but not bowed. Borrowing money to speculate, he made it back and set up an irrevocable trust with the profits that would be his sole support in later years. After losing repeatedly on the short side in 1923 and 1924, he exited stocks for commodities. Returning to Wall Street before the Crash, he made a couple of million, but lost it all when he went long too soon. He never attained his previous success, lived off his trust and, in 1940 after having his picture taken at the Stork Club, shot himself the next day in a New York hotel.

Barnard Baruch

Barnard Baruch accumulated part of his fortune through selling short—although, according to biographer James Grant, he was not significantly short during the Crash.

Baruch tells of his first notable short sale, Brooklyn Rapid Transit, in *My Own Story.* He began to follow the stock promotions of ex-governor Roswell P. Flower, who was a corporate turnaround artist with a large following of eager stock purchasers. After successfully reversing the fate of several companies (Chicago Gas and the Chicago, Rock Island and Pacific), Flower took charge of Brooklyn Rapid Transit Company; as revenues increased, so went the stock price. The governor touted the stock, said the price would go to $75, then $125, which it did—from a starting level of $20 when he took charge. Baruch watched, and noticed that "the company's statements were not as clear as such statements should be. I had a hunch that something was not quite right."[12] The stock had moved to $137 when a story circulated on the exchange that the governor was ill. It was denied in the press, but by night he was dead. The stock collapsed and was supported by pools, including Morgan, the Vanderbilts, and John D. Rockefeller. When it rallied to $115, the pools stepped out and the price again stalled, then sank for several months. Baruch shorted it at par; it never sold at that price again, and he made $60,000. In the best tradition of contemporary short selling, Baruch studied the financials, correctly identified a Wall Street hype, and waited for a trigger to take action. He said, "My confidence began to return."[13]

The next notable Baruch short sale episode shows him a master of supply and demand in the commodity market. In 1901 the Amalgamated Copper Company organizers attempted to corner the copper supply, and the stock moved to $130 with talk it would continue to $150 or $200. An acquaintance of Baruch—Herman Sielcken, a coffee merchant—thought that the high price of the commodity was suppressing demand and that the market would shortly become glutted, despite Amalgamated's attempt. Baruch shorted the stock in the face of advice from mentor Thomas Ryan, and he kept shorting as rumors circulated that insiders were also selling.

He was attacked for wicked short selling that would "tear down a constructive enterprise."[14] Baruch responded in his autobiography,

> All this was nonsense, of course. If the Amalgamated had not overcapitalized and then blown the stock up, it never would have risen to such heights or descended to the depths it afterward did. What was dropping the copper shares was the irresistible force of economic gravitation seeking its proper level. . . . In the face of these attacks, I sat silent, knowing that if I was right, I would win.[15]

The market consensus on Amalgamated was that the dividend was sound, but the directors cut it one Friday. The stock price dropped to just above $100 Saturday, and Baruch anticipated closing the short on Monday after another probable decline. His mother intervened, inviting him for Yom Kippur—which, of course, meant seclusion. Instead of covering after a two-point drop on Monday, he returned to the exchange on Tuesday to find the stock still lower. He rode it to an eventual profit of $700,000.

In 1913 Baruch assisted with a privately printed pamphlet supporting short sales, titled *Short Sales and Manipulation of Securities,* to attempt to explain the technique to hostile observers. The pamphlet was a compendium of quotations and historical incidences of short selling, with the recurrent sentiment that short selling steadied markets and prices and was a reflection of the judgment of the seller about prices rather than a dishonest manipulation.

His outspoken short politics came under fire after the panic of December 1916. Baruch and many other Wall Street operators were accused of trading on advance information about diplomatic affairs concerning American neutrality in the First World War. Republican representative William S. Bennett stated on the floor of the House that Baruch was responsible for leaking the information to Wall Street and shorting 15,000 U.S. Steel in advance of the December 21 market decline. Grant's biography recounts Baruch's distress over the charges and his ensuing congressional testimony. When responding to a question on abolition of short selling, Baruch answered:

> I believe that if you had a market without short selling, that when the break comes—of course, trees do not grow to heaven overnight—and when securities go up as we see them, and when they start to fall down there might be a crash that would engulf the whole structure, and there is also this, if I may add, that the short seller is the greatest critic of the optimist, who continuously calls the attention of the man who is long on securities or the individual who might become long, of the defects, you might say, of these securities, and you might in that way keep people from buying securities at extraordinary high prices.[16]

He had, in fact, shorted U.S. steel but early in December, and he had covered most of it on December 20 before the market panic. He was absolved.

September 1929 found Baruch in New York shorting Radio Corporation of America. He covered the Monday before Black Thursday. On November 15, he cabled Winston Churchill, "Financial storm definitely passed."[17] Grant estimates that by the end of 1931, Baruch's net worth had shrunk from $22 million in 1929 to $16 million. Although master of the short sale discipline, he missed the largest move in the history of the American markets.

Joseph Kennedy

Joseph Kennedy learned about short selling and security trading in the early 1920s while working at the Boston brokerage firm Hayden, Stone. He became adept at both sides of the market, managing a famous bull pool to defend Yellow Cab from bear raiders in 1924. It was rumored when the stock dropped precipitously a few months later that Kennedy had turned and led his own bear raid. His biographer David Koskoff suggests that the size of Kennedy's fortune was too small in the 1930s for him to have been a large short seller during 1929, although the press said he sold short $15 million during the panic.[18] When Franklin D. Roosevelt later appointed him head of the new Securities and Exchange Commission, it was popularly thought to be a case of the fox guarding the chicken coop. He proved to be a serendipitous choice for constructing rules and laws, since he was familiar with all phases of manipulation and market abuse.

Ben Smith

Ben Smith was tagged as one of the villains of Wall Street because of his reputed gains during the Crash. He suffered losses on his long positions in the first wave, then reversed and became an outspoken bear. At some point after November 29, 1929 he was said to have rushed into the boardroom of the brokerage house where he had an office and shouted, "Sell 'em all! They're not worth anything!" Thus his nickname, "Sell 'em" Ben Smith.

Albert Wiggin

The most appalling example of short selling was Albert H. Wiggin, the president of Chase Bank, "the most loved banker on Wall Street."[19] Wiggin, in addition to his duties at the bank, was also on the board of fifty-nine other corporations. The majority of his wealth came from a group of family corporations named after his daughters and their husbands, Shermar and Murlyn, and from three Canadian corporations that he also owned. He made prodigious amounts of money trading on insider information (legal in the 1920s) in his corporations and then used a loophole in the Canadian law to avoid capital gains taxes. As Ferdinand Pecora tells it in *Wall Street Under Oath,* if Shermar sold stock short, Murlyn bought the stock and loaned it to Shermar to cover. Shermar would not realize the gain, since the purchase had not been made by the corporation that shorted the stock.[20]

Wiggin starting selling Chase stock short September 19, 1929 and continued "until he covered on December 11, 1929 (using, by the way, borrowed money from the Chase to buy the stock to cover), to the tune of making $4,008,538, on which he paid no taxes."[21] Of the stock sold short, he was reputed to have sold some to the very pool of bankers (of which he was a member) that tried to support stock prices during the Crash with organized buying. He feathered his own nest at the expense of his colleagues and his employer.

The Union Industrial Bank Crowd

The most capricious incident of short selling during the 1920s bull market came from a speculative group of bankers in Flint, Michigan, at the Union Industrial Bank. Gordon Thomas and Max Morgan-Witts retell the sequence of events in *The Day the Bubble Burst.*[22] A group of employees, two stockholders and the president's son among them, embezzled bank funds as a group to speculate on the market in the late 1920s. At their weekly meeting in the bank boardroom, they tallied individual losses and perfected new methods of hiding the ebb of bank capital. They subverted money that customers sent to be loaned in the broker call money market in New York by wiring it out, then back in the next day without booking the return. The tellers also pocketed cash at the teller windows, and the group capitalized on teamwork in a faked note scheme in which they forged the necessary paperwork for bogus loans.

Problems ballooned since they were, individually and as a group, terrible investors. They sold short in 1928 and early 1929.

After egregious losses, they uniformly cried "uncle" and went long in 1929 buying Radio Corporation of America at the tail end of Michael Meehan's famous pool, bagged yet again. They had a run of successes on the long side, wiping out half their debit balance by the middle of 1929, but the tide turned again in September. By the end of October, they had lost $3.592 million, and margin calls continued until one of the group confessed to the president, who called the chairman of the board, Charles Stewart Mott. He replaced the stolen money from his personal account. The embezzlers were prosecuted and sentenced to short prison terms in adjoining cells, doubtless opponents of short selling for life.

Witch Hunts and Regulation

After a panic in the financial markets, politicians and business leaders institute panels and studies to place blame for the havoc that reigns when the bubble bursts. In the past, short sellers have been censored for deleterious activity. Incidents in Amsterdam, London, France, and Germany and the U.S. House investigation in 1916 were followed by similar discussions after the 1929 Crash. J. Edward Meeker, economist to the New York Stock Exchange, addressed many of the arguments against short sellers in his 1932 book, *Short Selling.* [23]

Meeker distills the arguments against short selling into several cogent points. Short sales, the critics say, establish an inflated supply and cause price declines. Bear raids generate margin calls, loan liquidation, and the sale of securities by customers who are long. Margined stock should not be lent to short sellers without the express approval of the client, since it may be contrary to the owner's interests.

In his defense of short selling, Meeker states that short selling stabilizes prices when no other buyers exist, reduces the risk of manipulation, deflates bubbles, and provides liquidity.

He reviews the history of the New York Stock Exchange regarding short selling in this century. In the 1919–21 bear market, there was no evidence of shorting. In the 1921–29 market, short sellers repeatedly lost money. In 1929 the volume of short sales was small and was judged of no importance in the overall drop.

Total number of shares short on the NYSE was only .001524 percent on November 1, 1929. In 1931 short sales were again analyzed by the exchange, and it was determined that liquidations, not short sales, were responsible for the drops, and that short selling steadied prices with buying.

Investigations concerning "bear raids," organized depression of prices caused by a great volume of share sales, were also made during 1929–31 by the NYSE. The exchange could find no evidence of conspiracy by unscrupulous bear operators. They found that short sales had been made after careful study of company prospects and business conditions. Large-volume sales were frequently the result of institutions' attempts to get similar prices on pools of managed accounts. Of the fifty or sixty large-block sales investigated, only one was a short sale, and that one was entered as an order to sell by scaling up on sale execution price so that the stock was not battered by the order.

In conclusion, Meeker says that "recent governmental attempts to regulate markets have shown their uneconomic character and their extreme danger to everyone. . . . The law of supply and demand cannot be contravened by laws artificially restricting marketing methods."[24] Or in the words of Bernard Baruch, "no law can protect a man from his own errors. The main reason why money is lost in stock speculations is not because Wall Street is dishonest, but because so many people persist in thinking that you can make money without working for it and that the stock exchange is the place were this miracle can be performed."[25]

Ferdinand Pecora, counsel for the Senate Banking and Currency Committee that investigated Wall Street after the 1929 Crash, said that the impetus for the months of testimony that led to the Securities Act of 1933, the Securities Exchange Act of 1934, and the formation of the SEC was concern over alleged market activity by short sellers. Apparently a concerned Republican senator, Frederic C. Walcott of Connecticut, received information that short sellers were planning a series of bear raids to discredit Herbert Hoover before the election that pitted Hoover against Roosevelt.[26] The committee investigation that ensued with Pecora at its head instead revealed that the old regime had used their collective power for personal gain and public detriment. The subsequent bills outlawed double dealing, deceptions, and manipulations by insiders in favor of full disclosure. So what began as a short seller witch hunt ended in the laws that form the base of current markets.

In 1938 the SEC adopted Rule 10a–1, under the Exchange Act of 1934, the "tick rule," which requires short sales on exchanges to be traded on plus ticks or zero-plus ticks. Congress previously, under Section 10(a), had granted the Securities and Exchange Commission the authority to regulate short sales on the national exchanges. The thrust of the law was to prevent short sellers from causing mercuric declines and accelerating an already declining market.

In 1986 the National Association of Securities Dealers (NASD) published the Pollack Report, a study of the need for additional regulation of short sales at NASDAQ. Irving Pollack's *Short Sale Regulation of NASDAQ Securities* is the most comprehensive source of information on short selling. The study concluded that most short selling was done by professionals (traders, market makers) to provide market liquidity and that there was no evidence of widespread abuse. It noted naked shorting, however, as a potential area for concern and suggested surveillance procedures. NASD implemented all the recommended actions as a result.

The Pollack Report also supported the SEC's findings that allegations of ruinous short selling were overblown. Many complaints were unfounded (short positions didn't exist), and a number of the companies later showed losses, fraud, or regulatory actions. The report commented: "While each situation was unique in important respects, it became clear that a valid basis existed for short selling in most of the selected securities. Given the benefit of hindsight, heavy short selling in these securities would have surprised no one."[27]

1989 House Subcommittee Hearing on Short Selling

After the 1987 crash, panels were again formed to study how the system failed and who pushed the stock market over the cliff. Congressman Doug Barnard, Jr., from Georgia chaired a House Committee to review the effects of short sellers on small companies and the need for regulation in the markets. The witness list included executives from three over-the-counter (OTC) companies, the editor of *OTC Review,* the chairman of Berkeley Securities, and representatives from NASD, the OTC Association (NAOTC), the NYSE, AMEX, and the SEC.

Barnard stated at the beginning of the hearings that the key questions were:

1. Does the market work for new, small companies to assist them in raising capital?
2. Do the differences in the exchanges make OTC stocks more vulnerable?
3. Is the SEC doing its job in regard to these issues?

Two ancillary abusive practices were also under investigation: naked shorting and rumor-mongering.

The editor of *OTC Review,* Robert J. Flaherty, summed up the concerns of the anti-short contingency: he felt short sellers needed more regulation and disclosure. He was supported by OTC companies, Carrington Labs, American City Business Journals, and IGI, Inc., all favorites of short sellers for the occasional absence of earnings. Flaherty agreed that legitimate short selling served a positive function in the marketplace—deflating bubbles of over-optimism and stabilizing markets. His main concern was bear raids by secret networks of short sellers.

The discussion centered around three issues: lack of an uptick rule on the over-the-counter markets (because it would be largely unenforceable), naked short selling, and disclosure of large short positions.

The NAOTC companies president, John Guion, presented his association's survey. Of a thousand companies surveyed, twenty-five answered that they had been subjected to abusive practices by short sellers. Thirteen companies said short selling had been accompanied by false rumors and negative information. Guion called for disclosure of short positions in excess of 5 percent of the stock shares.

The arguments were much the same as on the Amsterdam Bourse or during the Crash in Meeker's day. AMEX, NASDAQ, and NYSE testified that current regulations were sufficient to control reputed abuses. The AMEX representative expressed the concern that disclosure of large short positions would lead to further price declines as investors sold in tandem with shorts and, besides, a short position wasn't exactly a "controlling position" as the spirit of a 13D would imply. NASD testified that new rules had been implemented to further reduce incidents of naked short selling.

The SEC turned in a voluminous report again mentioning the positive attributes of short selling—market liquidity and pricing efficiency—and reviewed the history of the regulatory process.

Small companies countered that short selling, bear raids, and rumor-mongering inhibited capital formation for start-up companies.

A Mexican standoff resulted.

Notes

1. Quoted in James Edward Meeker, *Short Selling* (New York: Harper and Row, 1932), 205.

2. Quoted in ibid., 206.

3. Ibid., 207.

4. Ibid., 107.

5. Clement Juglar and Decourcy W. Thom, *A Brief History of Panics and Their Periodical Occurrence in the United States* (New York: Putnam, 1916), 4.

6. Meeker, *Short Selling,* 107.

7. Ibid., 219.

8. See Kenneth Ackerman, *The Gold Ring* (New York: Harper and Row, 1989) for details on the Erie manipulation and the attempted gold short squeeze.

9. Meeker, *Short Selling,* 188–93.

10. Ibid., 224–31.

11. Tom Shachtman, *The Day America Crashed* (New York: G. P. Putnam's 1979), 53.

12. Barnard M. Baruch, *My Own Story* (New York: Henry Holt, 1957), 125.

13. Ibid., 126.

14. Ibid., 129.

15. Ibid.

16. U.S. Congress, House of Representatives, Committee on Rules, Investigation Relating to Alleged Divulgence of President's Note to

Belligerent Powers, 64th Cong., 2d Sess., Washington, D.C., 9th of January, 1917, 173:212.

17. James Grant, *Bernard M. Baruch* (New York: Simon and Schuster, 1983), 241.

18. David E. Koskoff, *Joseph P. Kennedy: A Life and Times* (Englewood Cliffs, N.J.: Prentice Hall, 1974), 41.

19. Shachtman, *The Day America Crashed,* 43.

20. Ferdinand Pecora, *Wall Street Under Oath* (New York: Simon and Shuster, 1939), 131–61.

21. Shachtman, *The Day America Crashed,* 167.

22. See Gordon Thomas and Max Morgan-Witts, *The Day the Bubble Burst* (New York: Doubleday & Company, 1979) for a fuller description of the Union Industrial Bank embezzlement.

23. Meeker, *Short Selling,* 4–19.

24. Ibid., 18.

25. Baruch, *My Own Story,* 264.

26. Hillel Black, *The Watchdogs of Wall Street* (New York: Arno Press, 1975), 10.

27. Irving M. Pollack, *Short-Sale Regulation of NASDAQ Securities* (Washington, D.C.: The National Association of Securities Dealers, Inc., 1986), 67.

13

Six Pillars of Fundamental Short Selling

General methods of fundamental analysis can be gleaned from the short sellers and used to advantage by analysts, portfolio managers, and other serious observers of the stock market. The anecdotal information from previous chapters can be condensed into more a orderly framework applicable to any stock, short or long.

The Short Seller's Random Walk for Ideas

Short sellers get ideas from many sources. Some of the best ideas come from the most obvious places—*Barron's,* the *Wall Street Journal, Forbes, Financial World.* Frequently, the stocks drop immediately after a negative article and then pop back up. A good *Barron's* exposé used to make a great short a year later; it took that long for the termites to eat through the supports in a bull market. *Barron's* "Phoenix Descending" article was published in December 1988, and the stocks started dropping seriously in February 1989.

One more source is the short interest data published in the *Wall Street Journal* and *New York Times.* Frequently, middle-sized short positions (relative to the stock float) are good stocks to look at if the stock isn't an arbitrage play (a buyout or a common stock with a convertible). For example, Jan Bell Marketing had short interest of 576,500 in December 1989 with a float of 13-plus million shares and a percentage price increase for the year of 107. A look at Jan Bell's financials showed the inventories out of line and the valuation lofty. The subsequent short sale resulted in a quick profit when the stock crashed in January. A short interest of 300,000 to 500,000 shares means a professional short seller has already looked at the stock and shorted it. The short interest and the stock float are important: make sure the short interest isn't so high that a short squeeze can increase the risk relative to the return. In the stock market of early 1990, a short position in excess of 15 percent of the float seems to have generated buy-ins.

Another productive source is experience. If observation or business sense suggests that Wall Street might be blindsided, proceed in your analysis. Worlds of Wonder, an excellent example, was dramatically inflated from the wondrous talking bear, Teddy Ruxpin, in the fall of 1987. When a second product, Laser Tag, excited analysts even more, the stock price stayed at ludicrous valuations. Any toy-shopping parent could tell that the stock was a short when the stores didn't have the product before the key Christmas selling season. Production wasn't sufficient to fuel demand for a fad product with competition intensifying. Sure enough, Laser Tag couldn't pull in revenues to support manufacturing costs because the product wasn't in the stores—a hit turned into a colossal stumble. Toy-buying parents get important advance information on magnitude and availability of fads— consistently better than Wall Street scuttlebutt.

Reading the previous chapters should convince you that some industries are particularly conducive to financial manipulation. Franchises (chapter 4) have extensive potential for financial stumbles, and once you've analyzed one, it's easy to peruse a group of them. Look for types of businesses that eat money: financial services (chapters 6, 7, 9), cable (chapter 6), and real estate (chapter 9). Or look for companies with complex financial statements and blind pools of investments—the financial services sector is another solid choice in this category.

Once you target a company, analyze it with skepticism and

curiosity every time a new financial document is published. Although stock analysis is frequently an untidy business, these six pillars might provide structure for an open-ended task.

1. The Pessimist's Guide to Financial Statements

The financial statements are always the first stage for any serious student of stocks. Appearance is reality, or that's how most analysts perceive financial statements. Short sellers, on the other hand, attempt to discover what's behind the numbers, what drives the company, what the business prognosis is. The best source books on how to read financials are Leopold Bernstein's *Financial Statement Analysis,* anything written by Abraham Briloff, and Thornton O'glove's *Quality of Earnings.* These short sale guidelines do not presume to emulate an accounting textbook, but just to mark some guideposts in the search for quality.

To begin the financial quest, call the company and ask for the last six 10Qs, the last two 10Ks, proxies, and annuals, as well as any 8Ks (amendments to Ks and Qs). That gives you two years of quarterly data, enough to compare trends on inventories, receivables, and margins and three years of annual numbers. After studying these documents, you may need to go back farther chronologically.

Before we start pulling entrails from the cadaver, the point is to dissect, then to reassemble with a clearer knowledge of how the company works. Reading the financials is therefore a multi-step process.

Quality Control

The first look at the financials is with the intent of breaking the company into tiny pieces and checking to see if all those pieces are real. Is there anything funny about the numbers? The most useful part of the financials will, of course, be the footnotes. The other consistent keys are what's not there and what you can't understand.

Start with the last dated balance sheet. Look for bogus assets or assets for which the market value is less than the balance sheet value. Examples are:

- securities not marked to market;
- real estate at inflated values;
- inventories with obsolete products;
- receivables that have been booked too aggressively;
- receivables with loss provisions too low; and
- bad loans.

For example, ICH Corp. had an asset line of $101.6 million that read "the present value of future tax benefits."

Then test accounts receivable and inventories: look at the growth in receivables and inventories versus previous year and compare that to the growth in sales. If the difference is large, problems with earnings will be likely (unless, of course, an acquisition has reduced the numbers to noncomparable). (See National Education in chapter 5).

A frequent area of abuse is deferred charges. A company that pushes expenses into the future can experience an earnings reversal if revenues dry up. Examples of deferred charges are prepaid advertising and deferred commissions or sales charges. L. A. Gear had the most creative use of deferred charges in the February 28, 1989 10Q: the company added to earnings—$.20 with deferred advertising that hadn't been spent yet. That's a double negative for a positive.

Another category worthy of a jaundiced eye is goodwill and other intangible costs—potential clues that a company has overpaid for an acquisition or is failing to expense drilling costs or software development. Capitalizing routine expenses is another clue that a company is manipulating earnings. Capitalizing or deferring expenses like policy manuals and start-up costs may spread them over too long a period for the benefits of those expenses. Check the footnotes for exposition and see if the company discloses the schedule for expensing the policy manuals.

Next, look at the liability side of the balance sheet. Are any of the descriptions odd or unrecognizable as types of liabilities? Are any of the liabilities approximated or present valued with assumptions made by management? Check the footnotes and the notes on financial conditions to see if the company has any off-balance-sheet liabilities, any debt guarantees, or recourse-factored receivables. Is short-term debt growing? Is long-term debt up?

The quality-detecting exercise for the income statement is primarily carried out in the verbiage that explains earnings. For now, note all lines of revenues that appear to be nonrecurring:

- sale of equipment, land, and real estate;
- sale of securities;
- interest on securities or cash equivalents;
- tax credits; and
- change in accounting.

To dig this information out, flip to the footnotes to see the assumptions the company uses to book revenues, then read the notes explaining earnings in the current period. Make a subjective decision on what percentage of the business is stable and repeatable. If a company has had consistently real revenues and suddenly they hide a gain in an unlikely place—like J. Bildner's hidden cookie gain in chapter 4—look harder.

Don't forget that old Wall Street favorite, earnings per share. Earnings per share is an interesting test of Wall Street's viewpoint. Are earnings per share up only because there are fewer shares out? Compare using fully diluted shares outstanding, not just undiluted average shares.

Fully diluted shares outstanding is close to the toughest calculation required on financial statements, and that's why it's so frequently wrong. Take number of shares off the front of the 10Q, add in convertibles shares if they're close to conversion or likely to be converted, then try to determine how many options are close to being exercised, not to mention warrants. Add those all up for fully diluted shares outstanding.

Does the company appear to be trying to show a per share

trend to pander to the needs of the Street? (This is certainly not reprehensible in a savage environment for steady predictable growth in that number, but a point to be noted.)

A Bunch of Ratios

Then massage the numbers. Start with the balance sheet and look at capitalization: long-term debt to equity, total debt to total capital, long-term debt to capital. Compare several years of balance sheets to see the trend in these ratios.

Then look at the return ratios: return on equity, return on assets, and return on invested assets, which is a particularly worthwhile calculation. Income before interest and taxes, divided by equity plus all interest-paying debt, gives several useful types of data. When calculated for a sequence of years, it tells you the trend and volatility of returns over time. It also tells you by comparison what the company does relative to other companies in the same industry and whether a company earns more than its average and marginal cost of debt, currently and historically.

Keep track of valuation ratios. If the stock runs up, it's nice to have immediate access to numbers that quantify insanity. Price to earnings, price to book, price to revenue, and price to cash flow are the four key indicators. If a takeover occurs in a similar company, these ratios let the analyst calculate quick comparables. Valuations ratios are relative to specific industries, however. Price/revenue is higher for retail than for manufacturing. Price/earnings reflects growth potential. Price/cash flow is a buy-out indicator.

Checklist of Ratios

Capital structure:

- long term debt to equity
- total debt to total capital
- total debt to equity

Return ratios:

- return on equity

- return on assets
- return on invested assets

Valuation ratios:

- price to earnings
- price to revenues
- price to book
- price to operating cash flow

Then go to the income statement to common size the statement: put everything in percentage of revenues to see if the percentage relationships are changing. Is research and development or advertising declining as a percentage of revenue? If so, is the company deferring or not spending to the detriment of later business? Compare the anomalies to the balance sheet. If sales, general, and administrative (S, G, and A) is declining as a percent, are prepaid expenses or other assets rising? Is depreciation flat while fixed assets increase? Compare pretax operating profits. What's the sequential trend as well as the annual one? Does it make sense for the business? Look for deviations and trends.

Cash Flow Is King

The Statement of Changes is always the toughest of financial documents. It's frequently difficult to determine what's a necessary cost from a business point of view. Each company is different. The Financial Accounting Standards Board Statement no. 95 changed the way companies report cash flow in July 1988. The new three-part presentation of operating, investing, and financing flows has made the task easier. The quickest check is a look at the "Cash Flows from Financing" section. Does the company have to go to the markets repeatedly to keep afloat? Are short-term and long-term debt ever-escalating? Is there a stock or convertible issue every year?

The next step for the Statement of Changes is a back-of-the-envelope calculation on what the company actually spends (or takes in) to do business. Generally that calculation is some derivation of net income plus depreciation, amortization, and deferred taxes minus nonrecurring items (tax-adjusted, if possible) plus or minus changes in current assets (without cash, but broken out by lines to see what specifics are causing cash drain) plus or minus changes in other items perceived to be relevant (like some portion of capital expenditures).

What you're doing is editing the Statement of Changes by adjusting the "Cash Flow from Operations" section. Make sure operating income is adjusted by what you see as nonrecurring. What has the company put in the "investing" section that is a necessary expense of doing business, like buying property for a real estate company or programming expense for a media production company? Adjust for free cash flow by subtracting necessary capital expenditures (if the company tells you; if not, guess) and dividends. Is that number positive or negative? Look at the Statement of Changes versus previous years (then quarter by quarter, if necessary) to see if an expansion plan has made for a one-year anomaly or if the trend is appreciably worse. If it's a cyclical business, is the balance sheet strong enough to support needed cash infusions when operating flows dry up? Is the company in a financial position to meet the debt repayment schedule if the financing environment gets hostile to refinancing? Be sure to check PIKs (payment in kind), zero coupon bonds, and other odd-ball 1980s instruments.

Reading the Sleep-Inducing Verbiage

Now for the hard part. The first financial run-through was simply a test of your accounting skills and your ability to follow the footnote trail and understand accounting jargon. Read the 10K description of the business and the competition. See if you understand the financials in relation to that business plan. Try to determine what drives the company, what the two or three most relevant numbers are. What's the most important number to watch to identify a developing problem? If it's a low-margin business, the key is probably revenues and inventory turnover ratios. If it's a franchise, it may be system sales or same-store sales. Does the financial structure make sense for the business? (Don't leverage a cyclical company too much, don't build inventories too high if there's potential product obsolescence).

Think About It

Try to see the three financial statements as a 3-D chess game to judge how they interact and what tugs and pulls on what.

Conclusion: determining the key variables in the health of the company is the most complex part of analysis. It's almost a gift, not a learned skill. The people who do it easily have great success on the long side, as well as the short, because it gives them X ray vision to developing trends in a company using only the financial statements.

Backtrack and track the Qs and Ks over time in order—first to last—to see if anything changes for better or worse.

After that, read the Annual and see if what the officers say matches what you saw. Give it the buzz word test. Every company communicates its vision of itself in recurring use of certain phrases: synergism is a popular one for companies viewed by the Street as confusing. Literally count the pictures of babies. Too many babies in a drilling or defense company annual report suggest's that executives either don't know their business or are trying to imply that the company sells something they don't own. (California Energy had its fair share of babies one year, NCNB another.) Watch for auditor turnover. It's the one signal that is truly indicative of trouble.

Think about what's not there, what you didn't understand. Some popular items that are often not included are:

- description of nonrecurring revenues;
- information on explicit valuation procedures of odd assets;
- clear disclosure of revenue booking procedures;
- composition of fuzzy liabilities;
- breakout of blind pool assets (like loans);
- comprehensible breakout of divisions: revenues, income, assets; and
- description of effect of an acquisition on inventories and receivables.

The hardest part is determining what the relevant piece of information is: what runs or ruins the business. Experience as a business person helps more than analyst acumen.

2. In Search of Greed and Sleaze

The second step is easy and fun. It gives short sellers confidence in their financial analysis. It's also the step most frequently omitted by Wall Street.

The SEC requires companies to release all sorts of data about management and large stockholders. Among the most useful are:

Form 144. Key officers are required to file a Form 144 with the SEC when they place a sell order for their company stock with a broker—in other words, on or before the date of sale of stock. Some insider sales are reported in *Barron's* and the *Wall Street Journal.* Several services, including *Vickers* and the *Insider's Report,* also publish the list.

Form 4. Officers must also file a Form 4 listing purchases and sales of stock ten days after the last day of the month in which positions were increased or decreased. Form 4's lag the action by too much to be of use to a careful observer. They are, however, the only source, besides the proxy of management purchases.

13-D. Any entity that buys a controlling position in a stock, 5 percent or more, must file a 13-D with the SEC within ten days. These positions are usually publicized in the news, *Barron's, Vickers,* and the *Insider Report,* as well as in the proxy.

Best of all—proxies. Each year a company must file a proxy statement with the SEC. The annual meeting is the trigger for publication. The purpose of the proxy is to tell stockholders what they may vote on at the meeting. It also reveals how much stock management owns, what their salaries and employment contracts are, including options, bonuses, and some perks, and the stockholders who own over 5 percent. The proxy tells you who the accountants are, what the pending lawsuits are, and what other relationships and related transactions are pertinent.

Many money managers allow outside services to read proxies for their position stocks. These services vote the proxy issues for the manager, supposedly saving valuable time for portfolio managers. Shorts consider this an appalling custom: would you let a person who doesn't know that management earns 30 percent of company net income vote a proxy for you? They view it as one more indication that institutional investors don't know which facts are important and where to find them.

Management contracts have become incredibly creative in recent years. Read the proxies in search of greed in corporate America. A lot of the finer details (Ross Johnson's perks at RJR as outlined in Bryan Burrough's and John Helyav's *Barbarians at the Gate,* for example) are not delineated in the SEC filings, but you get the flavor in the notes on "certain transactions."

To give an idea of benchmarks, some favorite examples follow. Proxies are one of the best sources of information about management philosophy.

Pantheon of Stars or Pigs at the Trough?

Southmark, a company resplendent in multiple companies and affiliates, mirrors its corporate confusion with the toughest proxy to date. It's impossible to quantify the benefits absorbed by the key players. But there are a lot of them.

A few highlights from the January 1988 proxy: Gene Phillips, chairman of the board, president, and director, was also director or chairman of the board of eleven other Southmark-affiliated companies. He had stock options on three of them, use of the company aircraft, and $860,608 in cash compensation. Phillips and William Friedman, vice-chairman of the board, owned or controlled 23.45 percent of Southmark, as well as stock in most of the related companies. They pledged their Syntek Investment Properties shares and Syntek West shares to Southmark as security on loans of $8.5 million and a $1.5 million line of credit. The board authorized the loans so Phillips and Friedman would be able to meet any margin calls resulting from recent declines in the market price of the stock. The board felt that stock sales would depress the stock price and "distract" the sensitive execs.

Southmark loaned a lot of money to officers and officer partnerships: one in particular, to James Gilley, executive vice-president, was nonrecourse, secured by the Southmark stock purchased with the proceeds. It collected interest at a rate equal to the rate of dividend payments of the stock that secured the loan—a pretty good deal, if the stock were worth anything.

Partnerships were extremely creative. 1601 Partners, for example, had 190 officers and employees of Southmark as limited partners for only a nominal contribution. Phillips and Friedman were the general partners. Southmark was generous enough to loan 1601 $13.8 million unsecured. As of June 30, 1987, $1 million in interest had accrued and no interest had been paid; Southmark wisely discontinued accruing interest for financial purposes. Phillips had taxable losses on his partnership interests in 1985 and 1986 of $1.22 million.

The proxy goes on and on with similar loans and partnerships and transactions. No one who read the proxy could have escaped the point. In a partial denouement, on April 19, 1990 the creditors' committee of Southmark asked a federal judge to allow it to sue the company's former top two executives to recover more than $83 million in assets.

L. A. Gear and Bally Manufacturing get the honors for one of the highest ratios of salary plus bonus to net income. In fiscal 1989 the two top fashion sports shoe kings at L. A. Gear made a combined $10.6 million with net income of $55.059 million. Presumably the stockholders didn't care, since the stock price went up 185 percent.

Bally stockholders weren't quite as complacent in 1989. The Bally boys don't own much stock (3.2 percent in 1988, up to 4.1 percent in 1989 thanks to the generous incentive plan), but they paid themselves pretty well, relative to what stockholders have made in net and stock price appreciation. Cash compensation was $10 million total for the top ten in 1989, with net income to common shareholders of $9.4 million. Richard Gillman, president of Bally's Park Place, Inc. got cash of $4 million. Donahue Wildman, president and CEO of Bally's Health got cash compensation in 1989 of $1.925 million. The stock price went from $22.125 to $15.125 in 1989 with earnings per share from $1.12 to $.35.

Pinnacle West's chairman of the board, Keith Turley, led the company into a major real estate expansion in Arizona at the top of the market. The company paid him $601,694 in 1988 (plus $530,962 in his later retirement), to take earnings from

$233 million in 1986 to $4 million in 1988. He capped that record with a net loss of $551 million in 1989 and slashed the dividend, after giving one of the acquired subs, Merabank, to the taxpayers to bail out, despite its purchase by Pinnacle West under a "keep-well" agreement. One member of the Arizona Corporations Commission publicly termed Turley "a bozo." Some shareholders (Turley only owned 18,600 shares himself) might agree.

National Education has the most attractive severance package. Based on salary/bonus levels at the time of his departure, David Bright, chairman of the board and CEO, would have received severance payment of approximately $7.37 million. Alas, the departing officer is currently in litigation with the company over realization of his lovely parachute.

Medco Containment's Martin Wygod has the most creative bonus arrangement for finder's fees and corporate finance activity. He receives 1 percent of the consideration paid to the company for the sale of the company or any sub, or any piece of the business or the assets through merger, sale of assets, tender, sale of majority interest in the company, or liquidation. Just to cover all contingencies, he also gets 1 percent of the number of shares or rights to purchase shares offered or distributed for shares of the stock in subs. What a great incentive to form and reform the company! Wygod received deferred compensation of $3.893 million on the consummation of the merger of Medco and Porex, which was not payable until termination of his employment, death, disability, or change in position. That payment was accelerated and received in 1989.

Crazy Eddie and Integrated Resources share my regard as all-time favorites for scope and creativity of corporate perks. Chapters 6 and 10 detail the benefits for the Zises and Antars. The really big chunks of cash for both families came from sale of stock: many shareholders were not as astute in their market timing.

The rule of thumb when you study a proxy is if you have to read it three times, you've struck pay dirt. Try to determine if the company is run for the executives or the stockholders. When the company is run for the stockholders, the executives are compensated with more stock options, not immediately convertible into cash, less salary, and fewer benefits.

Checklist of Proxy Questions

Cash Compensation

1. Are executives paid exorbitant salaries? Look at cash compensation relative to company earnings.
2. Does the company pay big bonuses? What for? Is the bonus tied to extraordinary efforts or just for doing the job? Is the bonus for increased sales, return on equity, or some other measure or combination of measures?
3. Does the company pay a percentage of pretax profits to the primary officers in the form of bonuses? Or a percentage of revenues? Some bonuses are calculated on stock price appreciation.

Stock Options

4. Stock Grants vs. Stock Options vs. SARs. SARs, Stock Appreciation Rights, are the most generous for the executives, followed by grants. SARs give the grantee cash money, bankable now with no stock price suspense.
5. Does the company in any way pay for stock options?
6. Does the company pay a bonus for taxes on options?
7. Do the officers get any special deals if there is a stock/rights offering of company or a sub's stock?
8. What is the percentage of stock owned by the primary officers?

Parachutes

9. Does the company have an unusual severance pay contract, especially in case of merger or buy-out?
10. What are the terms of retirement contracts?

Extras

11. Are there extra perks such as large insurance policies, apartments, automobile use, plane use?

"Certain Transactions": Arm's Length, No Doubt

12. Does the company permit the primary officers to engage in other activities, such as owning other businesses associated with the company? Do they give favorable terms to the officers or give favorable contracts to businesses owned by officers?
13. Are many of the officers related to each other?
14. Does the company deal with any relatives of officers?
15. Does the company frequently loan money to the officers? If so, does the company charge interest?
16. If the company engages in limited partnerships, does it pay for the officers to become general partners or limited partners, or grant them bonuses for participation in partnerships, (or just give them the tax losses)?

Miscellaneous

17. Are there a lot of lawsuits, and what is the liability?
18. What is the age range of the primary officers—all old or all young?
19. Who else owns the stock?
20. Check the board biographies. Is it a rubber stamp, "good ol' boy" board or a working group? How independent is the board?

Some industries—entertainment and brokerage, for example—have higher salary/bonus plans. Even if the industry standards are relatively high, see if executives get bonuses for doing what they're paid to do before stockholders get paid. See what the top employees' total package is relative to net income.

Stock ownership is a great incentive, but cash payment disguised as stock ownership does the shareholders no favor. Option plans can be so generous and expensive that stockholders get diluted and deluded through their own largesse. Stockholders approve the number of shares set aside and the board sets the terms, vesting requirements, and payment conditions. A quick review of types:

- Incentive stock options are the most conservative, usually priced at fair market—the company doesn't get a deduction when exercised. A capital gain or loss is declared by the optionee at the time of disposition.

- Nonqualified stock options are issued at less than market, but at no less than 85 percent of the price. An optionee who exercises a nonqualified option recognizes ordinary income for the amount in excess of the fair market value, and the company takes the same amount as a business deduction.

- Stock appreciation rights are in essence gifts to the optionee, who receives shares or cash equal to the appreciated difference between the original grant price and the market value at the time of exercise. He does not have to purchase the stock. Upon exercise of the rights, the optionee recognizes ordinary income in the amount of the cash received. The company will generally be entitled to a tax deduction at the same time.

- Restricted stock options/stock option grants are outright distributions of stock or the cash equivalent with forfeiture clauses for termination.

Proxies also tell you which executives have disappeared if you compare several years of documents. Sometimes, attrition isn't well published except by default.

One more word on proxies. Of late, a bit of a hubbub has been raised about institutions not reading and voting proxies. In particular, the Labor Department appears to be concerned about dereliction of duty regarding ERISA accounts and proxies—fiduciary responsibilities. A survey by the Labor Department found that 39 percent of the investment managers didn't vote proxies and didn't know who did. Corporate clients appear to be equally fuzzy about assigning responsibility, but some executives are retaining the authority for themselves. Perhaps they should hire short sellers to read them.

3. The Bigger Puzzle

Step 3 is divided into two parts: research and store checks. The research segment starts in the library, whereas the second segment ends up watching the marketplace.

Research

Review the industry and the company's competitors and clients. The 10K should give you a good preview of how the company fits into its industry and the names of competitors, customers, and suppliers.

Start with the big picture and check the library and *Value Line* for industry information. Most public libraries have a copy of the *Standard and Poors Industry Surveys* to synopsize industry fundamentals. Next, see what trade publications are available and if a government office tracks data. Several services, like Washington Researchers, provide comprehensive information gathering on any topic.

Masses of industry data are available even without use of computer on-line searching facilities. For example, the *Poultry Times,* the U.S. Department of Agriculture economists, and state agriculture departments in poultry-producing states all supply volumes of information on chicken prices, including a hot line of daily trading data and projections of supply and demand.

Other publicly traded companies' financial statements can also provide a lot of data, so discover who else is in the business. Reading competitors' financials, comparing margins, return on invested assets, growth rates, and inventory and receivable turns can give an analyst an idea of who is out of line and what looks different.

Store Checks

Back in the first step you decided what the business of the company was and what the trigger numbers were. Use that information to check in the marketplace. If the key is store volume, visit a store and count customers, check average ticket size, talk to the store manager. If it's a hot new company with a to-die-for product, see if competitors have heard of the product yet. If it's an oil change franchise, count cars at peak hours to see if franchisees are hitting breakeven assumptions.

Don't base a conclusion on store checks alone; frequently one store or geographical area can be an outlyer in volume. Observing does, however, give the flavor of the business plan's execution.

4. Who Owns It?

Follow the trading patterns, volume in particular. Track the percentage of institutional ownership. (*Vickers On-Line Service* and *Spectrum* compile quarterly numbers and names of holders.) High institutional ownership and high Wall Street coverage can make for a quick collapse if something unexpected happens. Always follow the short sale numbers to tell you when a squeeze might develop, so the relative impact on the portfolio can be monitored. Watch option volume and relative pricing to note takeover speculation. Continue to pay attention to 13Ds and 144s.

5. Check the Water Temperature

Accumulate any brokerage reports to provide the company-think and Wall Street's attitude. Sometimes brokerage reports will supply pertinent industry data. Frequently, the company will send you brokerage reports with the financial statements, if you ask (particularly if they're favorable).

Remember, as you read Wall Street reports, the job description of analysts: they are not paid to make waves or to disagree or to be on the cutting edge of stock analysis. Analysts are relative: they're supposed to do a little better than their peers and charm the institutional clients who vote on the Institutional Investor all-star list. The problem is that some misinformed clients expect analysts to read the financials, even if their bosses do not. Use them for indications of Street-think and as conduits of management information. It's not good guys vs. bad guys, shorts against analysts; the point is how effectively you use the information presented to you.

Check the library periodical indexes for all past media references to the company and ancillary topics. *Forbes* and *Barron's* do good, strong, analytical factfinding. Nobody fires them if they make waves. Many indexes carry only two or three years of references, but make sure you have at least five, since ancient history is relevant to corporate hanky panky or to the firm's cultural tradition of hanky panky.

6. Pay Attention

If you decide not to short a stock after the preliminary analysis, it may be a great idea next year. If you do short it now, watch it. Events move so slowly in the financial world, it's hard to maintain concentration.

First watch for earnings releases. Note when they're expected to be published and what Street expectations are. The date of the earnings release is also statistically relevant: the later, the worse the numbers. Many companies will fax the PR release, together with the income statement and balance sheet. Quick information is important. If it's a large, Street-covered stock, small investors are at a disadvantage, since Street analysts get the faxes and phone calls first, little players sometimes not until days later.

Know when financials are expected out. 10Qs and 10Ks are read slowly by Wall Street, so quick attention can yield important data; you can make up for the delay on receipt of earnings release information. Waiting for new financials is like waiting for Christmas. It's fun to see if you were right and how things are developing. Go first to the key numbers, then the cash flow statement, and finally the verbiage. Read the Qs carefully.

Keep watching—once a potential target, always a possibility. If you know a company well, you may recognize a trigger, like the Zises' selling their Integrated stock or HBJ selling Shamu. Or J. Bildner's closing stores or running over expected costs and out of money.

Don't be surly about admitting defeat. If you shorted the stock because the inventories were too high and the 10Q shows the company has corrected the problem, cover. NOW.

Don't cover just because of price movements; wait until the

resolution of the scenario. If Integrated looks like death, wait till it's buried.

Short selling can be much like a cat waiting outside a mouse hole—the level of persistence, patience, and attentiveness is not for everyone, especially over sustained periods of time.

Concept Recap

The short sellers' credo can be summarized into several points:

1. Dissent is OK.
2. The facts are somewhere, free for the digging.
3. Hard work is outmoded, so if you do a little, you'll be far ahead. Analysts look at company PR rather than fundamentals and financials, and that provides opportunities and longer periods of market inefficiencies.
4. Computers confuse and build false confidence in portfolio managers, and that also provides opportunities.
5. Some accountants sanction almost everything, and that helps a lot, too.
6. Finally, Wall Street ices the inefficient cake with compulsive conformity. Everyone gets on the bandwagon and stays until the evidence is too compelling, then they all fall off with a jolt.

Conclusion

The key points to remember about selling, short selling, or simply not buying are several.

Never assume that the same paradigm applies to all stocks. Each company and industry is different so it's dumb to measure by the same scale if the yardstick isn't relevant. If a company owns land at 1932 prices, don't worry about earnings or price/earnings. Think about the business and decide what the market wants you to pay for (cash flow, assets, earnings). Then, after thoughtful consideration of the prospects, value the company according to your own analysis.

Don't genuflect in front of a business, an executive, or an analyst. Keep your distance and your objectivity. The stock market is about people disagreeing over stock prices. Short sellers are entitled to their opinions, as are executives and analysts. And so are you. Don't take it seriously; it's only money.

A short seller is a skeptic with a constructive, optimistic bent. If you're appalled when an executive lies about earnings prospects, don't just sell the stock, consider shorting it.

When the short interest peaks at a staggering percentage of total volume and the lemmings embrace pessimism, remember that the stories of short sale candidates are lessons in the antithesis of good company characteristics. Buying low and selling high remains the game, no matter what the order of the transaction.

Appendix

Margin Accounts and Short Selling

Short sellers of common stocks borrow stock from a brokerage house to sell in the organized markets. They are borrowing property, not money, and can short only through a margined account.

When a customer opens a margin account, an agreement must be signed. That form states that the customer is hypothecating (pledging) securities as collateral for a margin loan. Stocks deposited into a margin account are put into Street or nominee name, not client name. The broker can then rehypothecate a customer's securities, up to 140 percent of the debit balance, as collateral for further borrowings.

The current Federal Reserve requirement (Reg T, as it is known in the industry) is at 50 percent, meaning that a customer must initially put up 50 percent of the short sale price in cash or 100 percent in fully paid securities.

For a short sale, the broker obtains the to-be-borrowed stock from one of two places: from other customer margin accounts (if there are sufficient hypothecated shares), or from another broker dealer.

After the customer makes the short sale, the brokerage house marks the position to market: that is to say, the broker uses the closing security prices to compute a gain or loss. The account is then credited or debited for the price change. Usually, this is done on a weekly basis, but if the market begins to fluctuate actively, mark to markets are figured daily. Since the turmoil of late 1987, some brokers have begun marking to market daily regardless of trading activity.

If the price has moved above the original value, the short seller is required by the brokerage house to put up more collateral. Using the example in table 1.1, if the price of the stock rises to $12,000, the equity would then be $3,000, and the account becomes restricted, (technically, any account under the 50 percent equity level is considered restricted). Although the NYSE requires a minimum maintenance level of 30 percent, most brokers issue maintenance calls when an account goes below the 35 percent equity level. In this example, the equity is now at only 25 percent. To comply with NYSE regulations, the short seller would need to deposit an additional $600, or an additional $1,200 in securities, to bring the account up to the 35 percent level. Unlike Reg T calls, which must be paid for within seven days, maintenance calls are due immediately. Most carry a due deadline of forty-eight hours.

The NYSE and NASD also have a set of special maintenance rules for "cheap stocks." Stocks selling between $0 and $2.50 require minimum equity of $2.50 per share; those selling between $2.50 and $5 require 100 percent of per-share value, and those selling above $5 require $5 per share or 30 percent of per-share value, whichever is greater.

If the price moves down, the seller has use of the excess funds. Using the above example, if the stock falls to $80, the $2,000 excess can be used for other shorts or purchases or can be deposited in a money market account.